ESSENTIALS OF INTERNATIONAL RELATIONS

ESSENTIALS OF INTERNATIONAL RELATIONS

Second Edition

Karen A. Mingst

University of Kentucky

W • W • Norton & Company

New York • London

*The text of this book is composed in Fairfield with the
display set in Rundfunk and Benguiat Gothic.*
Editor: Roby Harrington
Copy Editor: Carol Loomis
Editorial Assistant: Rob Whiteside
Associate Managing Editor: Jane Carter
Production Manager: JoAnn Simony
Text Design: Jack Meserole
Art and Maps: John McAusland
Composition: UG / GGS Information Services, Inc.
Manufacturing: Courier Companies Inc.

Library of Congress Cataloging-in-Publication Data

Mingst, Karen A., 1947–
  Essentials of international relations / Karen Mingst.—2nd ed.
    p.cm.
  Includes bibliographical references and index.
  ISBN 0-393-97722-6 (pbk.)
    1. International relations. I. Title.

JZ1305 .M56 2001
327—dc21

                                                           2001030453

W. W. Norton & Company, Inc., 500 Fifth Avenue, New York, N.Y. 10110
                      www.wwnorton.com

W. W. Norton & Company Ltd., Castle House, 75/76 Wells Street, London W1T 3QT

4 5 6 7 8 9 0

CONTENTS

The State ~~100~~ 5

The Individual 131 6

The Quest for Global Governance 217 **9**

Globalizing Issues 251 **10**

MAPS

PREFACE

In the fall of 1995 Roby Harrington, the director of the college department at Norton, appeared at my door to talk about an idea for a series of textbooks on international relations and world politics. He believed that faculty were "clamoring for smart, short textbooks with a clear sense of what's essential and what's not." The plan was to offer faculty short, provocative books from which they could pick and choose to build their reading lists. I was asked to write the overview book based on that seminal idea. He thought that, because I had taught the introductory international relations course at several large public universities, I might have insight into students' knowledge and their needs, as well as an eye for how to present the material. Jack Snyder, the general editor of the series, signed on to write the book on nationalism; he was joined by Stephen Krasner writing on international political economy, Robert Bates on political economy of development, John Mearsheimer on power, and Bruce Russett and John Oneal on international institutions. Richard Harknett came on board to create a website for the series.

Having to think about how to present the rich and complex subject of international relations in a text of only 250 pages was a challenging and enlightening task—challenging, of course, because we academics always want to say more, not less, about our favorite topics, and enlightening because being forced to make difficult choices about what topics to address strengthened my belief in what the roots of the discipline are. I felt strongly about beginning with a discussion of the history of international relations, so that students can understand why we study the subject and how current scholarship is always informed by what has preceded it. This discussion leads naturally into Chapter 2, which traces the history of the state and the international system. The theoretical framework is presented in Chapter 3, which lays out the levels of analysis and the three schools of thought—liberalism, realism, and radicalism—I chose to organize the book around these three theories because they provide interpretive frameworks for understanding what is happening in the world. Each of the next three chapters is devoted to one of the levels of analysis—the international system, the state, and the individual. Chapters 7 and 8 focus on two topics that underlie all interactions between states—security and economics. The final chapter explores the ways in which countries try to work together through international organizations to resolve or prevent conflict.

Once I had established the organization of the book, I grappled with how to present the various topics concisely yet thoroughly. I soon realized that the effective use of visual tools would make the difference. Points made in the text are reinforced with tables, figures, and boxes. Each chapter opens with a set of central questions that not only alert students to key topics discussed in the chapter but also get students thinking—*questioning*—as political scientists do. Theory often scares students, especially in an introductory course. To make it more palatable, the text's "Theory in Brief" boxes break theory down to its basic parts, so that students can more easily grasp and remember the material. "In Focus" boxes are used to reinforce concepts presented in the text, from historical events to complex ideas, like collective security. In addition, maps are used throughout the text to help students locate the countries and regions discussed.

In addition to the pedagogical support provided in the text, students will benefit from a sophisticated and pedagogically driven website providing study help. The site features interactive quizzes, chapter summaries, and a searchable glossary, as well as case studies and role-playing material. An added resource for instructors is a test bank of multiple-choice and essay questions.

Writing this book proved to be a more-rewarding experience than I had ever envisioned. I was able to reflect on what has worked in my teaching and what has not. I had to pick and choose the material, knowing that a "smart, short textbook" could never include everything or please everyone. Much of the reward came from working closely with individuals, each thoroughly professional: Roby Harrington, who read and commented on each chapter at several stages; Sarah Caldwell, who also commented on and corrected subsequent drafts, devised art presentations, and guided me through the production process; and Traci Nagle, whose extensive copyediting deflated my ego but made a better book. At several junctures Craig Warkentin, then a graduate student at the University of Kentucky and now a Ph.D., provided valuable research assistance. He has also written the accompanying test bank. To my colleagues who provided extensive comments during the first review process—Bill Chittick (University of Georgia), Sumit Ganguly (Hunter College), Neil Richardson (University of Wisconsin), Dale Smith (Florida State University), and Nina Tannenwald (Brown University)—I owe special thanks.

This Second Edition of the book has been thoroughly updated and expanded. In particular, the introductory material has been reorganized both to introduce the different theoretical perspectives and to detail how the various theorists go about conducting research. In Chapter 3 the newer theory of constructivism is described, and throughout the text constructivism understandings are presented when appropriate. There is an expanded treatment of the causes of war in Chapter 7 and of globalization, multinational corporations, the North American Free Trade Agreement, and the World Trade Organization in Chapter 8. In several chapters, a more explicit consideration of feminist and gender issues is integrated into the discussions, illustrating the way that this perspective augments and amplifies the various theoretical perspectives. Most importantly, a new chapter on globalizing issues has been added. This chapter addresses how the globalizing issues have made the search for global governance imperative. It examines two issues in depth—the environment (including population, natural resources, and pollution) and human rights (with a special section on women's rights as human rights). Finally, the chapter examines the impact that the globalizing issues have on international bargaining, on international conflict, on key concepts like sovereignty, and on each of the theoretical perspectives.

My thanks go to Roby Harrington who provided the vision for the Norton series and has offered encouragement along the way. This Second Edition benefited substantively from the guidance of the editor Rob Whiteside who answered my many desperate queries, found able reviewers, and commented thoughtfully on the approach to be taken. He also offered gentle reminders about time throughout the writing. Thanks also to colleagues who used the First Edition and offered advice on what changes should be made. They included Doug Lemke (University of Michigan), Virginia Haufler (University of Maryland), Keith Shimko (Purdue University), Margaret Karns (University of Dayton), Douglas Borer (Virginia Tech University), James Marquardt (Colby College), Melissa Butler (Wabash College), and Marian Miller (University of Akron). Although I could not use all of their suggestions, I was guided by their experience and observations.

This edition is also designed as a core introductory text. Accompanying the book in the Norton series on world politics is a reader, coedited by the series editor Jack Snyder and myself, *Essential Readings in World Politics*. These readings have been selected to provide in depth analysis for students on certain questions, to offer competing views on controversial issues, and to provide policy relevance. The two books may also be usefully paired with other books in the Norton series.

During both editions of this book, I was involved in numerous other projects that stimulated me and provided distractions. These included writing original research papers and collaborating with colleagues; serving as department chair; enjoying a year's sabbatical, which took me to several different parts of the world; and functioning as wife and as a mother of two teenagers. Time is always precious and encouragement imperative. I have been fortunate to have received both.

KAREN MINGST

Lexington, Kentucky
June 1998; January 2001

Africa, 2000

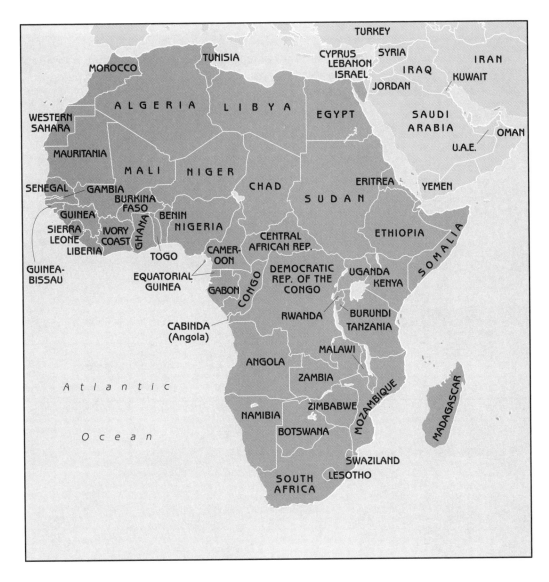

Asia, 2000

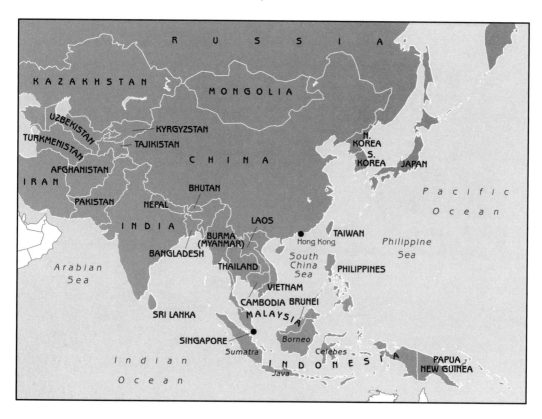

Europe, 2000

Latin America, 2000

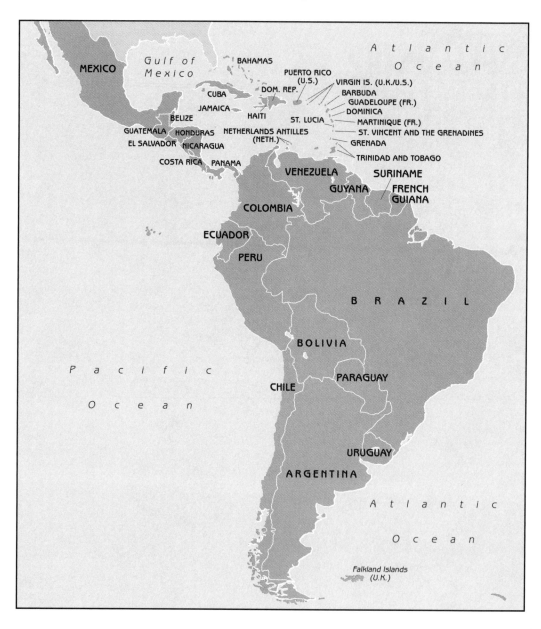

ESSENTIALS OF INTERNATIONAL RELATIONS

APPROACHES TO INTERNATIONAL RELATIONS

1

- *How does international relations affect you in your daily life?*
- *Why do we study international relations theory?*
- *How have history and philosophy been used to study international relations?*
- *What is the contribution of behavioralism?*
- *What alternative methods have challenged traditional methods? Why?*

INTERNATIONAL RELATIONS IN DAILY LIFE

Reading a daily newspaper and listening to the evening national news make us aware of international events far away from our everyday lives. But these events—bombings in Israel, starvation in Somalia and Mozambique, a summit meeting in Moscow, steep fluctuations in the value of the Japanese yen, and intense competition for investment opportunities in Vietnam— may seem to most of us to be distant and unrelated to our own lives.

Yet these seemingly remote events quickly can become both highly related and personally salient to any or all of us. Those bombings killed visiting students from your university; your sibling or your uncle was called into active duty in the National Guard to deliver food to Somalia; the price of the new computer or television set you want has plummeted because of the favorable dollar-yen exchange rate; Vietnam, once the symbol of protest and pain for your parents' generation, is now a hotly contested terrain for your employer's investment dollars. A slight change of the story line immediately transforms events "out there" to matters of immediate concern. Buyers of quality carpets and clothing learn that those goods often are produced by children in faraway lands, just as Mexican workers recognize that U.S. trade laws may affect their ability to provide food for their families.

Historically, international activities such as these were overwhelmingly the results of decisions taken by central governments and heads of state, not by ordinary citizens. Increasingly, however, these activities involve different actors, some of whom *you* directly influence. In all likelihood, you, too, will be participating in international relations as you travel to foreign lands, purchase products made abroad, or work for a multinational corporation headquartered in another country. You may be a member of a nongovernmental organization—Amnesty International, the Red Cross, or Greenpeace—with a local chapter in your community or at your college. With your fellow members around the globe, you may try to influence the local, as well as the national and international, agenda. Your city or state may be actively courting foreign private investment, competing against both neighboring municipalities and other countries. These activities can directly affect the job situation in your community, creating new employment possibilities or taking away jobs to areas with cheaper wages. As a businessperson, you may be liberated or constrained by business regulations—internationally mandated standards established by the World Trade Organization to facilitate the movement of goods and commerce across national borders.

Thus the variety of actors in international relations includes not just the 189 states recognized in the world today, and their leaders and government bureaucracies, but also municipalities, for-profit and not-for-profit private organizations, international organizations, and you. **International relations** is the study of the interactions among the various actors that participate in international politics, including states, international organizations, nongovernmental organizations, subnational entities like bureaucracies and local governments, and individuals. It is the study of the behaviors of these actors as they participate individually and together in international political processes.

IN FOCUS

FOUNDATIONAL QUESTIONS OF INTERNATIONAL RELATIONS

▶ How can human nature be characterized?
▶ What is the relationship between the individual and society?
▶ What is the relationship between societies?
▶ What are the characteristics of the state?
▶ What should be the role of the state?
▶ What ought to be the norms in international society?
▶ How might international society be structured to achieve order?

How, then, can we begin to study this multifaceted phenomenon called international relations? How can we understand why bombings occur in Israel, why the Somali people experienced such massive food shortages, what the agenda was during the latest summit meeting in Moscow, what structural factors account for the fluctuations of the Japanese yen, and why the once war-ravaged economy of Vietnam will become the investment bonanza of the twenty-first century? How can we begin to think theoretically about events and trends in international relations? How can we make sense of the seemingly disconnected events that we read about or hear on the news? How can we begin to answer the foundational questions of international relations?

THINKING THEORETICALLY

Political scientists develop theories or frameworks both to understand the causes of events that occur in international relations every day and to answer the foundational questions in the field. Although there are many contending theories, three of the more prominent theories are developed in depth in this book: liberalism and neoinstitutional liberalism, realism and neorealism, and radical perspectives whose origin lie in Marxism. Also introduced is the newer theory of constructivism.

In brief, liberalism is historically rooted in several philosophical traditions which posit that human nature is basically good. Individuals form into groups and later states. States generally cooperate and follow international norms and procedures that have been mutually agreed on. In contrast, realism posits that states exist in an anarchic international system. Each state bases its policies on an interpretation of national interest defined in terms of power. The structure of the international system is determined by the distribution of power among states. A third approach, radical theory, is rooted in economics. Actions of individuals are largely determined by economic class; the state is an agent of international capitalism; and the international system is highly stratified, dominated by an international capitalist system.

Theory development, however, is a dynamic process. Beginning in the late twentieth century, alternative critical approaches to international relations have challenged the traditional theories of liberalism and realism and substantially modified radicalism. Believing that a generalized theory based on historical, philosophical, or behavioral methods is impossible to achieve, critical theorists contend that theory is situated in a particular

time and place, conditioned by ideological, cultural, and sociological influences. There is no single objective reality, only multiple realities based on
individual experiences and perspectives.

Among the best-developed alternative theories are postmodernism and
constructivism. Postmodernists question the whole notion of states, which
they view as a fiction constructed by scholars and citizens alike. They contend that states do not act in regularized ways but are known only through
the stories told about them, filtered through the perspectives of the story-
teller. The task of postmodernist analysis is thus to deconstruct the basic
concepts of the field and to replace them with multiple realities.

Constructivists, following in the radical tradition because of attention
to the sources of change, argue that the key structures in the states system
are not material but instead are intersubjective and social. The interest of
states is not fixed but is malleable and ever changing. While constructivists, like the other theorists, differ among themselves, they share the
common belief that discourse shapes how political actors define interests,
and thus modify their behavior. Constructivism has assumed increasing
importance in twenty-first-century thinking about international relations.

Different theoretical approaches help us see international relations
from different viewpoints. As political scientist Stephen Walt explains,
"No single approach can capture all the complexity of contemporary world
politics. Therefore we are better off with a diverse array of competing
ideas rather than a single theoretical orthodoxy. Competition between theories helps reveal their strengths and weaknesses and spurs subsequent re-
finements, while revealing flaws in conventional wisdom."[1] We will
explore these competing ideas, their strengths and weaknesses, in the re-
mainder of the book.

DEVELOPING THE ANSWERS

How do political scientists find the answers to the questions posed? How
do they find information to assess the accuracy, relevancy, and potency of
their theories?

History

Answers have often been discovered in history. Without any historical
background, many of today's key issues are incomprehensible. History
tells us that the bombings in Israel are part of a dispute over territory be-

tween Arabs and Jews, a dispute with its origins in biblical times and with its modern roots in the establishment of Israel in 1948. The most immediate origins of the Somali famine of the early 1990s can be found in the breakdown of central authority after the overthrow of President Siad Barre in 1991, after which rival warlords, with weapons from both Soviet and U.S. Cold War stockpiles, vied for power, using food as one weapon of war. Yet periodic famine has been a fact of life in Somalia for centuries, as oral traditions recount. The Moscow summit meeting is one example of an approach to conducting diplomacy developed since World War II, although the specific issues discussed at a given meeting depend on a host of factors. The fluctuations in the value of the Japanese yen can be attributed, in part, to the very loosely regulated banking system in that country. Finally, those investing in Vietnam are hoping that country will duplicate the success of the newly industrializing countries (NICs) of Asia—South Korea, Taiwan, Hong Kong, and Singapore—whose rapid economic growth in the 1980s and 1990s was engineered by government policies favoring exports.

Thus, history provides a crucial background for the study of international relations. History has been so fundamental to the study of international relations that there was no separate international relations subdiscipline until the early twentieth century, especially in the United States. Before that time, especially in both Europe and the United States, international relations was simply diplomatic history in most academic institutions.

History invites its students to acquire detailed knowledge of specific events, but it also can be used to test generalizations. Having deciphered patterns from the past, students of history can begin to explain the relationship among various events. For example, having historically documented the cases when wars occur and described the patterns leading up to war, the diplomatic historian can search for explanations for, or causes of, war. The ancient Greek historian Thucydides (c. 460–401 B.C.) in *History of the Peloponnesian War,* uses this approach. Distinguishing between the underlying and the immediate causes of wars, Thucydides finds that what made that war inevitable was the growth of Athenian power. As that city-state's power increased, Sparta, Athens's greatest rival, feared its own loss of power. Thus, the changing distribution of power was the underlying cause of the Peloponnesian War.[2]

Many scholars following in Thucydides's footsteps use history in similar ways. But those using history must be wary. History may be a bad guide; the "lessons" of Munich and Allied appeasement of Germany before World War II or the "lessons" of the war in Vietnam are neither clear-cut nor agreed on. And periodically, fundamental changes in actors and in technology can make history obsolete as a guide to the present or the future.

Philosophy

Answers to international relations questions also incorporate classical and modern philosophy. Much classical philosophizing focuses on the state and its leaders—the basic building blocks of international relations—as well as on method. For example, the ancient Greek philosopher Plato (c. 427–347 B.C.) in *The Republic* concludes that in the "perfect state" the people who should govern are those who are superior in the ways of philosophy and war. Plato calls these ideal rulers "philosopher-kings."[3] While not directly discussing international relations, Plato introduces two ideas seminal to the discipline: class analysis and dialectical reasoning, both of which are bases for later Marxist analysts. Radicals, like Marxists, see economic class as the major divider in domestic and international politics; this viewpoint will be explored in depth in Chapters 3 and 8. Marxists also acknowledge the importance of dialectical reasoning—that is, reasoning from a dialogue or conversation that leads to the discovery of contradictions in the original assertions and in political reality. In contemporary Marxist terms, such an analysis reveals the contradiction between global and local policies, whereby, for example, local-level textile workers lose their jobs to foreign competition and are replaced by high-technology industries.

Just as Plato's contributions to contemporary thinking are both substantive and methodological, the contributions of his student, the philosopher Aristotle (384–322 B.C.), lie both in substance (the search for an ideal domestic political system) and in method (the comparative method). Analyzing 168 constitutions, Aristotle looked at the similarities and differences among states, becoming the first writer to use the comparative method of analysis. He came to the conclusion that states rise and fall largely because of internal factors—a conclusion still debated in the twentieth century.[4]

After the classical era, many of the philosophers of relevance to international relations focused on the notion of the basic characteristics of man and how those characteristics might influence the character of international society. The English philosopher Thomas Hobbes (1588–1679) in *Leviathan* imagines a state of nature, a world without governmental authority or civil order, where men rule by passions, living with the constant uncertainty of their own security. To Hobbes, the life of man is solitary, selfish, and even brutish. Extrapolating to the international level, in the absence of international authority, society is in a "state of nature," or anarchy. States left in this anarchic condition act as man does in the state of nature. For Hobbes the solution to the dilemma is a unitary state—a Leviathan—where power is centrally and absolutely controlled.[5]

The French philosopher Jean-Jacques Rousseau (1712–78) addressed the same set of questions but, having been influenced by the Enlightenment, saw a different solution. In "Discourse on the Origin of Inequality," Rousseau describes the state of nature as an egocentric world, with man's primary concerns being self-preservation—not unlike Hobbes's description of the state of nature. Rousseau posed the dilemma in terms of the story of the stag and the hare. In a hunting society, each individual must keep to his assigned task in order to find and trap the stag for food for the whole group. However, if a hare happens to pass nearby, an individual might well follow the hare, hoping to get his next meal quickly and caring little for how his actions will affect the group. Rousseau analogized between these hunters and states. Do states follow short-term self-interest, like the hunter who follows the hare? Or do they recognize the benefits of a common interest?[6]

Rousseau's solution to the dilemma posed by the stag and the hare is different from Hobbes's Leviathan. Rousseau's preference is for the creation of smaller communities in which the "general will" can be attained. Indeed, it is "only the general will," not the Leviathan, that can "direct the forces of the state according to the purpose for which it was instituted, which is the common good."[7] In Rousseau's vision, "each of us places his person and all his power in common under the supreme direction of the general will; and as one we receive each member as an indivisible part of the whole."[8]

Still another philosophical view of the characteristics of international society is set forth by the German philosopher Immanuel Kant (1724–1804) in both *Idea for a Universal History* and *Perpetual Peace*. Kant envisioned a federation of states as a means to achieve peace, a world order in which man is able to live without fear of war. Sovereignties would remain intact, but the new federal order would be both preferable to a "super-Leviathan" and more effective and realistic than Rousseau's small communities. Kant's analysis is based on a vision of human beings which is different from that of either Rousseau or Hobbes. While admittedly selfish, man can learn new ways of cosmopolitanism and universalism.[9]

The tradition laid by these philosophers contributes to the development of international relations by calling attention to fundamental relationships: those between the individual and society, between individuals *in* society,

TABLE
1.1

Contributions of Philosophers to International Relations Theory

Plato (427–347 B.C.)	Greek political philosopher who argues that the life force in man is intelligent. Only a few people can have the insight into what is good; society should submit to the authority of these philosopher-kings. Many of these ideas are developed in *The Republic.*
Aristotle (384–322 B.C.)	Greek political philosopher who addresses the problem of order in the individual Greek city-state. The first to use the comparative method of research, observing multiple points in time and suggesting explanations for the patterns found.
St. Thomas Aquinas (1225–74)	Italian theorist who wrote during the height of feudal Europe. In *Treatise of the Laws,* develops the framework of natural law—a fusion of classical philosophy, Christian theology, and Roman law. Natural law is followed by man instinctively and releases man's good tendencies.
Thomas Hobbes (1588–1679)	English political philosopher who in *Leviathan* describes life in a state of nature as solitary, selfish, and brutish. Individuals and society can escape from the state of nature through a unitary state, a Leviathan.
Jean-Jacques Rousseau (1712–78)	French political philosopher whose seminal ideas were tested by the French Revolution. In "Discourse on the Origin of Inequality," describes the state of nature in both national and international society. Argues that the solution to the state of nature is the social contract, whereby individuals gather in small communities where the "general will" is realized.
Immanuel Kant (1724–1804)	German political philosopher key to the idealist or utopian school of thought. In *Idea for a Universal History* and *Perpetual Peace,* advocates a world federation of republics bound by the rule of law.

and between societies. These philosophers had varied, often competing visions of what these relationships are and what they ought to be. Some of their more important contributions are summarized in Table 1.1. The early philosophers lead contemporary international relations scholars to the examination of the characteristics of leaders, to the recognition of the importance of the internal dimensions of the state, to the analogy of the state and nature, and to descriptions of an international community.

History and philosophy permit us to delve into the foundational questions—the nature of man and the broad characteristics of the state and of international society. They allow us to speculate on the **normative** (or moral) element in political life: What *should be* the role of the state? What *ought to be* the norms in international society? How *might* international society be structured to achieve order?

With its emphasis on normative questions, the philosophical tradition encourages examination of the role of law at both the societal and international levels. Indeed, St. Thomas Aquinas (1225–74), the Italian philosopher and theologian, was one of the first to make the connection. In *Treatise of the Laws,* he finds the universe to be governed by "divine reason" and argues that human law needs to be made compatible with this natural law. Aquinas posited the existence of a law of nations, derived from the natural law: "To the law of nations belong those things, which are derived from the law of nature as conclusions from premises, just buying and selling, and the like, without which men cannot live together, which is a point of the law of nature, since man is by nature a social animal, as is proved in the *Politics* of Aristotle."[10]

The study of law presumes a degree of order based on written and unwritten norms of behavior. The task of those employing the legal approach is not only to describe the "laws" and norms that govern behavior but to prescribe those laws that are most useful, fair, and just for states and societies seeking to achieve the normative goals elucidated by various philosophers. Whether international law has achieved these goals is discussed in Chapter 9.

Thus, from the beginning of time scholars interested in international relations became grounded in diplomatic history as a substantive focus, and also became thoroughly versed in philosophy, posing the foundational questions and seeking normative answers.

Behavioralism

In the 1950s, some scholars became dissatisfied with examining historic events as idiosyncratic cases. They become disillusioned with philosophical discourse. They pondered new questions: Are there subtle and perhaps more intriguing patterns to diplomatic history than those found in the descriptive historical record? Is individual behavior more predictable than the largely contextual descriptions of the historian? Is it possible to test whether the trends found through historical inquiry or the "oughts" proposed by the philosophers are actually possible? How do people—the foundation of the municipality, the state, and international society—actually behave? Is man as selfish as Hobbes and Rousseau posited? Are states as power-hungry as those who compare the anarchic international system to the state of nature would have us believe?

Scholars seeking answers to these new questions were poised to contribute to the behavioral revolution in U.S. social sciences during the 1950s and 1960s. **Behavioralism** proposes that individuals, both alone and in groups, act in patterned ways. The task of the behavioral scientist is to suggest plausible hypotheses regarding those patterned actions and to systematically and empirically test those hypotheses. Using the tools of the scientific method to describe and explain human behavior, these scholars hope ultimately to predict future behavior. Many will be satisfied, however, with being able to explain patterns, as prediction in the social sciences remains an uncertain enterprise.

The focus of the behavioral revolution is on developing appropriate methods to empirically test for the anticipated patterns. Although the methods of behavioralism have never been an end in themselves, only a means to improve explanation, during the 1980s and 1990s scholars have seriously questioned the behavioral approach. Their disillusionment has taken several forms. To some, many of the foundational questions—the nature of man and society—are neglected by behavioralists because they are not easily testable by empirical methods. These critics suggest returning to the philosophical roots of international relations. To others, the questions behavioralists pose are the salient ones, but their attention to methods has overwhelmed the substance of their research. Few would doubt the importance of J. David Singer and Melvin Small's initial excursion into the causes of war, but even the researchers themselves admitted losing sight of the important questions in their quest to compile data and hone research methods. Some scholars, still within the behavioralist orientation, suggest simplifying esoteric methods in order to refocus on the substantive questions, like those examined in the democratic peace debate. Others remain firmly committed to the behavioral approach, pointing to the lack of funding and time for their meager results.

Alternative Methods

Alternative theorists are dissatisfied with using history, philosophy, or behavioral approaches. They have relied on other methods. One group, the postmodernists, seek to deconstruct the basic concepts of the field, like the state, the nation, rationality, and realism, by searching the texts (or sources) for hidden meanings underneath the surface, in the subtext. Once those hidden meanings are revealed, the postmodernist seeks to replace the once-orderly picture with disorder, to replace the dichotomies with multiple portraits.

Researchers have begun to deconstruct core concepts and replace them with multiple meanings. Political scientist Cynthia Weber, for example, argues that sovereignty (the independence of a state) is neither well defined nor consistently grounded. Digging below the surface of sovereignty, going beyond evaluations of the traditional philosophers, she discovers that conceptualizations of sovereignty are constantly shifting, based on the exigencies of the moment and sanctioned by different communities. The multiple meanings of sovereignty are conditioned by time, place, and historical circumstances.[11] This analysis has profound implications for the theory and practice of international relations, which are rooted in state sovereignty and accepted practices that reinforce sovereignty. It challenges conventional understandings.

Postmodernists also seek to find the voices of the "the others," those individuals who have been disenfranchised and marginalized in international relations. Feminist Christine Sylvester illustrates her approach with a discussion of the Greenham Common Peace Camp, a group of mostly women who in the early 1980s left their homes and neighborhoods in Wales and walked more than a hundred miles to a British air force base to protest against plans to deploy missiles at the base. Although the marchers were ignored by the media—and thus were "voiceless"—they maintained a politics of resistance, recruiting other political action groups near the camp and engaging members of the military stationed at the base. The women learned how to maintain a peace camp, forcing down the barriers between the militarized and demilitarized and between women and men. In 1988, when the Intermediate Range Nuclear Force Treaty was signed, dismantling the missiles, the women moved on to another protest site, drawing public attention to the role of Britain in the nuclear era.[12]

Others like the constructivists have turned to discourse analysis to answer the questions posed. To trace the impact of ideas on shaping identities, they turn to an analysis of culture, norms, procedures, and social practices. They probe how identities are shaped and changed over time. They turn to texts, interviews, and archival material, as well as probe local practices by riding public transportation and standing in lines. By using multiple sets of data, they create thick description. The case studies found in Peter Katzenstein's edited volume *The Culture of National Security* utilize this approach. Drawing on case studies including Soviet foreign policy at the end of the Cold War, German and Japanese security policy from militarism to antimilitarism, and Arab national identity, the authors search for security interests defined by actors who are responding to changing cultural factors. These studies show how social and cultural factors shape national security policy in ways that contradict realist or liberal expectations.[13]

Clearly, international relations scholars use multiple methodologies to answer the core questions.

INTEGRATING THE ANSWERS

In actuality, political scientists have answered research questions by combining different methodologies. The Correlates of War project and the democratic peace debate are two prominent examples of such integration.

The Correlates of War project, research based at the University of Michigan, permits us to see the integration of methodologies in action. Beginning in 1963, political scientist J. David Singer and his historian colleague Melvin Small attacked one of the fundamental questions in international relations: Why is there war? As Singer himself later acknowledged, he was motivated by the normative philosophical concern—how can there be peace? The two scholars chose a different methodological approach than their historian colleagues. Rather than focusing on one war, one of the "big ones" that change the tide of history as Thucydides did in his study of the Peloponnesian War, they sought to find patterns among a number of different wars. Believing that there are generalizable patterns to be found across all wars, Singer and Small turned to statistical data to discover the patterns.

The initial task of the Correlates of War project was to collect data on international wars (not civil wars) between 1865 and 1965 in which 1,000 or more deaths had been reported. For each of the 93 wars that fit these criteria, the researchers found data on the magnitude, severity, and intensity of wars, as well as the frequency of war over time.[14] This data collection process proved a much larger task than Singer and Small had anticipated, employing a bevy of researchers and graduate students.

Once codified, the second task was to generate specific, testable hypotheses that might explain the outbreak of war. Is there a relationship between the number of alliance commitments in the international system and the number of wars experienced? Is there a relationship between the number of great powers in the international system and the number of wars? Is there a relationship between the number of wars over time and the severity of the conflict? In the Correlates of War studies and in subsequent studies using the same data, hundreds of such relationships have been verified, although the relative importance of some of these findings is questionable.

The ultimate goal of the project is to connect all the relationships that are found into a coherent theory of why wars occur. Which groups of factors are *most* correlated with the outbreak of war over time? And how are these factors related to one another? Although answering this question will never *prove* that a particular group of factors is the cause of war, it could suggest some high-level correlations that merit theoretical explanation. Are characteristics within specific warring states most correlated with the outbreak of war? What is the correlation between international system–level factors—such as the existence of international organizations—and the outbreak of war? If the Correlates of War project finds consistently high correlations between alliances and war or between international organizations and war, then it can explain why wars break out, and perhaps policymakers may be able to predict the characteristics of the actors and the location for future wars. That is the goal of that research project.

Another example of a research program that used behavioral methods to examine a set of philosophical questions is found in the "democratic peace" debate. Based on ideas expressed by Immanuel Kant, Jean-Jacques Rousseau, and Woodrow Wilson, the theory posits that democracies are more peaceful than nondemocracies. The research question is an old one: Are democracies more prone to peace? More specifically, do democracies fight each other more than nondemocracies do? Do democracies fight nondemocracies more than they fight each other? Gathering data on different kinds of warfare over several centuries, researchers have addressed these sets of questions. One study confirms the hypothesis that democracies do not go to war against one another: since 1789 no wars have been fought strictly between independent states with democratically elective governments. Another study finds that wars involving democracies have tended to be less bloody but more protracted, although between 1816 and 1965, democratic governments have not been noticeably more peace-prone or passive.[15] But the evidence is not that clear-cut and explanations are partial. Why are states in the middle of democratic transitions more prone to conflict? How can we explain that when democratic states have not gone to war, it may have had little to do with their democratic character?

Why have some of the findings on the democratic peace been divergent? Behavioralists themselves point to some of the difficulties. Some researchers use different definitions of the key variables—democracy and war; others examine different time periods. Such differences in research protocol might well lead to different research findings. Yet even with these qualifications, the basic finding from the research is that democracies do not engage in militarized disputes against each other. That finding *is* statistically significant; that is, it does not occur by random chance. Overall, democracies are not more pacific than nondemocracies; democracies just do not fight *each other*.

These two research projects suggest that scholars utilize all the available approaches to answer the questions posed. No important question of international relations today can be answered with exclusive reliance on any one approach. History, whether in the form of an extended case study (Peloponnesian War) or of a study of multiple wars (Correlates of War), provides useful answers to the foundational question. Philosophical traditions provided the framework for the democratic peace project to follow. And the newer uses of deconstructionism and thick description and discourse analysis provide an even richer base for the international relations scholar to utilize.

IN SUM: MAKING SENSE OF INTERNATIONAL RELATIONS

How can we, as students, begin to make sense of events in our daily lives? How have scholars of international relations helped us make sense of the world around us? In this chapter, major theories of international relations

TABLE 1.2

Approaches to Studying International Relations

Type of approach	Method
History	Examines individual or multiple cases.
Philosophy	Develops rationales from core texts and analytical thinking.
Behavioralism	Finds patterns in human behavior and state behavior using empirical methods.
Alternative	Deconstructs major concepts and uses discourse analysis to build thick description.

have been introduced, including the liberal, realist, radical, and constructivist frameworks. These theories provide alternative frameworks for asking and answering core foundational questions. To answer these questions, international relations scholars turn to many other disciplines, including history, philosophy, behavioral psychology, and critical studies. International relations is a quintessential pluralistic and eclectic discipline.

WHERE DO WE GO FROM HERE?

To understand the development of international relations theory, we need to examine general historical trends to show developments in the state and international systems, particularly events in Europe during the nineteenth and twentieth centuries. This "stuff" of diplomatic history is the subject of Chapter 2. Chapter 3 is designed to help us think about the development of international relations theoretically from several frameworks—liberalism, realism, radicalism, and constructivism. Chapters 4, 5, and 6 examine the three levels of analysis in international relations. Each of these chapters is organized around the theoretical frameworks. Thus, in Chapter 4 the international system is examined; in Chapter 5, the state; and in Chapter 6, the individual. In each of these chapters the focus is on comparing liberal, realist, and radical descriptions and explanations, augmented, when appropriate, with constructivism. In the last four chapters, the major issues of international relations are studied: in Chapter 7, war and strife; in Chapter 8, international political economy; in Chapter 9, the problem of global governance; and in Chapter 10, the globalizing issues of the twenty-first century.

NOTES

1. Stephen M. Walt, "International Relations: One World, Many Theories," *Foreign Policy*, no. 110 (Spring 1998), 30.
2. Thucydides, *History of the Peloponnesian War*, trans. Rex Warner (Rev. ed.; Harmondsworth, Eng.: Penguin, 1972).
3. Plato, *The Republic* (Harmondsworth, Eng.: Penguin, 1955).
4. Aristotle, *The Politics*, ed. Trevor J. Saunders, trans. T. A. Sinclair (Harmondsworth, Eng.: Penguin, 1981).

5. Thomas Hobbes, *Leviathan*, ed. C. B. Macpherson (Harmondsworth, Eng.: Penguin, 1968).

6. Jean-Jacques Rousseau, "Discourse on the Origin and Foundations of Inequality among Men," in *Basic Political Writings of Jean-Jacques Rousseau*, ed. and trans. Donald A. Cress (Indianapolis, Ind.: Hackett Publishing, 1987).

7. Jean-Jacques Rousseau, "On the Social Contract," Book 2, Ch. 1, in *Basic Political Writings of Jean-Jacques Rousseau*, Cress, 153.

8. Rousseau, "On the Social Contract," Book 1, Ch. 6, 148.

9. See Immanuel Kant, *Idea for a Universal History from a Cosmopolitan Point of View* (1784) and *Perpetual Peace: A Philosophical Sketch* (1795), both reprinted in *Kant Selections*, ed. Lewis White Beck (New York: Macmillan Co., 1988).

10. St. Thomas Aquinas, "Treatise of the Laws" (XCV:4), reprinted in *Great Books of the Western World*, vols. 19, 20, ed. Robert Maynard Hutchins (Chicago: Encyclopedia Britannica, 1952, 1986).

11. Cynthia Weber, *Simulating Sovereignty: Intervention, the State and Symbolic Interchange* (Cambridge, Eng.: Cambridge University Press, 1994).

12. Christine Sylvester, "Empathetic Cooperation: A Feminist Method for IR," *Millennium: Journal of International Studies* 23:2 (1994), 315–34.

13. Peter J. Katzenstein, ed, *The Culture of National Security. Norms and Identity in World Politics* (New York: Columbia University Press, 1996).

14. J. David Singer and Melvin Small, *The Wages of War, 1816–1965: A Statistical Handbook* (New York: Wiley, 1972).

15. See William J. Dixon, "Democracy and the Peaceful Settlement of International Conflict," *American Political Science Review* 88 (1994), 14–32; and Joe D. Hagan, "Domestic Political Systems and War Proneness," *Mershon International Studies Review* 38:2 (October 1994), 183–207.

THE HISTORICAL CONTEXT OF CONTEMPORARY INTERNATIONAL RELATIONS

2

- Which historical periods have most influenced the development of international relations?
- What are the historical origins of the state?
- Why is the Treaty of Westphalia used as a benchmark for international relations scholars?
- What are the historical origins of the European balance-of-power system?
- How could the Cold War be both a series of confrontations between the United States and the Soviet Union and a "long peace"?
- Why did the Cold War end?

Students of international relations need to understand the events and trends of the past. Theorists recognize that core concepts in the field—the state, the nation, sovereignty, power, balance of power—were developed and shaped by historical circumstances. Policymakers search the past for patterns and precedents to guide contemporary decisions. In large part, the major antecedents to the contemporary international system are found in European-centered Western civilization.

Great civilizations thrived in other parts of the world too, of course: India and China, among others, have had extensive, vibrant civilizations since long before the historical events covered below. But the European emphasis is justified on the basis that contemporary international relations, in both theory and practice, is rooted in the European experience, for better or worse. In this chapter, we will first look at the period before 1648 (a seminal year for students of international relations), then the post-Westphalian world after 1648, then Europe of the nineteenth century, and finally the major transitions in the twentieth century.

The purpose of this historical overview is to trace important trends over time—the emergence of the state and the notion of sovereignty, the development of the international state system, and the changes in distribution of power among key states. These trends have a direct impact on international relations theory and practice today.

THE PRE-WESTPHALIAN WORLD

Many international relations theorists date the contemporary system from 1648, the year of the Treaty of Westphalia ending the Thirty Years War. This treaty marks the end of rule by religious authority in Europe and the emergence of secular authorities. With secular authority came the principle that has provided the foundation for international relations ever since: the notion of the territorial integrity of states—legally equal and sovereign participants in an international system.

Greece and the City-State System of Interactions

The classical Greek city-state system provides one of the antecedents for the new Westphalian order. The Greeks, organized in independent city-states, were at the height of their power in 400 B.C. and engaged in classic power politics, as cataloged by Thucydides in *History of the Peloponnesian War*. As the militaries of the great city-states struggled, states carried on economic relations and trade with each other to an unprecedented degree. This environment clearly fostered the flowering of the strong philosophical tradition of Plato and Aristotle that we studied in Chapter 1. In this setting, city-states—each an independent unit—conducted peaceful relations with each other as they vied for power—a precursor of the modern state system.

Rome: Governing of an Empire

Many of the Greek city-states were eventually incorporated into the Roman Empire (50 B.C.–400 A.D.). The Roman Empire served as the precursor for larger political systems. Its leaders imposed order and unity by force on a large geographic expanse—covering much of Europe, the

Greece, c. 450 B.C.

Mediterranean portions of Asia, the Middle East, and northern Africa. Having conquered far-flung and diverse peoples, the Roman leaders were preoccupied with keeping the various units—tribes, kingdoms, and states—within their sphere of influence and ensuring that the fluid borders of the empire remained secure from the roving hordes to the north and east. Indeed, from the Roman experience comes the word *empire* itself, from the Latin *imperium*. The leaders imposed various forms of government, from Roman proconsuls to local bureaucrats and administrators, disseminating the Latin language to the far reaches of the empire. They

The Roman Empire, c. 117 A.D.

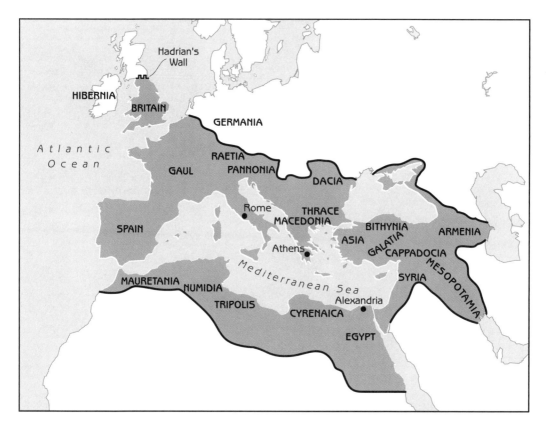

followed the practice of granting Roman citizenship to free peoples in the far-flung empire, while at the same time giving local rulers considerable autonomy to organize their own domain.

Roman philosophers provide an essential theoretical underpinning to the empire, as well as to future international relations theory. In particular, Marcus Tullius Cicero (106–43 B.C.) offered a mechanism for the uniting of the various parts of the empire. He proposed that men ought to be united by a law among nations applicable to humanity as a whole. But such a law among nations did not preclude Cicero's offering more practical advice to Rome's leaders: he emphasized the necessity of maintaining state security by expanding resources and boundaries, while at the same time ensuring domestic stability.[1] Above all, the Roman Empire itself and the writers it spawned provided the foundation for a larger geographic entity whose members, while retaining local identities, were united through the universalization of power.

The Middle Ages: Centralization and Decentralization

When the Roman Empire disintegrated in the fifth century A.D., power and authority became decentralized in Europe, but other forms of interaction flourished—travel, commerce, and communication, not just among the elites but also among merchant groups and ordinary citizens. By 1000 A.D. three civilizations had emerged from the rubble of Rome. First among them was the Arabic civilization, which had the largest geographic expanse, stretching from the Middle East and Persia through North Africa to the Iberian peninsula. United under the religious and political domination of the Islamic Caliphate, the Arabic language, and advanced mathematical and technical accomplishments, the Arabic civilization was a potent force. Second was the Byzantine Empire, located nearer the core of the old Roman Empire in Constantinople and united by Christianity. Third was the rest of Europe, where with the demise of the Roman Empire, central authority was absent, languages and cultures proliferated, and the networks of communication and transportation developed by the Romans were disintegrating.

Much of western Europe reverted to feudal principalities, controlled by lords and tied to fiefdoms that had the authority to raise taxes and exert legal authority. Lords exercised control over vassals, who worked for the lords in return for the right to work the land and acquire protection. Feudalism, which placed authority in private hands, was the response to the prevailing disorder. Power and authority were located at different overlapping levels.

The preeminent institution in the medieval period was the church; virtually all other institutions were local in origin and practice. Thus, authority was centered either in Rome (and in its agents, the bishops, dispersed throughout medieval Europe) or in the local fiefdom. Yet even the bishops seized considerable independent authority despite their overarching allegiance to the church. Economic life was also intensely local.

In the late eighth century, the church's monopoly on power was challenged by Carolus Magnus, or Charlemagne (742–814), the leader of the Franks in what is today France. Charlemagne was granted authority to unite western Europe in the name of Christianity against the Byzantine Empire in the east; the pope made him emperor of the Holy Roman

The Three Empires of the Early Middle Ages

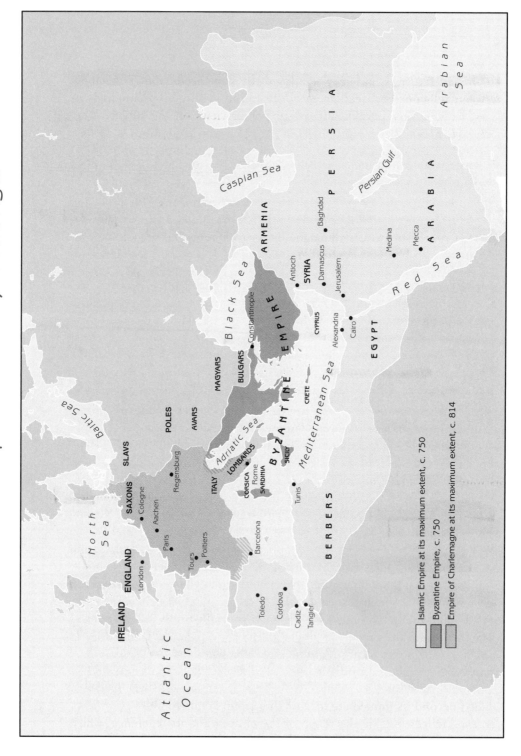

IRELAND

ENGLAND
London •

North
Sea

Atlantic
Ocean

SAXONS
Cologne •
• Aachen
Paris •
Tours •
• Poitiers

SLAVS

POLES

AVARS

Regensburg •

ITALY

LOMBARDS

CORSICA
SARDINIA
Rome •

Baltic Sea

MAGYARS

BULGARS

Constantinople •

Black Sea

Adriatic Sea

BYZANTINE EMPIRE

SICILY

CRETE

Mediterranean Sea

Tunis •

BERBERS

Barcelona •

Toledo •
Cordova •
Cadiz •
Tangier •

Caspian Sea

ARMENIA

Antioch •
SYRIA
Damascus • Baghdad •
Jerusalem •

CYPRUS

Alexandria •
Cairo •

EGYPT

Red Sea

PERSIA

Persian Gulf

Medina •

Mecca •

ARABIA

Arabian
Sea

Islamic Empire at its maximum extent, c. 750

Byzantine Empire, c. 750

Empire of Charlemagne at its maximum extent, c. 814

Empire. In return, Charlemagne offered the pope protection. The debate between religious and secular authority would continue for hundreds of years, with writers' periodically offering their views on the subject. One such writer was Dante Alighieri (1265–1321), who argued in *De Monarchia* that there should be a strict separation of the church from political life.[2] This question was not resolved until three hundred years later at the Treaty of Westphalia.

The Holy Roman Empire itself was a weak secular institution; as one famous saying goes, it was not very holy, very Roman, or much of an empire. Yet successors to Charlemagne did provide a limited secular alternative to the church. The contradictions remained, however: the desire on the part of the church for universalism versus the medieval reality of small, fragmented, diverse authorities. These small units, largely unconnected to each other, with dispersed populations, all served to prevent the establishment of centralized governmental authority.

The Late Middle Ages: Developing Transnational Networks

Although the intellectual debate was not resolved, after 1000 A.D. secular trends began to undermine both the decentralization of feudalism and the universalization of Christianity. Commercial activity expanded into larger geographic areas, as merchants traded along increasingly safer transportation routes. All forms of communication improved. New technology, such as water mills and windmills, not only made daily life easier but also provided the first elementary infrastructure to support agrarian economies. Municipalities, like the reinvigorated city-states of northern Italy—Genoa, Venice, Milan, Florence—established trading relationships, meeting at key locations, arranging for the shipment of commercial materials, and even agreeing to follow certain diplomatic practices to facilitate commercial activities. These diplomatic practices—establishing embassies with permanent staff, sending special consuls to handle commercial disputes, and sending diplomatic messages through specially protected channels— were the immediate precursors of contemporary diplomatic practice.

These economic and technological changes led to fundamental changes in social relations. First, a new group of individuals emerged—a transnational business community—whose interests and livelihoods extended beyond its immediate locale. This group acquired more cosmopolitan experiences outside the realm of the church and its teachings, which had so thoroughly dominated education up to this point. The individual

Europe, c. 1360

members developed new interests in art, philosophy, and history, acquiring considerable economic wealth along the way. They believed in themselves, becoming the individualists and humanists of the Renaissance. Second, writers and other individuals rediscovered classical literature and history, finding sustenance and revelation in Greek and Roman thought.

The Italian philosopher Niccolo Machiavelli (1469–1527), more than any other writer, illustrates the changes taking place and the ensuing gulf between the medieval world of the church and secular institutions. In *The Prince* Machiavelli elucidated the qualities that a leader needs to maintain the strength and security of the state. Realizing that the dream of unity in Christianity was unattainable (and probably undesirable), Machiavelli called on leaders to articulate their own political interests. Having no universal morality to guide them, leaders must act in the state's interest, answerable to no moral rules. The cleavage between the religiousness of medieval times and the humanism of the later Renaissance was thus starkly drawn.[3]

The desire to expand economic intercourse even further, coupled with the technological inventions that made ocean exploration safer, fueled a period of European territorial expansion. Individuals from Spain and Italy were among the earliest of these adventurers— Christopher Columbus sailing to the New World in 1492, Hernán Córtes to Mexico in 1519, Francisco Pizarro to the Andes in 1533. During this age of exploration European civilization spread to distant shores. For some theorists, it is these events—the gradual incorporation of the underdeveloped peripheral areas into the world capitalist economy and the international capitalist system—that mark the beginning of history relevant for contemporary international relations.

In the 1500s and 1600s, as explorers and even settlers moved into the New World, the old Europe remained unsettled. In some key locales such as France, England, and Aragon and Castile in Spain, feudalism was replaced by an increasingly centralized monarchy. The move toward centralization did not go uncontested; the masses, angered by taxes imposed by newly emerging states, rebelled and rioted. New monarchs needed the tax funds to build armies; they used their armies to consolidate their power internally and conquer more territory. Other parts of Europe were mired in the secular-versus-religious controversy, and Christianity itself was torn by the Catholic and Protestant split. In 1648, that controversy inched its way toward resolution.

IN FOCUS

KEY DEVELOPMENTS BEFORE 1648

▶ The Greek city-states are sovereignties at the height of their power in 400 B.C.; they carry out cooperative functions through diplomacy and classic power politics.

▶ The Roman Empire (50 B.C.–400 A.D.) originates imperialism, develops the practice of expanding territorial reach. The empire is united through law and language, while allowing some local identity.

▶ The Middle Ages (400–1000) witness the centralization of religious authority in the church, with decentralization in political and economic life.

▶ The Late Middle Ages (1000–1500) foster the development of transnational networks during the age of exploration.

THE EMERGENCE OF THE WESTPHALIAN SYSTEM

The formulation of **sovereignty**—a core concept in contemporary international relations—was one of the most important intellectual developments leading to the Westphalian revolution. Much of the development of the notion is found in the writings of the French philosopher Jean Bodin (1530–96). To Bodin, sovereignty is the "absolute and perpetual power vested in a commonwealth."[4] It resides not in an individual but in a state; thus it is perpetual. Sovereignty is "the distinguishing mark of the sovereign that he cannot in any way be subject to the commands of another, for it is he who makes law for the subject, abrogates law already made, and amends obsolete law."[5]

Although absolute, sovereignty, according to Bodin, is not without limits. Leaders are limited by divine law or natural law: ". . . all the princes on earth are subject to the laws of God and of nature." They are also limited by the type of regime—"the constitutional laws of the realm"—be it a monarchy, an aristocracy, or a democracy. And last, leaders are limited by covenants, contracts with promises to the people within the commonwealth, and treaties with other states. There is no supreme arbiter in relations among states.[6] Thus, Bodin provided the conceptual glue of sovereignty that would emerge with the Westphalian agreement.

The Thirty Years War (1618–48) devastated Europe; the armies plundered the central European landscape, fought battles, and survived by ravaging the civilian population. But the treaty that ended the conflict had a profound impact on the practice of international relations. First, the **Treaty of Westphalia** embraced the notion of sovereignty. With one stroke, virtually all the small states in central Europe attained sovereignty. The Holy Roman emperor was dead. Monarchs in the west realized that religious conflicts had to be stopped, so they agreed not to fight on behalf of either Catholicism or Protestantism. Instead, the monarch gained the authority to choose the version of Christianity for his or her people. This meant that monarchs, and not the church, had religious authority over their populations. This development implied the general acceptance of sovereignty—that the sovereign enjoyed exclusive rights within a given territory. With the power of the pope and the emperor stripped, the notion of the territorial state was accepted.

IN FOCUS

KEY DEVELOPMENTS AFTER WESTPHALIA

▶ Notion and practice of sovereignty develops.
▶ Centralized control of institutions under military grows.
▶ Capitalist economic system emerges.

Europe, c. 1648

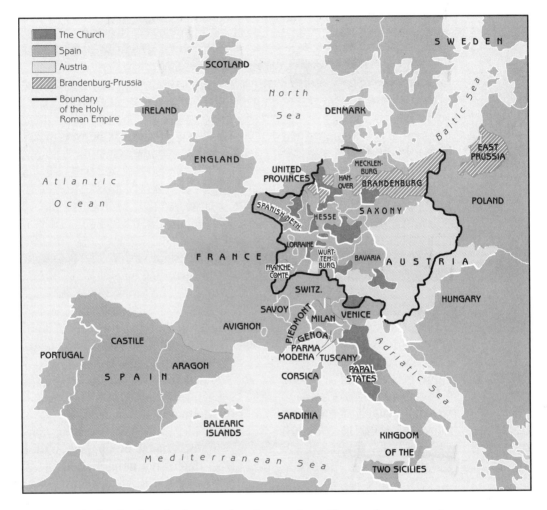

Second, the leaders had seen the devastating effects of mercenaries fighting wars. Thus, after the Treaty of Westphalia, the leaders sought to establish their own permanent national militaries. The growth of such forces led to increasingly centralized control, as the state had to collect taxes to pay for these militaries and the leaders assumed absolute control over the troops. The state with a national army emerged, its sovereignty acknowledged, and its secular base firmly established. And that state became increasingly more powerful. Larger territorial units gained an advantage as armaments became more sophisticated.

Third, the Treaty of Westphalia established a core group of states that dominated the world until the beginning of the nineteenth century: Austria, Russia, Prussia, England, France, and the United Provinces (the area now comprising the Netherlands and Belgium). Those in the west—England, France, and the United Provinces—underwent an economic revival under the aegis of capitalism, while those in the east—Prussia and Russia— reverted to feudal practices. In the west, private enterprise was encouraged. States improved infrastructure to facilitate commerce, and great trading companies and banks emerged. In contrast, in the east, serfs remained on the land and economic change was stifled. Yet in both regions, absolutist states dominated: Louis XIV of France (1638–1715), Peter the Great of Russia (1672–1725), and Frederick II of Prussia (1712–86). Until the end of the eighteenth century, European politics was dominated by multiple rivalries and shifting alliances. These rivalries were also played out in regions beyond Europe, where contending European states vied for power, most notably Great Britain and France in North America.

The most important theorist of the time was the Scottish economist Adam Smith (1723–90). In *An Inquiry into the Nature and Causes of the Wealth of Nations,* Smith argued that the notion of a market should apply to all social orders. Individuals—laborers, owners, investors, consumers— should be permitted to pursue their own interests, unfettered by state regulation. According to Smith, each individual acts rationally to maximize his or her own interests. With groups of individuals pursuing self-interests, economic efficiency is enhanced and more goods and services are produced and consumed. At the aggregate level, the wealth of the state and that of the international system are similarly enhanced. What makes the system work is the so-called invisible hand of the market; when individuals pursue their rational self-interests, the system (the market) operates effortlessly.[7] Smith's explication of how competing units enable capitalism to work to ensure economic vitality has had a profound effect on states' economic policies and political choices, which we shall explore in Chapter 8. But other ideas of the period would also dramatically alter governance in the nineteenth and twentieth centuries.

EUROPE IN THE NINETEENTH CENTURY

Two revolutions ushered in the nineteenth century—the American Revolution (1776) against British rule and the French Revolution (1789) against absolutist rule. Each revolution was the product of Enlightenment thinking as well as social contract theorists. During the Enlightenment, thinkers began to see individuals as rational, capable of understanding the laws governing them and of working to improve their condition in society.

The Aftermath of Revolution: Core Principles

Two core principles emerged in the aftermath of the American and French Revolutions. The first is that absolutist rule is subject to limits imposed by man. In *Two Treatises on Government*, the English philosopher John Locke (1632–1704) attacks absolute power and the notion of the divine right of kings. Locke argues that the state is a beneficial institution created by rational men in order to protect both their natural rights (life, liberty, and property) and their self-interests. Men freely enter into this arrangement. They agree to establish government to ensure natural rights for all. The crux of Locke's argument is that political power ultimately rests with the people, rather than with the leader or the monarch. The monarch derives his legitimacy from the consent of the governed.[8]

The second core principle that emerged at this time is that nationalism, wherein the masses identify with their common past, their language, customs, and practices, is a natural outgrowth of the state. Nationalism leads people to participate actively in the political process. For example, during the French Revolution, a patriotic appeal was made to the masses to defend the nation and its new ideals. This appeal forged an emotional link between the masses and the state. These two principles—legitimacy and nationalism—rose out of the American and French Revolutions to provide the foundation for politics in the nineteenth and twentieth centuries.

Peace at the Core of the European System

Following the defeat of Napoleon in 1815 and the establishment of peace by the Congress of Vienna, the five powers of Europe—Austria, Britain, France, Prussia, and Russia—ushered in a period of relative peace in the international political system, the so-called Concert of Europe. No major wars among these great powers were fought after the demise of Napoleon until the Crimean War in 1854, and in that war both Austria and Prussia remained neutral. Other local wars of brief duration were fought in which some of the five major powers remained neutral. Held together by a series of ad hoc conferences, all five powers were never involved in conflict simultaneously.

Europe, c. 1815

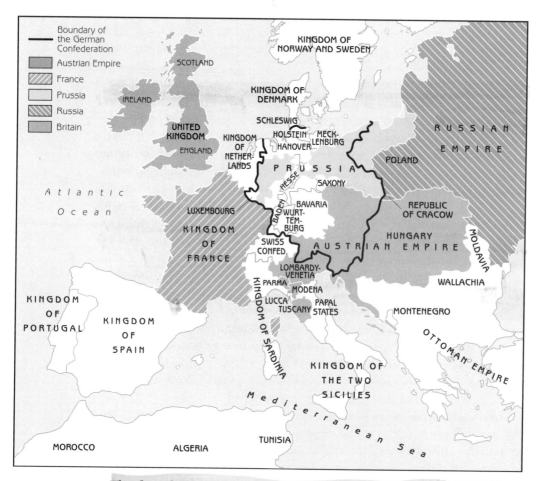

The fact that general peace prevailed during this time is surprising, since major economic, technological, and political changes were radically altering the landscape. The population growth rate soared and commerce surged as transportation corridors were strengthened. Political changes were dramatic: Italy was unified in 1870; Germany was formed out of thirty-nine different fragments in 1871; Holland was divided into the Netherlands and Belgium in the 1830s; and the Ottoman Empire gradually disintegrated, leading to independence for Greece in 1829 and for Moldavia and Wallachia (Romania) in 1856. With such dramatic changes under way, what factors explain the peace? At least three factors explain this phenomenon.

First, the European states enjoyed a solidarity among themselves, based on their being European, Christian, "civilized," and white. These traits differentiated "them"—white Christian Europeans—from the "other"—the rest of the world. With their increasing contact with the colonial world, Europeans saw more than ever their commonalities, the uniqueness of being European. This was, in part, a return to the unity found in the Roman Empire and in Roman law, a secular form of medieval Christendom, and a larger Europe as envisioned in the writings of Kant and Rousseau. The Congress of Vienna and the Concert of Europe gave form to these beliefs.

Second, European elites were united in their fear of revolution from the masses. In fact, at the Congress of Vienna, the Austrian diplomat Klemens von Metternich (1773–1859), the architect of the Concert of Europe, believed that Europe could best be managed by returning it to the age of absolutism. Elites envisioned grand alliances that would bring European leaders together to fight revolution from below. In the first half of the century, these alliances were not altogether successful in their battle against mass uprisings. In the 1830s, Britain and France sided together against the three eastern powers (Prussia, Russia, and Austria), and in 1848, all five powers were confronted by the masses with demands for reform. But in the second half of the century, European leaders acted in concert, ensuring that mass revolutions did not move from state to state. In 1870, Napoleon III was isolated quickly for fear of a revolution that never occurred. Fear from below thus united European leaders, making interstate war less likely.

Third, two of the major issues confronting the core European states were internal ones: the unification of Germany and Italy. Both German and Italian unification had powerful proponents and opponents among the European powers. For example, Britain supported Italian unification, making possible Italy's annexation of Naples and Sicily; Austria, on the other hand, was preoccupied with the increasing strength of Prussia and thus did not actively oppose what may well have been against its national interest—the creation of two sizable neighbors out of myriad independent units. German unification was acceptable to Russia as long as its interest in Poland was respected, and German unification got support from the dominant middle class in Britain, as they viewed a stronger Germany as a potential counterbalance to France. Thus, although the unification of both were finally solidified through small local wars, a general war was averted until the rise of an even more powerful Germany in the twentieth century.

Industrialization, a critical development at the time, was a double-edged sword. In the second half of the nineteenth century, all attention was focused on the processes of industrialization. Great Britain was the leader, outstripping all rivals in the output of coal, iron, steel, and export of manufactured goods. In addition, Britain became the source of finance capital, the banker for the Continent and, in the twentieth century, for the world. Industrialization romped through virtually all areas of western Europe as the masses flocked to the cities and entrepreneurs and middlemen scrambled for economic advantage.

This wave of imperialism began in the 1870s. The industrial revolution provided the European states with the military and economic capacity to engage in territorial expansion. Some imperial states were motivated by economic gains, as they sought new external markets for manufactured goods and obtained, in turn, raw materials to fuel their industrial growth. For others, the motivation was cultural and religious—to spread the Christian faith and the ways of white "civilization" to the "dark" continents and beyond. To still others, the motivation was political. Since the European balance of power prevented direct confrontation in Europe, European state rivalries were played out in Africa and Asia. At the Congress of Berlin in 1884–85, the Europeans divided Africa, hoping to appease Germany's Bismarck by satisfying his imperial ambitions and to prevent direct competition among themselves.

By the end of the nineteenth century, 85 percent of Africa was under the control of European states. In Asia, only Japan and Siam (Thailand) were not under direct European or U.S. control. China had been carved into spheres of influence. And the United States was an imperial power, having won the 1898 Spanish-American War, pushing the Spanish out of the Philippines, Puerto Rico, Cuba, and other small islands. By 1914, Europeans controlled four-fifths of the world.

The struggle for economic prowess led to heedless exploitation of the colonial areas, particularly in Africa and Asia. But the five European powers did not fight major wars directly against each other. By the end of the century, however, this economic competition became destabilizing, as European states coalesced into two competing alliance systems.

Balance of Power

How was this period of relative peace in Europe managed and preserved for so long? The answer lies in a concept called the **balance of power.** In the nineteenth century the *balance of power* meant that the independent

Europe, 1878

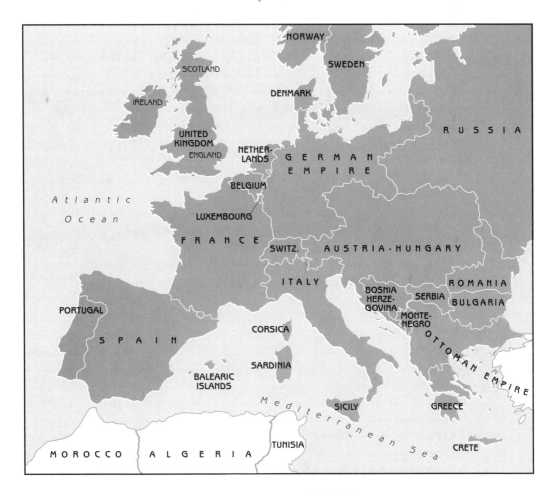

European states, each with relatively equal power, feared the emergence of any predominant state (**hegemon**) among them. Thus, they formed alliances to counteract any potentially more powerful faction—creating a balance of power. The treaties signed after 1815 were designed not only to quell revolution from below but to prevent the emergence of a hegemon, such as France under Napoleon had become. Britain and Russia, at least later in the century, could have assumed a dominant leadership position—Britain because of its economic prowess and naval capability, and Russia because of its relative geographic isolation and extraordinary manpower—but neither sought to exert hegemonic power.

Britain and Russia did play different roles in the balance of power. Britain most often played the role of balancer. For example, by intervening on behalf of the Greeks in their independence from the Turks in the late 1820s, on behalf of the Belgians during their war of independence against Holland in 1830, on behalf of Turkey against Russia in the Crimean War in 1854–56 and again in the Russo-Turkish war in 1877–78, Britain ensured that other states did not interfere and that Europe remained balanced. Russia's role was as a builder of alliances. The Holy Alliance of 1815 kept Austria, Prussia, and Russia united against revolutionary France, and Russia used its claim on Poland to build a bond with Prussia. Russian interests in the Dardanelles, the strategic waterway linking the Mediterranean Sea and the Black Sea, and in Constantinople (today's Istanbul) overlapped with those of Britain. Thus, these two states, located at the margins of Europe, played key roles in making the balance-of-power system work.

During the last three decades of the nineteenth century, the Concert of Europe frayed, beginning with the Russian invasion of Turkey in 1877. Alliances began to solidify. Outside of the core European region, conflict escalated. All the Central and South American states had won their independence from Spain and Portugal by 1830, and the United States and Great Britain prevented further European competition in South America. But the European colonial powers—Britain, France, Holland, Belgium, and Italy—fought wars to conquer and retain their colonies in Africa and Asia. And the United States, competing against Japan, among others, acquired its own colonial empire, gaining Cuba, the Philippines, Guam, and Puerto Rico as a result of the Spanish-American War of 1898.

In Europe, German ambitions for new territories, and its chancellor Otto von Bismarck's desire for increased prestige, could not be fulfilled in an already crowded Europe without upsetting the precarious balance of power. To satisfy Germany's ambitions, the major powers during the Congress of Berlin in 1885 divvied

IN FOCUS

KEY DEVELOPMENTS IN NINETEENTH-CENTURY EUROPE

▶ From revolutions emerge two concepts: absolutist rule subject to limitations, and nationalism.
▶ Peace is at the core of a system managed by the balance of power. Elites are united in fear of the masses, and domestic concerns are more important than foreign policy.
▶ European imperialism in Asia and Africa helps to maintain the European balance of power.
▶ The balance of power breaks down due to solidification of alliances, resulting in World War I.

up Africa, giving Germany a sphere of influence in East Africa (Tanganyika), West Africa (Cameroon and Togo), and southern Africa (South-West Africa). European imperialism provided a convenient outlet for Germany's aspirations as a unified power without endangering the delicate balance of power within Europe itself.

Thus was peace preserved in Europe during the nineteenth century. The only ideological preference exhibited by the major powers was the shared one of thwarting revolution from below. United by European characteristics and by the imperial enterprise, and fearful of any one country gaining the upper hand, nineteenth-century Europe is viewed as a classic balance-of-power system.

The Breakdown: Solidification of Alliances

By the waning years of the nineteenth century, that balance-of-power system had weakened. Whereas previously alliances had been fluid and flexible, with allies changeable, now alliances had solidified. Two camps emerged: the Triple Alliance (Germany, Austria, and Italy) in 1882, and the Dual Alliance (France and Russia) in 1893. In 1902, Britain broke from the "balancer" role, joining in a naval alliance with Japan to prevent a Russo-Japanese rapprochement in China. This alliance marked a significant turn: for the first time, a European state (Great Britain) turned to an Asian one (Japan) in order to thwart a European ally (Russia). And in 1904, Britain joined with France in the Entente Cordiale.

The end of the balance-of-power system, as well as the historic end of the nineteenth century, came with World War I. The two sides were enmeshed in a struggle between competitive alliances, made all the more dangerous by the German position. Germany had not been satisfied with the solutions meted out at the Congress of Berlin in 1885. They still sought additional territory; if that meant European territory, then the map of Europe would have to be redrawn. Being a "latecomer" to the core of European power, Germany did not receive the diplomatic recognition and status its leaders desired. Thus, with the assassination of Archduke Franz Ferdinand, the heir to the throne of the Austro-Hungarian Empire, in 1914 in Sarajevo, Germany encouraged Austria to crush Serbia. After all, Germany did not want to see the disintegration of the Austro-Hungarian Empire, its major ally.

Under the system of alliances, once the fateful shot had been fired, states honored their commitments to their allies, sinking the whole continent in warfare. Through support for Serbia, the unlikely allies of Russia, France, and Great Britain became involved; through Austria-Hungary, Germany

Europe, 1914

entered the fray. It was anticipated that the war would be short and decisive, but it was neither. Between 1914 and 1918, soldiers from more than a dozen countries endured the persistent degradation of trench warfare and the horrors of gas warfare. More than 8.5 million soldiers and 1.5 million civilians lost their lives. Symbolically, the nineteenth century had come to a close: the century of relative peacefulness ended in a systemwide confrontation.

THE INTERWAR YEARS AND WORLD WAR II

The end of World War I denotes critical changes in international relations. First, three European empires were strained and finally died during or near the end of World War I. With those empires went the conservative social order of Europe; emerging in its place was a proliferation of nationalisms. Russia exited the war in 1917, as revolution raged within its territory. The czar was overthrown and eventually replaced by not only a new leader (Vladimir I. Lenin) but a new ideology that would have profound implications for the rest of the twentieth century. Second to disintegrate was the Austro-Hungarian Empire, replaced by Austria, Hungary, Czechoslovakia, part of Yugoslavia, and part of Romania. Third to be reconfigured was the Ottoman Empire. The Ottomans, who had been allied with the Triple Alliance powers, were ousted from Europe.

The end of the empires produced proliferating nationalisms. In fact, one of President Woodrow Wilson's Fourteen Points in the treaty ending World War I called for self-determination, the right of national groups to self-rule. The nationalism of these various groups (Austrians, Hungarians) had been stimulated by technological innovations in the printing industry, which made it easy and cheap to publish material in the multitude of different European languages, and so offer differing interpretations of history and national life. Yet in reality, many of these newly created entities had neither shared histories nor compatible political histories, nor were they economically viable.

Second, Germany emerged out of World War I an even more dissatisfied power. Not only had Germany been defeated on the military battlefield and its territorial ambitions been thwarted, the Treaty of Versailles, which formally ended the war, made the subsequent generation of Germans pay the economic cost of the war through reparations—$32 billion for wartime damages. This dissatisfaction provided the climate for the emergence of Adolf Hitler, dedicated to righting the wrongs that had been imposed on the German people.

Third, enforcement of the Versailles Treaty was given to the League of Nations, the intergovernmental organization designed to prevent all future wars. But the organization itself did not have the political weight, the legal instruments, or the legitimacy to carry out the task. The political weight of the League was weakened by the fact that the United States, whose president had been the principal architect of the League, itself refused to join, retreating instead to a unilateralist foreign policy. Nor did Russia join, nor were any of the vanquished of the war permitted to participate. The League's legal authority was weak, and the instruments it had for enforcing the peace were ineffective.

Fourth, a vision of the post–World War I order had clearly been expounded, but it was a vision stillborn from the start. The first of Wilson's Fourteen Points called for open diplomacy—"open covenants of peace, openly arrived at, after which there shall be no private international un-

Europe, 1939

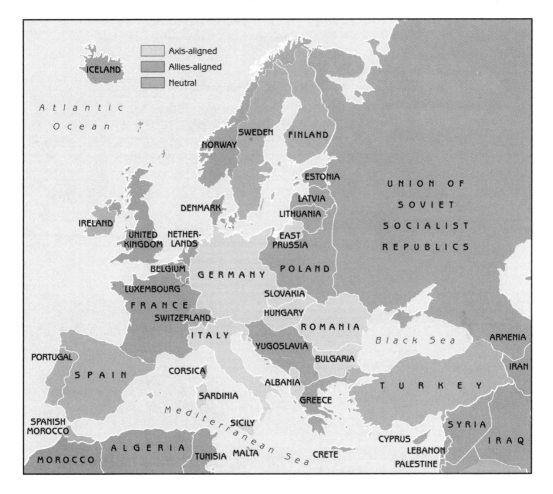

derstandings of any kind but diplomacy shall proceed always frankly and in public view."[9] Point three was a reaffirmation of economic liberalism, the removal of economic barriers among all the nations consenting to the peace. And, of course, the League, as a "general association of nations," was designed to ensure that war would never occur again. But that vision was not to be: "The characteristic feature of the twenty years between 1919 and 1939 was the abrupt descent from the visionary hopes of the first decade to the grim despair of the second, from a utopia which took little account of reality to a reality from which every element of utopia was rigorously excluded."[10] Liberalism and its utopian and idealist elements were to be replaced by realism—fundamentally divergent theoretical perspectives that are developed in Chapter 3.

And the world that the realists experienced was a turbulent one: a world economy in collapse; a German economy's imploding; the U.S. stock market's plummeting; Japan's marching into Manchuria in 1931 and into the rest of China in 1937; Italy's overrunning Ethiopia in 1935; fascism, liberalism, and communism's clashing. These were the symptoms of the interwar period.

Germany proved to be the real challenge. Having been rearmed under Hitler in the 1930s, buoyed by helping the Spanish fascists during the Spanish Civil War, and having been successful in reuniting ethnic Germans from far-flung territories, Germany was ready to right the "wrongs" imposed by the Treaty of Versailles. For various reasons, Britain and France acquiesced to Germany's resurgence. Britain agreed in 1938 to let Germany occupy Czechoslovakia, in the hope of averting more general war. But this was an idle hope. German fascism uniquely mobilized the masses in support of the state. It drew on the belief that war and conflict were noble activities, from which ultimately superior civilizations would be formed. It drew strength from the belief that certain racial groups were superior, others inferior, and mobilized the disenchanted and the economically weak on behalf of its cause.

The power of fascism—German, Italian, and Japanese versions—led to the uneasy (unholy) alliance between the communist Soviet Union and the liberal United States, Great Britain, and France, among others. That alliance was intended to check the Axis powers, by force if necessary. Thus, when World War II broke out, those fighting against the Axis acted in unison, regardless of ideological divergence.

The allies were successful. Both the German Reich and imperial Japan lay in ruins, the former by traditional firepower and the latter by the new

IN FOCUS

KEY DEVELOPMENTS IN THE INTERWAR YEARS

▶ Three empires are weakened: Russia by revolution, the Austro-Hungarian Empire by dismemberment, and the Ottoman Empire by external wars and internal turmoil. This leads to a resurgence of nationalisms.

▶ German dissatisfaction with the World War I settlement leads to fascism. Germany finds allies in Italy and Japan.

▶ A weak League of Nations is unable to respond to Japanese, Italian, and German aggression, nor does it respond to widespread economic unrest.

instrument of atomic warfare. The end of World War II meant a major redistribution of power (the victorious United States would now be pitted against the equally victorious Soviet Union) and changed political borders (the Soviet Union absorbed the Baltic states and portions of Finland, Czechoslovakia, Poland, and Romania; Germany and Korea were divided; and Japan was ousted from much of Asia). Each of these changes contributed to the new international conflict: the Cold War.

THE COLD WAR

The leaders of the "hot" World War II, Britain's prime minister Winston Churchill, the United States president Franklin Roosevelt, and the Soviet Union's premier Joseph Stalin planned during the war for the postwar order. Indeed, the Atlantic Charter of August 14, 1941, called for collaboration on economic issues and prepared for a permanent system of security. These plans were consolidated in 1943 and 1944 and came to fruition in the United Nations in 1945. Yet several other outcomes of World War II provided the foundation for the **Cold War** that followed.

Origins of the Cold War

The most important outcome of World War II was the emergence of two **superpowers**—the United States and the Soviet Union—as the primary actors in the international system, and the decline of Europe as the epicenter of international politics. Both the United States and the Soviet Union were reluctant powers. Neither had been anxious to fight; each entered the war only after a direct attack on its territory. But by the end of the war, each had become a military superpower.

The second outcome of the war was the recognition of fundamental incompatibilities between these two superpowers in both national interests and ideology. Differences surfaced immediately over geopolitical national interests. Russia, having been invaded from the west on several occasions, including during World War II, used its newfound power to solidify its sphere of influence in the buffer states of Eastern Europe—Poland, Czechoslovakia, Hungary, Bulgaria, and Romania. The Soviet leadership believed that ensuring friendly neighbors on its western borders was vital to Soviet national interests. As for the United States, as early as 1947, U.S. policymakers argued that U.S. interests lay in containing the Soviet Union. The diplomat and historian George Kennan published in *Foreign Affairs*

Europe during the Cold War

the famous "X" article, in which he argued that because the Soviet Union would always feel military insecurity, it would conduct an aggressive foreign policy. Containing the Soviets, Kennan therefore wrote, should become the cornerstone of the United States's postwar foreign policy.[11]

The United States put the notion of **containment** into action in the Truman Doctrine of 1947. Justifying material support in Greece against the communists, President Truman asserted, "I believe that it must be the policy of the United States to support free peoples who are resisting attempted subjugation by armed minorities or by outside pressures. I believe that we must assist free peoples to work out their own destinies in their own way."[12] But almost immediately, the United States retreated from containment, drastically reducing the size of its armed forces in hopes of returning to a more peaceful world. Then in 1948, when the Soviets blocked Western transportation corridors to Berlin, the German capital divided by the Cold War, the United States realized that its interests were broader. Thus, containment, based on U.S. geostrategic interests, became the fundamental doctrine of U.S. foreign policy during the Cold War.

The United States and the Soviet Union also had major ideological differences. These differences pitted two contrasting visions of society and of the international order. The United States's democratic liberalism was based on a social system that accepted the worth and value of the individual, a political system that depended on the participation of individuals in the electoral process, and an economic system, **capitalism,** that provided opportunities to individuals to pursue what was economically rational with little or no government interference. At the international level, this logically translated into support for other democratic liberal regimes and support of capitalist institutions and processes, including, most critically, free trade.

Soviet communist ideology also affected that country's conception of the international system and state practices. The Soviet state embraced Marxist ideology, which held that one class (the bourgeoisie) controls the ownership of the means of production and uses its institutions and authority to maintain that control. The solution to the problem of class rule, according to Marxism, is revolution, wherein the exploited proletariat takes control from the bourgeoisie by using the state to seize the means of production. Thus, capitalism is replaced by **socialism.** The leaders of the Soviet Union saw themselves in an interim period—after the demise of the capitalist state and before the victory of socialism. This ideology had critical international elements, as well: capitalism will try to extend itself through imperialism in order to generate more capital, larger markets, and greater control over raw materials. Soviet leaders thus felt themselves surrounded by a hostile capitalist camp and argued that the Soviet Union "must not weaken but must in every way strengthen its state, the state organs, the organs of the intelligence service, the army, if that country does not want to be smashed by the capitalist environment."[13] Internationally, they believed, it must support movements whose goals are both to undermine the capitalists and to promote a new social order.

Differences between the two superpowers were exacerbated by mutual misperceptions. Kennan cites powerful examples of misperceptions on the part of each superpower:

The Marshall Plan, the preparations for the setting up of a West German government, and the first moves toward the establishment of NATO [the North

Atlantic Treaty Organization] were taken in Moscow as the beginnings of a campaign to deprive the Soviet Union of the fruits of its victory over Germany. The Soviet crackdown on Czechoslovakia [1948] and the mounting of the Berlin blockade, both essentially defensive ... reactions to these Western moves, were then similarly misread on the Western side. Shortly thereafter there came the crisis of the Korean War, where the Soviet attempt to employ a satellite military force in civil combat to its own advantage, by way of reaction to the American decision to establish a permanent military presence in Japan, was read in Washington as the beginning of the final Soviet push for world conquest; whereas the active American military response, provoked by this move, appeared in Moscow ... as a threat to the Soviet position in both Manchuria and in eastern Siberia.[14]

While such misperceptions did not cause the Cold War, they certainly added fuel to the confrontation.

The third outcome of the end of World War II was the beginning of the end of the colonial system, a development which few predicted. The defeat of Japan and Germany led to the immediate end of their respective imperial empires. For the other colonialists, spurred by the U.N. Charter's endorsement of the principle of national self-determination, faced with the reality of their economically and politically weakened position, and confronted with indigenous movements for independence, the European states granted independence to their former colonies, beginning with Indian independence from Great Britain in 1947. For France, it took military defeat in Indochina in the early 1950s to bring decolonialization in that part of the world. African states, too, became independent between 1957 and 1963. While the process of decolonialization occurred over an extended time period, it was a relatively peaceful transition. The Europeans, together with their U.S. ally, were more interested in fighting communism than in retaining control of their colonial territories.

The fourth outcome was the realization that the differences would be played out indirectly, on third-party stages, rather than through direct confrontation between the two protagonists. As the number of newly independent states proliferated in the postwar world as the result of decolonization, the superpowers vied for influence with these new states as the way to project power to areas outside of their traditional spheres of influence. Thus, the Cold War resulted in the globalization of conflict to all continents. International relations became truly global.

Other parts of the world did not just react to Cold War imperatives. They developed new ideologies or recast the dominant discourse of Europe in ways that addressed their own experiences. Nowhere was this more true than in Asia. Both Ho Chi Minh of Vietnam and Chou En-lai of China had lived in Europe, where they joined Communist parties. Returning home, they imported communist ideology, reinterpreting it in ways compatible with their national circumstances. For example, in China, the beginning of the communist revolution predated World War II. Taking to the countryside to build a revolution of agrarian peasants, Chou En-lai and his colleague Mao Zedong insisted that China was a semifeudal society in which the proletariat was the rural peasantry. The Chinese Communist party became the vanguard of his group and the People's Army its instrument for guerrilla action. Mao's revolution was successful: the communists took control of mainland China in 1949 and established the People's Republic of China.

IN FOCUS

KEY DEVELOPMENTS IN THE COLD WAR

▶ Two superpowers emerged—the United States and the Soviet Union. They were divided by national interests, ideologies, and mutual misperceptions. These divisions were projected into different geographic areas.

▶ The Cold War produced a series of crises—Berlin (1948–49), Korean War (1950–53), Cuban missile crisis (1962), Vietnam (1965–73), Afghanistan (1979).

▶ The Cold War was a long peace sustained by mutual deterrence.

The globalization of post–World War II politics thus meant the rise of new contenders to power. Although the United States and the Soviet Union retained their dominant positions, new alternative ideologies acted as powerful magnets for populations in the independent and developing states of Africa, Asia, and Latin America. Later in the 1970s, these countries developed a new economic ideology, summarized in the program of the New International Economic Order.

The Cold War as a Series of Confrontations

The Cold War itself (1945–89) can be characterized as forty-five years of overall high-level tension and competition between the superpowers but with no direct military conflict. The advent of nuclear weapons created a bipolar stalemate, in which each side acted cautiously, only once coming close to the precipice of war. Each state backed down from particular confrontations, either because its national interest was not sufficiently strong to risk a nuclear confrontation or because its ideological resolve wavered in light of military realities.

The Cold War, then, was a series of events that directly or indirectly pitted the superpowers against each other. Some of those events were confrontations just short of war, while others were confrontations between proxies (North Korea vs. South Korea, North Vietnam vs. South Vietnam, Ethiopia vs. Somalia) that, in all likelihood, neither the United States nor the Soviet Union had intended to escalate further. Still other confrontations were fought over words; these usually ended in treaties and agreements. Some of these confrontations involved only the United States and the Soviet Union, but more often than not, the allies of each became involved. Thus, the Cold War comprised not only superpower confrontations but confrontations between two blocs of states: the United States, with Canada, Australia, and much of Western Europe (allied in the **North Atlantic Treaty Organization,** or NATO); and the Soviet Union, with its **Warsaw Pact** allies in Eastern Europe. Over the life of the Cold War, these blocs loosened, and states sometimes took positions different from that of the dominant power. But for much of the time period, bloc politics was operative. Table 2.1 shows a time line of major events during the Cold War.

One of those high-level, direct confrontations between the superpowers took place in Germany. Germany had been divided immediately after World War II into zones of occupation. The United States, France, and Great Britain administered the western portion; the Soviet Union, the eastern. Berlin, Germany's capital, was similarly divided but lay within Soviet-controlled East Germany. In the 1949 Berlin blockade, the Soviet Union blocked land access to Berlin, prompting the United States and Britain to airlift supplies for thirteen months. In 1949 the separate states of West and East Germany were declared. In 1961 East Germany erected the Berlin Wall around the West German portion of the city in order to stem the tide of East Germans trying to leave the troubled state; U.S. president John F. Kennedy responded with "Ich bin ein Berliner," committing the United States to Berlin at any cost. Not surprisingly, it was the crumbling of that same wall in November 1989 that symbolized the end of the Cold War.

In Asia, Korea became the symbol of the Cold War. It, too, was divided geographically—between north and south—and ideologically—between communist and noncommunist states. The first Asian confrontation came in 1950 as communist North Korean troops, prodded by the Soviet military (hoping to improve its defensive position), marched into a weak South Korea. The Soviets never fought directly, but the United States (under the aegis of the United Nations) and the Chinese (acting on behalf of the

Year	Event
1945–48	Soviet Union establishes communist regimes in Eastern Europe.
1947	Announcement of Truman Doctrine; United States proposes Marshall Plan for the rebuilding of Europe.
1948	Tito separates Yugoslavia from the Soviet bloc.
1948–49	Soviets blockade Berlin; United States and allies carry out airlift.
1949	Soviets test atomic bomb, ending U.S. nuclear monopoly; Chinese communists under Mao win civil war, establish People's Republic of China; United States and Allies establish NATO.
1950–53	Korean War.
1953	Death of Stalin leads to internal Soviet succession crisis.
1956	Soviets invade Hungary; Nasser of Egypt nationalizes the Suez Canal, leading to confrontation with Great Britain, France, and Israel.
1957	Soviets launch Sputnik, symbolizing superpower scientific competition.
1960–63	Congo crisis and U.N. action to fill power vacuum.
1960	The United States's U-2 spy plane shot down over Soviet territory, leading to the breakup of the Paris summit meeting.
1961	Bay of Pigs invasion of Cuba, sponsored by the United States, fails; Berlin Wall constructed.
1962	United States and Soviet Union brought to the brink of nuclear war following the discovery of Soviet missiles in Cuba; eventually leads to thaw in superpower relations.
1965	United States begins large-scale intervention in Vietnam.

TABLE 2.1

Important Events during the Cold War

Soviet Union) did. The North Korean offensive was eventually repelled, and the two sides became mired in a three-year stalemate. The war finally ended in 1953. But as in Berlin and Germany, that one event was to be followed over the years by numerous diplomatic skirmishes over the basing of U.S. troops in South Korea, the use of the demilitarized zone between north and south, and North Korean attempts to become a nuclear power even after the end of the Cold War.

The 1962 Cuban missile crisis represents a high-profile direct confrontation between the superpowers in yet another area of the world. Originally devised by the Soviet Union to compensate for its lagging missile program, the Soviets took the bold move of installing missiles in Cuba, 90

Important Events during the Cold War (continued)

Year	Event
1967	Israel defeats Egypt, Syria, and Jordan in the Six-Day War; Glassboro summit signals detente, loosening of tensions between the superpowers.
1968	Czech government liberalization halted by Soviet invasion; Nuclear Nonproliferation Treaty (NPT) signed.
1972	Nixon visits China and Soviet Union; United States and Soviet Union sign SALT I arms limitation treaty.
1973	United States ends official military involvement in Vietnam; Arab-Israeli War leads to energy crisis.
1975	Proxy and anticolonial wars fought in Angola, Mozambique, Ethiopia, and Somalia.
1979	Shah of Iran, a U.S. ally, overthrown by Islamic revolution; United States and Soviet Union sign SALT II; Soviet Union invades Afghanistan; U.S. Senate does not ratify SALT II.
1981–89	Reagan Doctrine provides basis for U.S. support of "anticommunist" forces in Nicaragua and Afghanistan.
1983	United States invades Grenada.
1985	Gorbachev starts economic and political reforms in Soviet Union.
1989	Peaceful revolutions in Eastern Europe replace communist governments; Berlin Wall is dismantled.
1990	Germany reunified.
1991	Resignation of Gorbachev; Soviet Union collapses.
1992–93	Russia and other former Soviet republics become independent states.

miles from U.S. shores. Once the missiles were discovered through high-altitude flights by the U.S. Central Intelligence Agency, the Cubans and the Soviets claimed they were for defensive purposes only. The United States, however, saw the installation of the missiles as a direct threat to its territory: no weapons of a powerful enemy had ever been located so close to U.S. shores. The way in which the crisis was resolved suggests unequivocally that neither party sought a direct confrontation. The United States chose to blockade Cuba to prevent further Soviet shipments of missiles; importantly, it rejected as first options more coercive military alternatives—land invasion or air strikes—although those options were never entirely foreclosed. Through behind-the-scenes unofficial contacts in Washington and direct communication between President Kennedy and Soviet premier Nikita Khrushchev, the crisis was defused and war was averted.

Vietnam provided a test of a different kind. The Cold War was played out there not in one dramatic crisis but in an extended civil war, in which communist North Vietnam and its Chinese and Soviet allies were pitted against the "free world"—South Vietnam, allied with France, the United States, and assorted supporters including South Korea, the Philippines, and Thailand. To most U.S. policymakers in the late 1950s and early 1960s, Vietnam represented yet another test of the containment doctrine: communist influence must be stopped, they argued, before it spread like a chain of falling dominos through the rest of Southeast Asia and beyond (thus the term **domino effect**). Thus, the United States supported the South Vietnamese dictators Ngo Dinh Diem and Nguyen Van Thieu against the rival communist regime of Ho Chi Minh in the north, which was underwritten by both the People's Republic of China and the Soviet Union. But as the South Vietnamese government and military faltered on its own, the United States stepped up its military support, increasing the number of U.S. troops on the ground and escalating the air war over the north.

In the early stages the United States was fairly confident of victory; after all, a superpower with all its military hardware and technically skilled labor force could surely beat a poorly trained guerrilla force. Policymakers in the United States were quickly disillusioned, however, as U.S. casualties mounted and the U.S. public grew disenchanted. Should the United States use all of its conventional military capability to prevent the "fall" of South Vietnam and stave off the domino effect? Should the United States fight until victory was guaranteed for liberalism and capitalism? Or should it extricate itself from the unpopular quagmire? Should the United States capitulate to the forces of ideological communism? These questions, posed in both geostrategic and ideological terms, defined the middle years of the Cold War, from the Vietnam War's slow beginning in the late 1950s until the dramatic departure of U.S. officials from the South Vietnamese capital, Saigon, in 1975, symbolized by U.S. helicopters leaving the U.S. embassy with hordes of Vietnamese trying to grab on and escape with them.

The U.S. effort to avert a communist takeover in South Vietnam failed, yet contrary to expectations, the domino effect did not occur. Cold War alliances were shaken on both sides: the friendship between the Soviet Union and China had long before degenerated into a geostrategic fight and a struggle over the proper form of communism, especially in

Third World countries. But the Soviet Union was left relatively unscathed. The U.S.-led Western alliance was seriously jeopardized, as several U.S. allies (including Canada) strongly opposed U.S. policy toward Vietnam. The bipolar structure of the Cold War international system was shattered. Confidence in military alternatives was shaken in the United States, undermining for over a decade the United States's ability to commit itself militarily. The power of the United States was supposed to be righteous power, but in Vietnam there was neither victory nor righteousness.

Not always where one of the superpowers acted did the other side respond. In some cases, the other side chose not to act, or at least not to respond in kind, even though it could have escalated the conflict. For example, the Soviet Union invaded Hungary in 1956 and Czechoslovakia in 1968, both sovereign states and allies in the Warsaw Pact. The United States verbally condemned these aggressive actions by the Soviets, which under other circumstances may have been met with counterforce, but the actions themselves went unchecked. In 1956, the United States, preoccupied with the Suez Canal crisis, kept quiet, aware that it was ill prepared to respond militarily. In 1968, the United States was mired in Vietnam and beset by domestic turmoil and a presidential election. So, too, was the United States relatively complacent, although angry, when the Soviets invaded Afghanistan in 1979. The Soviets likewise kept quiet when the United States took aggressive action within its sphere of influence, invading Grenada in 1983 and Panama in 1989. Thus, during the Cold War, even blatantly aggressive actions by one of the superpowers did not always lead to a response by the other.

Many of the events of the Cold War involved the United States and the Soviet Union only indirectly; proxies fought in their place. Nowhere has this been as true as in the Middle East. For both the United States and the Soviet Union, the Middle East is a region of vital importance, because of its natural resources (including approximately one-third of the world's oil and more than one-half of the world's oil reserves), its strategic position as a transportation hub between Asia and Europe, and its cultural significance as the cradle of three of the world's major religions. Not surprisingly, since the establishment of Israel in 1948, recognized diplomatically first by the United States, the region has been the scene of superpower confrontation by proxy: between a U.S.-supported Israel and the Soviet-backed Arab states of Syria, Iraq, and Egypt. During the Six-Day War in 1967, Israel crushed the Soviet-equipped Arabs in six short days, seizing the strategic territories of the Golan Heights, Gaza, and the West Bank. In 1973 during the Yom Kippur War, the Israeli victory was

The Middle East, 2000

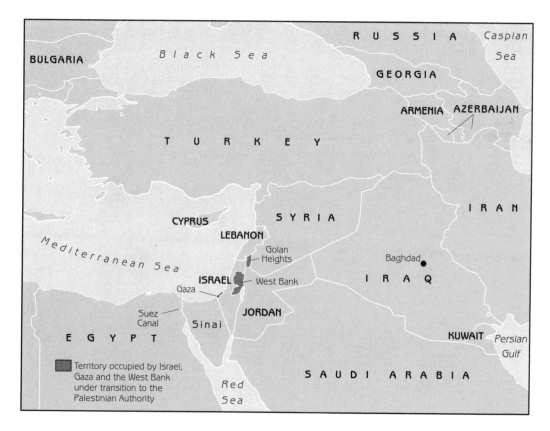

not as overwhelming, as the United States and the Soviets negotiated a cease-fire before more damage could be done. But throughout the Cold War, these "hot" wars were followed by guerrilla actions committed by all parties. As long as the basic balance of power was maintained between Israel (and the United States) on one side and the Arabs (and the Soviets) on the other, the region was left alone; when that balance was threatened, the superpowers acted through proxies to maintain the balance.

In parts of the world that are of less strategic importance, confrontation through proxies was even more the modus operandi during the Cold War. Events in Africa present numerous examples of this fact. When the colonialist Belgians abruptly left the Congo in 1960, a power vacuum arose. Civil war broke out, as various contending factions sought to take power and bring order out of the chaos. One of the contenders, the Congolese premier Patrice Lumumba (1925–61), appealed to the Soviets for help in fighting Western-backed insurgents and received both diplomatic support and military supplies. However, Lumumba was dismissed by the Congolese president, Joseph Kasavubu, an ally of the United States. Still others, such as Moise Tshombe, leader of the copper-rich Katanga province, who was also closely identified with Western interests, fought for control. The three-year civil war could have become another proxy war between the United States and the Soviet Union for influence in this emerging continent. However, the United Nations averted the proxy confrontation by sending in supposedly neutral peacekeepers, whose primary purpose was to fill the vacuum and prevent the superpowers from making the Congo yet another terrain of the Cold War.

In both Angola and the Horn of Africa (Ethiopia and Somalia), however, participants in civil wars were able to transform their struggles into Cold War confrontations by proxy, thereby gaining military equipment and technical expertise from one of the two superpowers. Such proxy warfare served the interests of the superpowers, permitting them to project power and support geostrategic interests (oil in Angola, transportation routes around the Horn) and ideologies without directly confronting each other.

The Cold War was also fought and moderated in words, at **summits** (meetings between leaders) and in treaties. Some Cold War summits were relatively successful: the 1967 Glassboro summit (between U.S. and Soviet leaders) began the loosening of tensions known as **detente**, but the meeting between President Dwight Eisenhower and Premier Khrushchev in Vienna in 1960 ended abruptly when the Soviets shot down a U.S. U-2 spy plane over Russian territory. Treaties between the two parties placed self-imposed limitations on nuclear arms. For example, the first Strategic Arms Limitations Treaty (SALT I), in 1972, placed an absolute ceiling on the numbers of intercontinental ballistic missiles (ICBMs), deployed nuclear warheads, and multiple independently targetable reentry vehicles (MIRVs) and limited the number of antiballistic missile sites maintained by each superpower. So the superpowers did enjoy periods of accommodation, when they could agree on principles and policies.

The Cold War as a Long Peace

If the Cold War is largely remembered as a series of crises and some direct and indirect confrontations, why then has the Cold War been referred to as the "long peace"? The term itself was coined by diplomatic historian John Lewis Gaddis to dramatize the absence of war between great powers.

Just as general war was averted in nineteenth-century Europe, so too has general war been avoided since World War II. Why?

Gaddis attributes the long peace to five factors, no single explanation's being sufficient. Probably the most widely accepted explanation revolves around the role of nuclear **deterrence.** Once both the United States and the Soviet Union had acquired nuclear weapons, neither was willing to use them, since their very deployment jeopardized both states' existence. This argument will be elaborated further in Chapter 7. Another explanation attributes the long peace to the **bipolar** split in power between the United States and the Soviet Union. Such an equal division of power led to stability in the international system, as will be explained in Chapter 4. However, since the advent of nuclear weapons occurred simultaneously with the emergence of the bipolar system, it is impossible to disentangle one explanation from the other.

A **third** explanation for the long peace is the stability imposed by the hegemonic economic power of the United States. Being in a superior economic position for much of the Cold War, the United States willingly paid the price of maintaining stability. It provided military security for Japan and much of northern Europe, and its currency was the foundation of the international monetary system. Yet while this argument explains why the United States acted to enhance postwar economic stability, it does not explain Soviet actions.

A **fourth** explanation gives credit for maintaining the peace not to either of the superpowers but to economic liberalism. During the Cold War, the liberal economic order solidified and became a dominant factor in international relations. Politics became **transnational** under liberalism—based on interests and coalitions across traditional state boundaries—and thus great powers became increasingly obsolete. Cold War peace is therefore attributed to the dominance of economic liberalism.

Finally, Gaddis explores the possibility that the long peace of the Cold War was predetermined, as just one phase in a long historical cycle of peace and war. He argues that every 100 to 150 years, war occurs on a global scale; these cycles are driven by uneven economic growth. This explanation suggests that the Cold War is but a blip in one long cycle, and specific events or conditions occurring during the Cold War offer no explanatory power.[15]

Whatever the "right" combination of explanations, international relations theorist Kenneth Waltz has noted the irony in the long peace: that both the United States and the Soviet Union, "two states, isolationist by tradition, untutored in the ways of international politics, and famed for impulsive behavior, soon showed themselves—not always and everywhere, but always in crucial cases—to be wary, alert, cautious, flexible, and forbearing."[16] The United States and the Soviet Union, wary and cautious of each other, were also now predictable and familiar to each other. Common interests had overcome the long adversarial relationship.

THE POST–COLD WAR ERA

The fall of the Berlin Wall in 1989 symbolized the end of the Cold War, but actually its end was gradual. The Soviet premier, Mikhail Gorbachev, and other Soviet reformers set in motion two domestic processes—*glasnost* (political openness) and *perestroika* (economic restructuring)—as early as the mid-1980s. Glasnost opened the door to criticism of the political system, culminating in the emergence of a multiparty system and the massive reorientation of the once-monopolistic Communist party. Perestroika undermined the foundation of the planned economy, an essential part of the communist system. At the outset, Gorbachev and his reformers sought to save the system, but once initiated, these reforms led to the dissolution of the Warsaw Pact, Gorbachev's resignation in December 1991, and the disintegration of the Soviet Union itself in 1992–93.

Gorbachev's domestic reforms also led to changes in the orientation of Soviet foreign policy. Needing to extricate the country from the political quagmire and economic drain of the war in Afghanistan, yet seeking to "save face," Gorbachev suggested that the permanent members of the U.N. Security Council "could become guarantors of regional security."[17] Afghanistan was a test case, where a small group of U.N. observers monitored and verified the withdrawal of more than one hundred thousand Soviet troops—an action that would have been impossible during the height of the Cold War. Similarly, the Soviets agreed to and supported the February 1988 withdrawal of Cuban troops from Angola. The Soviet Union had retreated internationally from commitments near its borders, as well as in far-flung places. Most important, the Soviets agreed to cooperate in multilateral activities to preserve regional security.

These changes in Soviet policy and the eventual demise of the empire itself mark the post–Cold War era and are the subject of much study in international relations today. What explains these remarkable changes? Did the West's preparations for war or its strong alliance system force the Soviet Union into submission? Was Western power and policy responsible for the Soviet demise and thus the end of the Cold War? Was it Western military strength that led the Soviets to become less bellicose and less threatening? Or did events within the Soviet Union itself lead to its demise? Was it the fault of communism, an impractical economic structure? Was it due to the resistance of those who opposed communism in Soviet domestic politics? Or was it the fact that communism not only failed to deliver on its promises but actually led to more poverty and more political repression? Or was it the failure of the Soviet bureaucratic system that led to the country's ultimate disintegration?

Did the United States, too, exhaust its capacity to carry on global confrontation, as Russian realists contend? Is the ideology—the collapse of international communism—responsible for the end of the confrontation? Was communism just too inefficient to survive? Or were protesters in the Soviet Union and Eastern Europe really seeking a system of more-limited government, which the United States exemplified? No single answer suffices; there were elements of each.

IN FOCUS

KEY DEVELOPMENTS IN THE POST–COLD WAR ERA

▶ Changes are made in Soviet/Russian foreign policy, with withdrawal from Afghanistan and Angola in the late 1980s as monitored by the United Nations.

▶ Iraqi invasion of Kuwait in 1990 and the multilateral response unites the former Cold War adversaries.

▶ Glasnost and perestroika continue in Russia, as reorganized in 1992–93.

▶ The former Yugoslavia disintegrates into independent states; civil war ensues in Bosnia and Kosovo, leading to U.N. and NATO action.

The first post–Cold War test of the so-called New World Order came in response to Iraq's invasion and annexation of Kuwait in August 1990. Despite the Soviets' long-standing relationship with Iraq, the Soviet Union (and later Russia), along with the four other members of the U.N. Security Council, agreed first to take economic sanctions against Iraq. Then they agreed in a Security Council resolution to support the means to restore the status quo—to oust Iraq from Kuwait with a multinational military force. Finally, they supported sending the U.N. Iraq-Kuwait Observer Mission to monitor the zone, and permitted the U.N. to undertake humanitarian intervention and create safe havens for the Kurdish and Shiite populations of Iraq. Although forging the consensus on each of these actions (or in the case of China, convincing them to abstain) was difficult, the coalition held, a unity unthinkable during the Cold War.

The end of the Cold War denotes a major change in international relations, the end of one historical era and the beginning of another (as yet unlabeled). Just as pathbreaking as the end of the Roman Empire or the development of the nineteenth-century European balance of power have been events that have occurred during the last several years—within our immediate memory—the outbreak of civil wars and ethnic conflicts and the response of humanitarian intervention.

IN SUM: LEARNING FROM HISTORY

Will the post–Cold War era be characterized by cooperation among the great powers? Does the post–Cold War world signal a return to the **multipolar** system of the nineteenth century? Or is this era to be the "**unipolar moment**" of U.S. domination, comparable to the British hegemony of the nineteenth century? How can we begin to predict what the current era is or what the future will bring?

We have taken the first step toward answering these questions by looking to the past. Our examination of the development of contemporary international relations has focused on how core concepts of international relations have emerged and evolved over time, most notably the state, sovereignty, the nation, and the international system. These concepts, developed within a specific historical context, provide the building blocks for contemporary international relations. The state is well established, but its sovereignty may be eroding from without (Chapter 9) and from within (Chapter 5). The principal characteristics of the contemporary international system are in the process of change as the bipolarity of the Cold War ends (Chapter 4).

To help us understand the trends of the past and how those trends influence contemporary thinking and to predict future developments, we turn to theory. Theory gives order; it takes specific events and provides generalized explanations. In Chapter 3 we will look at three competing theories and perspectives about international relations. These theories view the past from quite different perspectives.

NOTES

1. Cicero, *Res Publica: Roman Politics and Society according to Cicero*, trans. W. K. Lacey and B. W. J. G. Wilson (London: Oxford University Press, 1970).
2. Dante, "De Monarchia," in *The Portable Dante*, ed. Paolo Milano (New York: Penguin, 1977).

3. Niccolo Machiavelli, *The Prince and the Discourses* (New York: Random House, 1940).

4. Jean Bodin, *Six Books on the Commonwealth* (Oxford, Eng.: Basil Blackwell, 1967), 25.

5. Ibid., 28.

6. Ibid.

7. Adam Smith, *An Inquiry into the Nature and Causes of the Wealth of Nations* (New York: Modern Library, 1937).

8. John Locke, *Two Treatises on Government* (Cambridge, Eng.: Cambridge University Press, 1960).

9. A. C. Walworth, *Woodrow Wilson* (Baltimore: Penguin, 1969), 148.

10. Edward Hallett Carr, *The Twenty Years' Crisis, 1919–1939: An Introduction to the Study of International Relations* (New York: Harper Torchbooks, 1939, rep. 1964), 224.

11. George F. Kennan ["X"], "The Sources of Soviet Conduct," *Foreign Affairs* 25 (July 1947), 566–82.

12. Charles W. Kegley, Jr., and Eugene R. Wittkopf, *World Politics: Trend and Transformation,* (5th ed.; New York: St. Martin's, 1995), 94.

13. Josef Stalin, "Reply to Comrades," *Pravda,* August 2, 1950.

14. George F. Kennan, "The United States and the Soviet Union, 1917–1976," *Foreign Affairs* 54 (July 1976), 683–84.

15. John Lewis Gaddis, "The Long Peace: Elements of Stability in the Postwar International System," *International Security* 10:4 (Spring 1986), 92–142.

16. Kenneth N. Waltz, *Theory of International Politics* (Reading, Mass: Addison-Wesley, 1979), 173.

17. Mikhail Gorbachev, "Secure World," as reported in Foreign Broadcast Information Service, *Daily Report, Soviet Union,* September 17, 1987, 25.

CONTENDING PERSPECTIVES: HOW TO THINK ABOUT INTERNATIONAL RELATIONS THEORETICALLY

3

- *What is the value of studying international relations from a theoretical perspective?*
- *Why do scholars pay attention to the levels-of-analysis problem?*
- *What are the major theoretical underpinnings of liberalism and its newer variant, neoliberal institutionalism? Of realism and neorealism? Of radicalism? Of constructivism?*
- *Can you analyze a contemporary event by using the alternative theoretical perspectives?*

THINKING THEORETICALLY

How can theory help us make sense of international relations? In this chapter we will use the example of the Gulf War to explore major international relations theories and their explanations for political events.

In August 1990, Iraq invaded and successfully annexed Kuwait, an action almost universally condemned, even by the Soviet Union despite its long-standing relationship with Iraq. Between August and November, the U.N. Security Council approved twelve successive resolutions in an effort to secure Iraqi withdrawal. Those resolutions imposed comprehensive, mandatory sanctions on Iraq, declared Iraq's annexation null and void, legalized enforcement of an embargo against Iraq, and demanded the release of hostages. January 15, 1991, was set as the deadline for Iraq's compliance. Iraq did not comply. On January 16, a U.S.-led multinational coalition launched a war against Iraq. The major events of the crisis and the war are given in Table 3.1.

Why did Iraq invade Kuwait in the first place? Why did Iraq refuse to comply with the demands of the international community when it was universally condemned for the action? What motivated the U.S.-led coalition to launch the counterattack? We begin to answer these questions by describing historical circumstances, using the methods of traditional diplomatic history. The description needs also to include information about the specific government actions taken (Iraq's invasion and the U.S. response), reports on the public and private positions of those involved (Saddam Hussein's promises to the U.S. ambassador, April Glaspie, and her assurances to Saddam; statements by U.S. president George Bush, British prime minister Margaret Thatcher, U.N. secretary-general Boutros Boutros-Ghali), and the detailed knowledge of experts. Compiling such information enables us to reconstruct the context in which the events of 1990–91 occurred.

However, description of the surrounding context of the event may not explain *why* the sequence of events occurred. Why did Saddam invade? What motivated the United States and the coalition to respond? To find explanations, scholars often search the past for similar behaviors or comparable cases. After all, small states (Kuwait) with critical economic re-

TABLE 3.1

Major Events during the Gulf War	
Date	**Event**
August 2, 1990	Iraq invades and occupies Kuwait; Bush condemns Iraq.
August 6, 1990	U.N. Security Council passes resolution to embargo trade with Iraq.
August 6–7, 1990	Buildup of U.S., British, and allied Arab troops begins in Saudi Arabia.
November 29, 1990	U.N. resolution authorizes use of force against Iraq, sets January 15, 1991 as deadline for Iraqi withdrawal.
January 12, 1991	U.S. Congress passes resolution to use force against Iraq.
January 15, 1991	U.N. deadline passes without Iraqi withdrawal.
January 16, 1991	Allied forces begin bombing Iraq.
February 24, 1991	Allied ground troops begin assault on Iraqi troops in Kuwait; Iraqi soldiers surrender in droves.
February 28, 1991	Cease-fire accepted by both sides.

sources (oil) are always militarily vulnerable when located near a contending regional power (Iraq). Potential aggressor states (like Iraq) must be assured that their actions will provoke a massive counterresponse or else they will be inclined to act as they please (invade). Given these conditions, a student of international relations might find explanation for the invasion in the ambiguous statement made by Ambassador Glaspie supporting Iraqi intentions in the region, which may have led Saddam to think an invasion might not provoke a military response. A number of possible explanations for Iraq's actions is given in Box 3.1.

While these explanations provide a piece of the puzzle, other pieces are missing: information on Saddam's state of mind, how he actually interpreted Glaspie's statements, or what Glaspie herself meant by her assurances to Saddam. Moreover, social scientists want to go beyond explanations, to theories that can explain not just why Saddam invaded tiny Kuwait but why any state invades another state more generally across time and space.

A **theory** is a set of propositions and concepts that seeks to explain phenomena by specifying the relationships among the concepts; theory's

---

BOX 3.1

POSSIBLE EXPLANATIONS FOR IRAQI INVASION OF KUWAIT

1. Saddam Hussein is an aggressive person.
2. Saddam Hussein is insecure domestically, so he uses war to strengthen his popularity and tighten his grip on society.
3. Iraq is striving to counter Iran, its sworn enemy and primary antagonist in the region.
4. Authoritarian states like Iraq will always act aggressively.
5. The statements by the U.N. Security Council warning Saddam Hussein about the dire consequences of aggressive action were not credible.
6. Iraq needed more oil resources in order to pay its debts and develop economically.
7. The Arab League (an important organization in the Middle East) will never condemn actions taken by a fellow Arabic state.
8. The international community is preoccupied with other events and so will not respond to an act committed against a small state.
9. Saddam Hussein surrounds himself with advisers and military personnel who are afraid to tell him the possible consequences of his actions.
10. Saddam Hussein miscalculates the probable reaction of other states, including Saudi Arabia and the United States.

ultimate purpose is to predict phenomena. Good theory generates groups of testable **hypotheses:** specific statements positing a particular relationship between two or more variables. By testing groups of interrelated hypotheses, theory is verified and refined and new relationships are found that demand subsequent testing.

Moving from description to explanation to theory and from theory to testable hypotheses is not a unilinear process. Although theory depends on a logical deduction of hypotheses from assumptions, and a testing of the hypotheses, as more and more data are collected in the empirical world, theories have to be revised or adjusted. This is, in part, a creative exercise, in which one must be tolerant of ambiguity, concerned about probabilities, and distrustful of absolutes.

International relations theories come in a variety of forms. In this chapter, we introduce three general theories, or theoretical perspectives, in the study of international relations: liberalism (and its newest variant, neoliberal institutionalism), realism (and neorealism), and the radical critique based in Marxism. In addition, we present an overview of constructivism as one of the newest theoretical perspectives in international relations. Before we examine these theories more closely, we must consider the various levels at which we can analyze events and trends.

THEORY AND THE LEVELS OF ANALYSIS

Why did Iraq invade Kuwait? The list of possible explanations given in Box 3.1 can be organized according to three **levels of analysis** (see Figure 3.1). In this categorization, first used by Kenneth Waltz and amplified by J. David Singer, three different sources of explanations are offered. If the *individual level* is the focus, then the personality, perceptions, choices, and activities of individual decisionmakers (Saddam Hussein, George Bush) and individual participants (Ambassador Glaspie, Saddam's advisers) provide the explanation. If the *state level*, or domestic factors, are the focus, then the explanation is derived from characteristics of the state (democracy vs. authoritarian governments), the type of economic system (capitalist vs. socialist), interest groups within the country, or even the national interest. If the *international system* level is the focus, then the explanation rests with the anarchic characteristics of that system or with international and regional organizations and their strengths and weaknesses.[1] Box 3.2 categorizes the explanations from Box 3.1 according to these three levels of analysis. Of course, explanations from all three levels probably contributed

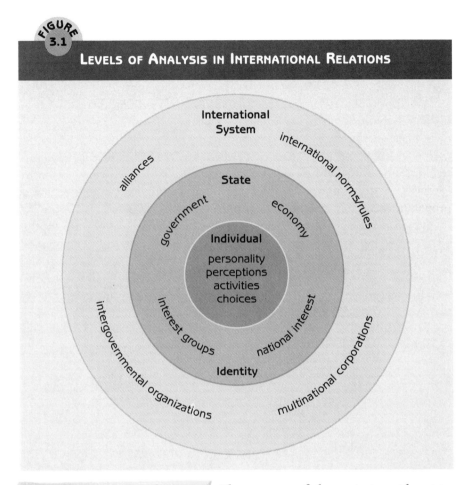

FIGURE 3.1

LEVELS OF ANALYSIS IN INTERNATIONAL RELATIONS

International System

international norms/rules

alliances

State

government

economy

Individual

personality
perceptions
activities
choices

interest groups

intergovernmental organizations

national interest

Identity

multinational corporations

to the decision to invade Kuwait. The purpose of theory is to guide us toward an understanding of which of these various explanations are the necessary and sufficient explanations for the invasion.

There are good reasons to pay attention to the levels of analysis. They help orient our questions and suggest the appropriate type of evidence to explore. Most importantly, using levels of analysis enables us to avoid several logical fallacies. For example, one cannot infer individual behavior from system-level characteristics. In other words, we cannot say that Saddam is aggressive because the international community is preoccupied with other events. Similarly, system-level behavior cannot be reduced to or explained in terms of individual behavior. Thus we cannot conclude that since the Arab League does not condemn actions of a fellow Arabic state, Saddam is aggressive. Paying attention to levels of

EXPLAINING IRAQ'S INVASION OF KUWAIT BY LEVEL OF ANALYSIS

INDIVIDUAL LEVEL

1. Saddam Hussein is aggressive and insecure.
9. Saddam Hussein surrounds himself with advisers and military personnel who are afraid of him.
10. Saddam Hussein miscalculates the responses of other states.

STATE LEVEL

2. Saddam is insecure domestically, so he uses war to tighten his grip on society.
3. Iraq is striving to counter its enemy Iran.
4. Authoritarian states like Iraq always act aggressively.
6. Iraq needs more oil resources to pay debts and to develop its economy.

INTERNATIONAL LEVEL

5. Statements made by the U.N. Security Council warning Saddam about the consequences of taking aggressive action are not credible.
7. The Arab League will never condemn actions by a fellow Arabic state.
8. The international community is preoccupied with other events and so will not respond to an act committed against a small state.

analysis helps us make logical deductions and enables us to explore all categories of explanation.

Although all scholars acknowledge the utility of paying attention to levels of analysis, they differ on how many levels are useful. Most political scientists use between three and six levels. Although adding more layers may provide more descriptive context, it makes explanation and prediction more problematic. The most important differentiation in theory must be made between the international level and the domestic level. In this book we will use the three levels explained above: individual, state, and system.

Good theory, then, should be able to explain phenomena at a particular level of analysis; better theory should also offer explanations across different levels of analysis. The general theories outlined in the rest of this chapter are all comprehensive, meaning they incorporate all the different levels of analysis. Yet each of the theories is not as simple or as unified as presented. Different authors have introduced variations, modifications, and problematics, and even the same authors have changed positions over time. Thus, the theories are discussed in terms of their essential characteristics.

LIBERALISM AND NEOLIBERAL INSTITUTIONALISM

Liberalism holds that human nature is basically good and that innate goodness makes societal progress possible. Evil or unacceptable human behavior, such as war, is, according to liberals, the product of inadequate or corrupt social institutions and of misunderstandings among leaders. Thus, liberals believe that war or any other aggressive behavior is not inevitable and can be moderated through institutional reform. Through collective action, states can cooperate to eliminate the possibility of war.

The origins of liberal theory are found in Enlightenment optimism, nineteenth-century political and economic liberalism, and twentieth-century Wilsonian idealism. The contribution of the eighteenth-century Enlightenment to liberalism rests on the Greek idea that individuals are rational human beings, able to understand the universally applicable laws governing both nature and human society. Understanding such laws means that people have the capacity to improve their condition by creating a just society. If a just society is not attained, then the fault rests with inadequate institutions, the result of a corrupt environment.

The writings of the French philosopher Baron de La Brède et de Montesquieu (1689–1755) reflect Enlightenment thinking. He argued that human nature is not defective and that problems are created as man enters civil society and forms separate nations. War is a product of society, not an attribute inherent in individuals. To overcome defects in the society, education is imperative; it prepares one for civil life. Groups of states are united according to the law of nations, which regulates conduct even during war. Montesquieu optimistically states that "different nations ought in time of peace to do one another all the good they can, and in time of war as little harm as possible, without prejudicing their real interests."[2]

Likewise, the writings of Immanuel Kant (discussed in Chapter 1) form the core of Enlightenment beliefs. International anarchy can be overcome through some kind of collective action—a federation of states in which sovereignties would be left intact. Kant offers hope that humans will learn ways to avoid war, though as he admits, the task will not be easy.[3]

Nineteenth-century liberalism took the rationalism of the eighteenth-century Enlightenment and reformulated it by adding a preference for democracy over aristocracy and for free trade over national economic self-sufficiency. Sharing the Enlightenment's optimistic view of human nature, nineteenth-century liberalism saw man as capable of satisfying his natural needs and wants in rational ways. These needs and wants could be achieved most efficiently by each individual's pursuing his own freedom and autonomy, unfettered by excessive state structures. According to liberal thought, individual freedom and autonomy can best be realized in a democratic state that is based on the economic system of free trade. Thus, the best society is that which permits the maximum of individual freedom.

Twentieth-century idealism also contributed to liberalism, finding its greatest adherent in U.S. president Woodrow Wilson, who authored the covenant of the League of Nations—hence the term "Wilsonian idealism." The basic proposition of this idealism is that war is preventable; more than half of the League covenant's twenty-six provisions focused on preventing war. The covenant even included a provision legitimizing the notion of **collective security**, wherein aggression by one state would be countered by collective action, embodied in a "league of nations."

Thus, the League of Nations illustrated the importance that liberals place on international institutions to deal with war, and the opportunity for collective problem solving in a multilateral forum. Liberals also place faith in international law and legal instruments—mediation, arbitration, and international courts. Still other liberals think that all war can be eliminated through disarmament. Whatever the specific prescriptive solution, the basis of liberalism remains firmly embedded in the belief of the rationality of humans and in the unbridled optimism that through learning and education, humans can develop institutions to bring out their best characteristics.

During the interwar period, when the League of Nations proved incapable of maintaining collective security, and during World War II, when human atrocities made many question the basic goodness of the species, liberalism came under intense scrutiny. Was man inherently good? How could an institution fashioned under the best assumptions have failed so miserably? Liberalism as a theoretical perspective fell out of favor.

Since the 1970s, liberalism has been revived under the rubric of **neoliberal institutionalism**. Neoliberal institutionalists like the political scientists Robert Axelrod and Robert O. Keohane ask *why* states choose to cooperate most of the time in the anarchic condition of the international system. One answer is found in the simple but profound story of the prisoner's dilemma.[4]

The **prisoner's dilemma** is the story of two prisoners, each being interrogated separately for an alleged crime. The interrogator tells each prisoner that if one of them confesses and the other does not, the one who confessed will go free and the one who kept silent will get a long prison term. If both confess, both will get somewhat reduced prison terms. If neither confesses, both will receive short prison terms based on lack of evidence. The solution to the prisoner's dilemma? Both prisoners will confess, and thus each will serve a longer sentence than if they had cooperated and kept silent.

Why did cooperation fail to occur? Each prisoner is faced with a one-time choice. Neither prisoner knows how the other will respond; the cost of not confessing if the other confesses is extraordinarily high. So both will confess, leading to a less-than-optimal outcome.

But if the game is repeated, the possibility of **reciprocity** makes it rational to cooperate. Had the two prisoners cooperated with each other by both remaining silent, then the outcome would have been much better for both. It was actually in the self-interest of each to cooperate! Similarly, states are not faced with a one-time situation; they confront each other over and over again on specific issues. Neoliberal institutionalists do not believe that individuals naturally cooperate out of any innate characteristics of the species. The prisoner's dilemma provides neoliberal institutionalists with a rationale for mutual cooperation in an environment where there are no rules for such cooperation.

Neoliberal institutionalists arrive at the same result as liberals do—cooperation—but their explanation for why cooperation occurs is different. For classical liberals, cooperation emerges from man's establishing and reforming institutions that permit cooperative interactions and prohibit coercive actions. For neoliberal institutionalists, cooperation emerges because for actors having continuous interactions with each other, it is in the self-interest of each to cooperate. Institutions may be established, affecting the possibilities for cooperation, but they do not guarantee cooperation.

For neoliberal institutionalists, security is essential, and institutions help to make security possible. Institutions provide a guaranteed framework of interactions; they suggest that there will be an expectation of future interactions. These interactions will occur not just on security issues but on a whole suite of international issues including human rights (a classic liberal concern), the environment, immigration, and economics.[5]

With the end of the Cold War in the 1990s, liberalism as a general theoretical perspective has achieved new credibility. Two particular areas stand out. First, researchers of the democratic peace (discussed in Chapter 1) are trying to determine *why* democracies do not fight each other. A variety of liberal explanations provide the answer. One argument is that democracies are pacific toward each other because democratic norms and culture inhibit the leaders; the leaders hear from a multiplicity of voices that tend to restrain decisionmakers and therefore lessen the chance of war. Another argument is that transnational and international institutions that bind democracies together through dense networks act to constrain behavior. Each explanation is based on liberal theorizing. Yet democratic peace scholars do not always rely on liberal explanations. According to another view, the democracies did not fight each other after World War II because they had a common enemy, the Soviet Union. This is an explanation rooted in realist theory.

Second, post–Cold War theorists like the scholar and former policy analyst Francis Fukuyama see not just a revival but a victory for international liberalism, in the absence of any viable theoretical alternatives. He admits that some groups, such as Palestinians and Kurds, Sikhs and Tamils, or Armenians and Azeris, will continue to have grievances against each other. But large-scale conflict is less frequent than in earlier eras. For the first time, Fukuyama argues, the possibility exists for the "universalization of Western liberal democracy as the final form of human governance."[6] Indeed, political scientist John Mueller makes the liberal argument even stronger. Just as dueling and slavery, once acceptable practices, have become morally unacceptable, war is increasingly seen in the developed world as immoral and repugnant. The terrifying moments of World Wars I and II have led to the obsolescence of war, says Mueller.[7]

As liberalism as a theoretical perspective has waxed and waned, so too has realism, the major theoretical counterpoint to liberalism.

Theory in Brief

LIBERALISM / NEOLIBERAL INSTITUTIONALISM

Key actors	States, nongovernmental groups, international organizations
View of the individual	Basically good; capable of cooperating
View of the state	Not an autonomous actor; having many interests
View of the international system	Interdependence among actors; international society; anarchy
Beliefs about change	Probable; a desirable process
Major theorists	Montesquieu, Kant, Wilson, Keohane, Mueller

REALISM AND NEOREALISM

Realism, like liberalism, is the product of long historical and philosophical tradition, even though its direct application to international affairs is of more recent vintage. Realism is based on a view of the individual as primarily selfish and power seeking. Individuals are organized in states, each of which acts in a unitary way in pursuit of its own **national interest**, defined in terms of power. These states exist in an anarchic international system, characterized by the absence of an authoritative hierarchy. Under this condition of anarchy, states in the international system can rely only on themselves. Their most important concern, then, is to manage their insecurity, which arises out of the anarchic system. They rely primarily on the balance of power and deterrence to keep the international system intact and as nonthreatening as possible.

At least four of the essential assumptions of realism are found in Thucydides's *History of the Peloponnesian War*. First, for Thucydides, the state (Athens or Sparta) is the *principal actor* in war and in politics in general, just as latter-day realists posit. While other actors, such as international institutions, may participate, they are not important.

Second, the state is assumed to be a **unitary actor**: although Thucydides includes fascinating debates among different officials from the same state, once a decision is made to go to war or capitulate, the state speaks and acts with one voice. There are no subnational actors trying to overturn the decision of the government or subvert the interests of the state.

Third, decisionmakers acting in the name of the state are assumed to be **rational actors**. Like most educated Greeks, Thucydides believed that individuals are essentially rational beings and that they make decisions by weighing the strengths and weaknesses of various options against the goal to be achieved. Thucydides admits that there are potential impediments to rational decisionmaking, including wishful thinking on the part of leaders, confusing intentions and national interest, and misperceiving the characteristics of the counterpart decisionmaker. But the core notion that rational decisionmaking leads to the pursuit of the national interest remains. Likewise for modern realists, rational decisions advance the national interest—the interests of the state—however ambiguously that national interest is formulated.

Fourth, Thucydides, like contemporary realists, was concerned with security issues—protecting the state from enemies both foreign and domestic. A state augments its security by increasing its domestic capacities, building up its economic prowess, and forming alliances with other states based on similar interests. In fact, Thucydides found that before and during the Peloponnesian War, it was fear of a rival that motivated states to join alliances, a rational decision on the part of the leader.[8] In the Melian dialogue, a section of *History of the Peloponnesian War,* Thucydides poses the classic dilemma between realist and liberal thinking. Do states have rights based on the conception of an international ethical or moral order, as liberals suggest? Or is a state's power, in the absence of an international authority, the deciding factor?

Thucydides did not identify all the tenets of realism. Indeed, the tenets and rationale of realism have unfolded over centuries, and not all realists agree on what they are. For example, six centuries after Thucydides lived, the Christian bishop and philosopher St. Augustine (345–430 A.D.) added a fundamental assumption, arguing that man is flawed, egoistic, and selfish, although not predetermined to be so. St. Augustine blames war on this basic characteristic of man.[9] Although subsequent realists dispute the biblical explanation for man's flawed, selfish nature, few realists dispute the fact that man is basically power seeking and self-absorbed.

The implications of man's flawed nature for the state are developed further in the writings of the Italian political philosopher Niccoló Machiavelli (1469–1527). He argues in *The Prince* that a leader needs to be ever mindful of threats to his personal security and the security of the state. Machiavelli promotes the use of alliances and various offensive and defensive strategies to protect the state.[10]

The central tenet accepted by virtually all realist theorists is that states exist in an anarchic international system. This tenet was originally articulated by Thomas Hobbes (see Chapter 1). Hobbes maintains that just as individuals in the state of nature have the responsibility and the right to preserve themselves, so too does each state in the international system. Hobbes depicts a state of international anarchy, where the norm for states is "having their weapons pointing, and their eyes fixed on one another."[11] In the absence of international authority, there are few rules or norms that restrain states.

In the aftermath of World War II, at the height of disillusionment with liberalism, international relations theorist Hans Morgenthau (1904–80) wrote the seminal synthesis of realism in international politics and offered a methodological approach for testing the theory. For Morgenthau, just as for Thucydides, Augustine, and Hobbes, international politics is a struggle for power. That struggle can be explained at the three levels of analysis: 1) the flawed individual in the state of nature struggles for self-preservation; 2) the autonomous and unitary state is constantly involved in power struggles, balancing power with power and reacting to preserve what is in the national interest; and 3) because the international system is anarchic—there is no higher power to put the competition to an end—the struggle is continuous. Because of the imperative to ensure a state's survival, leaders are driven by a morality quite different from that of ordinary individuals. Morality, for realists, is to be judged by the political consequences of a policy.[12]

Morgenthau's textbook, *Politics among Nations*, became the realist bible for the years following World War II. Policy implications flowed naturally from the theory: the most effective technique for managing power is balance of power. Both George Kennan (1904–), writer and chair of the State Department's Policy Planning Staff in the late 1940s and later the U.S. ambassador to the Soviet Union, and Henry Kissinger (1923–), scholar, foreign policy adviser, and secretary of state to Presidents Richard Nixon and Gerald Ford, are known to have based their policy recommendations on realist theory.

As we saw in Chapter 2, Kennan was one of the architects of the U.S. Cold War policy of containment, an interpretation of balance of power. The goal of containment was to prevent Soviet power from extending into regions beyond that country's immediate, existing sphere of influence (Eastern Europe). Containment was achieved by balancing U.S. power against Soviet power. Henry Kissinger, during the 1970s, encouraged the classic realist balance of power by supporting weaker powers like China to exert leverage over the Soviet Union, or Pakistan to offset India's growing power (India was an ally of the Soviets). Realist theory, then, offers clear policy prescriptions.

Among the various reinterpretations of realism, the most powerful is **neorealism** (or structural realism), as delineated in Kenneth Waltz's *Theory of International Politics*.[13] This reinterpretation was undertaken in order to make political realism a more rigorous theory of international politics. Neorealists are so bold as to propose general laws to explain events: they therefore attempt to simplify explanations of behavior in anticipation of being better able to explain and predict general trends.

Neorealists give precedence to the international system structure over the states emphasized by traditional realists and over explanations that focus on the innate characteristics of human beings. According to Waltz, the most important unit to study is the international structure. The structure of a particular system is determined by the ordering principle, namely the absence of overarching authority, and the distribution of capabilities among states. Those capabilities define a state's position in the system. The international structure is a force in itself; it constrains state behavior, and states may not be able to control it. The international structure, rather than the characteristics of individual states, determines outcomes.[14]

As in classical realism, balance of power is a core principle of neorealism. But unlike earlier realists, neorealists believe that the balance of power among states is largely determined by the structure of the system. In such a system, the possibilities for international cooperation are logically slim:

> When faced with the possibility of cooperating for mutual gain, states that feel insecure must ask how the gain will be divided. They are compelled to ask not "Will both of us gain?" but "Who will gain more?" If an expected gain is to be divided, say, in the ratio of two to one, one state may use its disproportionate gain to implement a policy intended to damage or destroy the other. Even the prospect of large absolute gains for both parties does not elicit their cooperation so long as each fears how the other will use its increased capabilities.[15]

Although the insecurity of each party in the anarchic international system impedes cooperation, interdependence among the parties may facilitate cooperation. But in an atmosphere of insecurity, states are wary of becoming too dependent on others. That explains why states seek greater control and self-sufficiency.

Scholars have developed other interpretations of realism in addition to neorealism. While neorealism simplifies the theory and focuses on a few core concepts (structure and balance of power), other reinterpretations add increased complexity to realism. Princeton University professor Robert Gilpin, in *War and Change in World Politics,* offers one such reinterpretation. Accepting the realist assumptions that states are the principal actors, decision makers are basically rational, and the international system structure plays a key role in determining power, Gilpin examines 2,400 years of history, finding that "the distribution of power among states constitutes the principal form of control in every international system."[16] What Gilpin adds is the notion of dynamism, of history as a series of cycles—cycles of birth, expansion, and demise of dominant powers. Whereas classical realism offers no satisfactory rationale for the decline of powers, Gilpin does, on the basis of the renewed importance of economic power. Hegemons decline because of three processes: the increasingly marginal returns of empire, a state-level phenomenon; the tendency for economic hegemons to consume more over time and invest less, also a state-level phenomenon; and the diffusion of technology, a system-level phenomenon through which new powers challenge the hegemon. As Gilpin explains, "disequilibrium replaces equilibrium, and the world moves toward a new round of hegemonic conflict."[17]

Whereas Gilpin adds dynamism to a largely static theory of realism, the feminist political scientist Ann Tickner and her colleagues add gender, and hence complexity, to realism. Classical realism is based on a very limited notion of both human nature and power, according to Tickner. She argues that human nature is not fixed and inalterable; it is multidimensional and contextual. Power cannot be equated exclusively with control and domination. Tickner thinks that realism must be reoriented toward a more inclusive notion of power, where power is the ability to act in concert (not just conflict) or to be in a symbiotic relationship (instead of outright competition). In other words, power can be a concept of connection rather than one of autonomy.[18]

In short, there is no single tradition of political realism; there are "realisms." Although each is predicated on a key group of assumptions, each attaches different importance to the various core propositions. Yet what unites proponents of realist theory—their emphasis on the unitary autonomous state in an international anarchic system—distinguishes them clearly from both the liberals and the radicals.

Theory in Brief	
REALISM/NEOREALISM	
Key actors	International system, states
View of the individual	Power seeking; selfish; antagonistic
View of the state	Power seeking; unitary actor; following its national interest
View of the international system	Anarchy; stability in balance-of-power system
Beliefs about change	Low change potential; slow structural change
Major theorists	Thucydides, St. Augustine, Machiavelli, Hobbes, Morgenthau, Waltz, Gilpin

THE RADICAL PERSPECTIVE

Radicalism offers the third overarching theoretical perspective to international relations. Whereas there is widespread agreement concerning the appropriateness of the liberal and realist labels, there is no such agreement on radicalism. There is, however, a group of core beliefs that unite those espousing a radical, largely Marxist, perspective.

The first set of beliefs in radicalism is found in historical analysis. Whereas for most liberals and realists, history provides various data points from which generalizations can be gleaned when appropriate, radicals see historical analysis as fundamental. Of special relevance is the history of the production process. During the evolution of the production process from feudalism to capitalism, new patterns of social relations are developed. Radicals are concerned most with explaining the relationship between production, social relations, and power.

The writings of Karl Marx (1818–83) are fundamental to radical thought, even though he did not directly address all the issues of today. Marx theorized on the evolution of capitalism on the basis of economic change and class conflict: the capitalism of nineteenth-century Europe emerged out of the earlier feudal system. In capitalism, private interests control labor and market exchanges, creating bondages from which certain classes try to free themselves. A clash inevitably arises between the controlling, capitalist bourgeois class and the controlled workers, called the proletariat. It is from this violent clash that a new socialist order is born.[19]

Contemporary interpretations begin with the writings of Marx, but they have developed ideas in quite different directions. Sociologist Immanuel Wallerstein (1930–), for one, links history and the rise of capitalism, in what is known as the world-capitalist system perspective. In *The Modern World-System,* he carefully and systematically examines the emergence of capitalism in Europe since the sixteenth century. At each stage of the historical process, he identifies core geographic areas (not necessarily states) where development is most advanced and the agricultural sector is able to provide sustenance for the industrial workers. Wallerstein identifies peripheral areas as well, where raw materials are extracted for the developed core and unskilled labor is mired in less-productive activities. These areas are prevented from developing by the developed core, which maintains its position at the expense of the periphery. In between the core and periphery lies the semiperiphery, where a mix of different activities occurs.[20]

Wallerstein's rendering of history intrinsically recognizes change. States of the semiperiphery can at another historic period move into the core, and occasionally vice versa. For example, in the 1980s and 1990s semiperipheral countries like South Korea and Taiwan moved into the core, and a few members of the periphery like Thailand and Malaysia entered the semiperiphery. Thus, for Wallerstein and his disciples, as for most radicals, attention is riveted on the changes in the systemwide phenomenon of capitalism. No political configuration can be explained without reference to the underlying structure of capitalism: "If there is one thing which distinguishes a world-system perspective from any other, it is its insistence that the unit of analysis is a *world*-system defined in terms of *economic* processes and links, and not any units defined in terms of juridical, political, cultural, geographical, or other criteria."[21]

Basing history on the importance of the production process, a second group of radical beliefs assumes the primacy of economics for explaining virtually all other phenomena. This clearly differentiates radicalism from either liberalism or realism. For liberals, economic interdependence is one possible explanation for international cooperation, but only one among many factors. For realists and neorealists, economic factors are one of the ingredients of power, one component of the international structure. In neither theory, though, is economics the determining factor. In radicalism, on the other hand, economic factors assume primary importance. For example, radical feminists based in the Marxist tradition suggest that the roots of oppression against women are found in the exploitive capitalist system.

A third group of radical beliefs centers on the structure of the global system. That structure, in Marxist thinking, is hierarchical and is largely the by-product of imperialism, or the expansion of certain economic forms into other areas of the world. The British economist John A. Hobson (1858–1940) theorized that expansion occurs because of three conditions: overproduction of goods and services in the more developed countries, underconsumption by workers and the lower classes in developed nations because of low wages, and oversavings by the upper classes and bourgeoisie in the dominant developed countries. In order to solve these three economic problems, states historically have expanded abroad, and radicals argue that developed countries still see expansion as a solution: goods find new markets in underdeveloped regions, workers' wages are kept low because of foreign competition, and savings are profitably invested in new markets rather than in improving the lot of the workers. Imperialism leads to rivalry among the developed countries, evoking, in the realist's interpretation, a "scramble" to balance power.[22]

To radicals, imperialism produces the hierarchical international system, in which there are opportunities for some states, organizations, and individuals and significant constraints on behavior for others. Developed countries can expand, enabling them to sell goods and export surplus wealth that they cannot use at home. Simultaneously, the developing countries are increasingly constrained and dependent on the actions of the developed world. Hobson, who condemned imperialism as irrational, risky, and potentially conflictual, did not see it as necessarily inevitable.

Radical theorists emphasize the techniques of domination and suppression that arise from the uneven economic development inherent in the capitalist system. Uneven development empowers and enables the dominant states to exploit the underdogs; the dynamics of capitalism and economic expansion make such exploitation necessary if the top dogs are to maintain their position and the capitalist structure is to survive. Whereas realists see balance of power and diplomacy as the mechanisms for gaining and maintaining power, Marxists and radicals view the economic techniques of domination and suppression as the means of power in the world; the choices for the underdog are few and ineffective.

The Russian revolutionary and communist leader V. I. Lenin (1870–1924), in *Imperialism: The Highest Stage of Capitalism*, argues that imperialism inevitably leads to war. Lenin believed that capitalist countries have to expand through imperialism; it is not a choice, but a necessity. Once the developing markets have been subdivided among the capitalist states, then war among capitalist states over control of those markets becomes inevitable. War, then, is an outcome of capitalist economic competition.[23]

Latter-day radicals recognize that capitalists can use other, more-sophisticated techniques of control. Contemporary radicals, such as **dependency theorists,** attribute primary importance to **multinational corporations** and international banks based in developed countries in exerting fundamental controls over

Theory in Brief

RADICALISM/DEPENDENCY THEORY

Key actors	Social classes, transnational elites, multinational corporations
View of the individual	Actions determined by economic class
View of the state	An agent of the structure of international capitalism and the executing agent of the bourgeoisie
View of the international system	Highly stratified; dominated by international capitalist system
Beliefs about change	Goal of radical change
Major theorists	Hobson, Marx, Wallerstein, Lenin

the developing countries. These organizations are seen as key players in establishing and maintaining dependency relationships; they are agents of penetration, not benign actors, as liberals would characterize them, or marginal actors, as realists would. These organizations are able to forge transnational relationships with elites in the developing countries, so that domestic elites in both exploiter and exploited countries are tightly linked in a symbiotic relationship.

Dependency theorists, particularly those from Latin America (Raul Prebisch, Enzo Faletto, Fernando Henrique Cardoso), believe that options for states on the periphery are few. Since the basic terms of trade are unequal, these states have few external options. And they have few internal options either, since their internal constraints are just as real: land tenure and social and class structures.[24] Thus, like the realists, dependency theorists are rather pessimistic about the possibility of change.

Finally, radicals are uniformly normative in their orientation. They evaluate the hierarchical capitalist structure as "bad," its methods exploitative. They have clear normative and activist positions about what should be done to ameliorate inequities—ranging from the radical revolution and revolutionary organizations supported by Leninists to more incremental changes suggested by dependency theorists.

In some quarters, radicalism has been discredited as an international relations theory. Radicalism could not explain why there was emerging cooperation even before the end of the Cold War between capitalist and socialist states. And it could not explain why there was such divisiveness among noncapitalist states. Neither could radicalism explain why and how some of the developing countries have been able to adopt a capitalist approach and escape from economic and political dependency. Radicalism could not have predicted such developments. And radicalism just like liberalism and realism did not foresee or predict the demise of the Soviet Union, arguably one of the most significant changes in the twentieth century. Each theory, despite claims of comprehensiveness, has significant shortcomings.

In other circles, radicalism has survived as a theory of economic determinism and as a theory advocating major change in the structure of the international system. Radicalism helps us understand the role of economic forces both within and between states and to explain the dynamics of late-twentieth-century economic globalization. In the following chapters, we will provide support for this view.

One of the changes that has occurred in radicalism is an adaptation which is called constructivism. Constructivism has clearly added new vigor to the study of international relations.

CONSTRUCTIVISM

Constructivism has returned international scholars to the foundational questions, including the nature of the state and the concepts of sovereignty and citizenship. New substantive areas of inquiry have been opened, such as the roles of gender and ethnicity, which have been largely absent from international relations approaches.

Like liberalism, realism, and radicalism before it, constructivism is not a uniform theory. Some question whether it is a substantive theory at all. Indeed, many of the variables in the theory are loosely defined. But constructivists do share the position that since the world is so complicated, no overarching theory in international relations is possible.

The major theoretical proposition that all constructivists subscribe to is that state behavior is shaped by elite beliefs, identities, and social norms. Individuals in collectivities forge, shape, and change culture through ideas and practices. State and national interests are the result of the social identities of these actors. Thus, the object of study is norms and practices of individuals and the collectivity, without distinguishing between domestic politics and international politics.[25] Ted Hopf offers a simple analogy:

> The scenario is a fire in a theater where all run for the exits. But absent knowledge of social practices of constitutive norms, structure, even in this seemingly overdetermined circumstance, is still indeterminate. Even in a theater with just one door, while all run for that exit, who goes first? Are they the strongest or the disabled, the women or the children, the aged or the infirm, or is it just a mad dash? Determining the outcome will require knowing more about the situation than about the distribution of material power or the structure of authority. One will need to know about the culture, norms, institutions, procedures, rules, and social practices that constitute the actors and the structure alike.[26]

Constructivists eschew structures. One of the most well-known constructivist theorists, Alexander Wendt, argues that political structure, whether of anarchy or material capabilities, explains nothing. It tells us little about state behavior. "It does not predict whether two states will be friends or foes, will recognize each other's sovereignty, will have dynastic ties, will have revisionist or status quo powers, and so on."[27] What we need to know is identity, and identities change by engaging in cooperative behavior and by learning. Whether the system is anarchic depends on the distribution of identities, not the distribution of military capabilities as the realist would have us believe. If the state identifies only with itself, then the system may be anarchic. If the state identifies with others, then there is no anarchy.

Like the realists and neoliberal institutionalists, constructivists see power as important. But whereas the former just see power in material terms (military, economic, political), constructivists also see power in discursive terms—the power of ideas, culture, and language. Power exists in every exchange among actors and the goal of constructivists is to find the sources of power. Their unique contribution may well be in elucidating the sources of power in ideas and in showing how ideas shape and change identity.

For all the renewed intellectual vigor that constructivism has fostered, this approach has been criticized. With no objective reality, where "the world is in the eye of the beholder," there are no right or wrong answers, only individual perspectives. With no authoritative texts, all texts are equally valid—the musings of the elites and the practices of everyday men and women. In this book, selective examples from constructivist scholarship will allow you to see the approach in use and to begin to develop a feel for this theoretical alternative.

THEORY IN ACTION: ANALYZING THE GULF WAR

The contending theoretical perspectives discussed in the preceding sections see the world and even specific events quite differently. What theorists and policymakers choose to see, what they each seek to explain, and what implications they draw—all these elements of analysis can vary, even though the facts of the event may be the same. Analyzing the Gulf War by using these different theories allows us to compare and contrast the theories in action.

Liberals would tend to focus on two features of the Gulf War. First, a liberal explanation for why the war occurred would concentrate on the individual and state levels of analysis. Thus Saddam Hussein misperceived the international community and did not realize that it would respond with a collective use of force. He was seeking to redress what he perceived to be an illegal situation inherited from the British colonial empire—the fact that part of the Kuwaiti oil fields had historically been a part of the southern Iraqi province of Basra. He was also reacting to difficulties within Iraq itself—the poor economic situation resulting from Iraq's 1980–88 war with Iran, reduced oil revenues, and the Kuwaiti refusal to increase oil outflow to make up for that decline in revenues. Iraq may also have been responding to basic underlying cultural differences between it-self and the West.

Second, a liberal analysis would emphasize the relative success of the in-ternational collectivist response elicited by Iraq's invasion of Kuwait. To many liberals, the response by the United Nations and the multinational coalition were excellent illustrations of a New World Order in which the major powers, as well as many of the developing states, united against an aggressor state. The international community had to accept U.S. leadership, yet the United States was also constrained in its actions—it could not do exactly as it pleased—because it had to serve the needs of the world community.

In contrast, a realist version of the Gulf War would emphasize the in-ternational system of anarchy, where there are few effective constraints on national power save other states. The Gulf War represents yet another case where both major protagonists—Iraq and the United States—were acting out of their respective state interests. Iraq saw its vital security in access to the Persian Gulf; it saw its internal economic problems exacer-bated by the fall in oil revenues. One way out of these dilemmas was to take over Kuwait, an altogether rational response considering advance hints that the United States would be reluctant to get directly involved.

Once Iraq did invade and successfully overrun Kuwait, the U.S. re-sponse was also consistent with its own national interest, according to re-alist thinking. Kuwait's oil resources (and also neighboring Saudi Arabia's) were crucial to the United States; these resources had to be kept under the control of friendly powers. The job of the United States, as leader of the multinational coalition against Iraq, was to convince other states (most importantly Japan, Great Britain, and France) that it was also in their respective national interests to oust Iraq from Kuwait and punish Iraq for aggressive action.

In realist thinking, the balance of power between the United States and the Soviet Union during the Cold War enhanced stability in the Mid-dle East. The various clients of the superpowers were constrained in their actions by the superpowers. The demise of Soviet power, particularly its unwillingness or inability to support Iraq, thus led the Iraqis to try desper-ate measures that they would not have attempted during the Cold War. Realists do not see any new world order, but rather continued instability in an anarchic system. States must be ready and willing to use their full resources to check power with power.

A radical interpretation, like the realist one, would tend to focus on the international system structure. That system structure, for radicals, is embedded in the historical colonial system and its contemporary legacies.

CONTENDING THEORETICAL PERSPECTIVES

	Liberalism/ Neoliberal Institutionalism	Realism/ Neorealism	Radicalism/ Dependency	Constructivism
Key actors	States, non-governmental groups, international organizations	International system, states	Social classes, transnational elites, multinational corporations	Individuals, collective identities
View of the individual	Basically good; capable of cooperating	Power seeking; selfish; antagonistic	Actions determined by economic class	Major unit, especially elites
View of the state	Not an autonomous actor; having many interests	Power seeking; unitary actor; following its national interest	Agent of the structure of international capitalism; executing agent of the bourgeoisie	State behavior shaped by elite beliefs; collective norms; social identity
View of the international system	Interdependence among actors; international society; anarchy	Anarchy; stability in balance-of-power system	Highly stratified; dominated by international capitalist system	Nothing explained by international structures alone
Beliefs about change	Probable; a desirable process	Low change potential; slow structural change	Need for radical change	Explanation of major changes

Political colonialism spawned an imperialist system in which the economic needs of the capitalist states were paramount. In the Middle East, that meant imperialism by the West to secure oil resources. In colonial times, imperialism was state organized; today imperialism is practiced by multinational corporations. Thus, the international petroleum companies, directly threatened by Iraq's takeover of Kuwait, pushed the West to counter Iraq's aggression with force.

Radicals, especially world-system and dependency theorists, would not be surprised at all that the core states of the capitalist system—the United States and its allies—responded with force when Iraq threatened their critical interests in oil. Nor would they expect that the end of the Cold War made any difference in the structure of the system. The major changes in international power relationships that radical seek have not yet come.

Constructivists explain the Gulf War as a conflict between two identities and two loose institutions: Pan-Arabism on the one hand and state sovereignty on the other. Pan-Arabism posits the unity of the Arab world; security and power is in the hands of the collectivity, namely the Arab world, not specific sovereign states. Arab identity has been forged historically through numerous contacts among various members of Arab communities. Thus Pan-Arabism represents one nation with common interests and an identity which is distinct from the West. On the other hand is state sovereignty, a practice forged historically in which states are prohibited from interfering in the domestic affairs of other states. In the Arab Middle East, there is a continual tension between these two identities.

In the Persian Gulf War, Iraq's Saddam Hussein miscalculated. Saudi Arabia was perceived as a Pan-Arab nation rather than a sovereign state. Iraq anticipated that Saudi Arabia would never allow U.S. forces on Arab territory to repel the Iraqi aggression in Kuwait. If Iraq had understood Saudia Arabia as a sovereign state, then Iraq would have expected U.S. military intervention and been deterred from naked aggression in the first place. In Saddam's view, he was uniting a part of the Arab world, and he did not expect to find significant opposition to his actions. The clash between the two identities was responsible for the conflict.[28]

IN SUM: SEEING THE WORLD THROUGH THEORETICAL LENSES

How each of us sees international relations depends on our own theoretical lenses. Do we see things through a realist framework, are we inclined toward a liberal interpretation, or do we adhere to a radical or constructivist view of the world? These lenses differ not only in who they identify as key actors, but in their views about the individual, the state, and the international system—the three levels of analysis. Equally important, these perspectives hold different views about the possibility and desirability of change in the international system.

In the next three chapters, we examine in more detail how each of these three dominant perspectives sees the international system, the state, and the individual. Where applicable, constructivist interpretations will also be included. First we will examine the most general level of analysis—the international system.

NOTES

1. Kenneth N. Waltz, *Man, the State and War* (New York: Columbia University Press, 1954); and J. David Singer, "The Levels of Analysis Problem," *International Politics and Foreign Policy*, ed. James N. Rosenau (Rev. ed.; New York: Free Press, 1961), 20–29.

2. Baron de La Brède et de Montesquieu, *The Spirit of the Laws*, vol. 36, ed. David Wallace Carrithers (Berkeley: University of California Press, 1971), 23.

3. Immanuel Kant, *Perpetual Peace*, ed. Lewis White Beck (New York: Macmillan Co., 1957).

4. Robert Axelrod, and Robert O. Keohane, "Achieving Cooperation under Anarchy: Strategies and Institutions," *Cooperation under Anarchy*, ed. Kenneth Oye (Princeton, N.J.: Princeton University Press, 1986), 226–54.

5. Robert O. Keohane and Joseph Nye, *Power and Interdependence* (3d ed.; New York: Longman, 2001); and Robert O. Keohane and Joseph Nye, "Transnational Relations and World Politics," *International Organization* 25:3 (Summer 1971), 329–50, 721–48.

6. Francis Fukuyama, "The End of History?" *National Interest* 16 (Summer 1989), 4.

7. John Mueller, *Retreat from Doomsday: The Obsolescence of Major War* (New York: Basic Books, 1989).

8. Thucydides, *History of the Peloponnesian War*, trans. Rex Warner (Rev. ed.; Harmondsworth, Eng.: Penguin, 1972).

9. St. Augustine, "Confessions" and "City of God," in *Great Books of the Western World*, vol. 18, ed. Robert Maynard Hutchins (Chicago: Encyclopedia Britannica, 1952, 1986).

10. Niccoló Machiavelli, *The Prince and the Discourses* (New York: Random House, 1940).

11. Thomas Hobbes, *Leviathan*, ed. C. B. Macpherson (Harmondsworth, Eng.: Penguin, 1968), 13.

12. Hans J. Morgenthau, *Politics among Nations* (5th ed. rev.; New York: Knopf, 1978).

13. Kenneth N. Waltz, *Theory of International Politics* (Reading, Mass: Addison-Wesley, 1979).

14. Kenneth N. Waltz, "Realist Thought and Neorealist Theory," in *Controversies in International Relations Theory: Realism and the Neoliberal Challenge,* ed. Charles W. Kegley, Jr. (New York: St. Martin's, 1995), 67–82.

15. Waltz, *Theory of International Politics,* 105.

16. Robert Gilpin, *War and Change in World Politics* (Cambridge, Eng.: Cambridge University Press, 1981), 29.

17. Ibid., 210.

18. Ann Tickner, "Hans Morgenthau's Principles of Political Realism: A Feminist Reformulation," *Millennium: Journal of International Studies* 17:3 (1988), 429–40.

19. Karl Marx, *Capital: A Critique of Political Economy* (New York: Random House, n.d.).

20. Immanuel Wallerstein, *The Modern World-System,* vol. 2, *Mercantilism and the Consolidation of the European World-Economy, 1600–1750* (New York: Academic Press, 1980).

21. Terence K. Hopkins et al., "Patterns of Development in the Modern World-System," in *World-Systems Analysis: Theory and Methodology,* ed. Terence K. Hopkins et al. (Beverly Hills, Calif.: Sage, 1982), 72. Emphasis in the original.

22. John A. Hobson, *Imperialism: A Study,* ed. Philip Siegelman (Ann Arbor: University of Michigan Press, 1965).

23. V. I. Lenin, *Imperialism: The Highest Stage of Capitalism* (New York: International Publishers, 1939).

24. Tony Smith, "The Underdevelopment of the Development Literature: The Case of Dependency Theory," *World Politics* 31:2 (January 1979), 247–88.

25. Stephen M. Walt, "International Relations: One World, Many Theories," *Foreign Policy,* no. 110 (Spring 1998), 29–46.

26. Ted Hopf, "The Promise of Constructivism in International Relations Theory," *International Security,* 23:1 (Summer 1998), 172.

27. Alexander Wendt, "Anarchy Is What States Make of It: The Social Construction of Power Politics," *International Organization,* 46:2 (Spring 1992), 396. For a more complete analysis, see Alexander Wendt, *Social Theory of International Politics.* (Cambridge, Eng.; Cambridge University Press, 1999).

28. Michael Barnett, "Institutions, Roles, and Disorder: The Case of the Arab States System," *International Studies Quarterly* 37:3 (September 1993), 271–96.

THE INTERNATIONAL SYSTEM

4

- *Why is the concept of a system a powerful descriptive and explanatory device?*
- *How would a liberal theorist view the international system?*
- *What concepts do realists employ to analyze the international system?*
- *How do radicals view the international system?*
- *How do each of the contending theoretical perspectives explain change in the international system?*

THE NOTION OF A SYSTEM

Each of the contending theoretical perspectives examined in Chapter 3 described an international system. For realists and radicals, the concept of an international system is vital to their analyses, whereas for liberals, the international system is less precise and less consequential and, for constructivists, system structure is irrelevant.

To understand the international system, the notion of a system itself must be clarified. A **system** is an assemblage of units, objects, or parts united by some form of regular interaction. Systems are essential to the physical and biological sciences; they are composed of different interacting units, whether at the micro (cell, plant, animal) or the macro (natural ecosystem or global climate) level. Because these units interact, a change in one unit causes changes in all others. Systems, with their interacting parts, tend to respond in regularized ways; there are patterns to their actions. Boundaries separate one system from another, but there can be exchanges across these boundaries. A system can break down, meaning that changes become so significant that in effect a new system emerges.

In the 1950s the behavioral revolution in the social sciences and growing acceptance of political realism in international relations led scholars to conceptualize international politics as a system. Beginning with the supposition that men and women act in regularized ways and that their patterns of interaction with each other are largely habitual, both realists and behavioralists made the conceptual leap that international politics is a system whose major actors are individual states.[1] This notion of a system is embedded in the thoughts of the three dominant theoretical schools of international relations.

THE INTERNATIONAL SYSTEM ACCORDING TO LIBERALS

The international system is not central to the view of liberals. It is therefore not surprising to find at least three different conceptions of the international system in liberal thinking.

The first conception sees the international system not as a structure but as a process, in which multiple interactions occur among different parties and where various actors learn from the interaction. Actors in this process include not only states but also international governmental institutions (such as the United Nations), nongovernmental organizations (such as Human Rights Watch) and multinational corporations, and substate actors (such as parliaments and bureaucracies). Each different type of actor has interactions with all of the other ones. With so many different kinds of actors, a plethora of national interests characterizes the liberal international system. While security interests, so dominant for realists, are still important for liberals, other interests such as economic and social issues are also considered, depending on time and circumstance. In their book *Power and Interdependence*, political scientists Robert O. Keohane and Joseph Nye describe the international system as an interdependent system in which the different actors are both sensitive to (affected by) and vulnerable to (suffering costly effects from) the actions of others. In interdependent systems, there are multiple channels connecting states; these channels exist between governmental elites and among nongovernmental elites and transnational organizations, as well. Multiple issues and agendas arise in the international system, but the issues have no hierarchy. The use of military force is generally avoided. Implicit in the notion of interdependence is a system.[2]

A second liberal conception of the international system comes from the English tradition of international society. According to two of the principal architects of this tradition, scholars Hedley Bull and A. Watson, while the international system comprises a group of independent political communities, an **international society** is more than that. In an international society, the various actors communicate; they consent to common rules and institutions and recognize common interests. Actors in international society share a common identity, a sense of "we-ness"; without such an identity, a society cannot exist. This conception of the international system has normative implications: liberals view the international system as an arena and process for positive interactions.[3]

A third view of the international system is that of neoliberal institutionalism, a view that comes closer to realist thinking. Neoliberal institutionalists see the international system as an anarchic one in which each individual state acts in its own self-interest. But unlike many realists, they see the product of the interaction among actors as a potentially positive one, where institutions created out of self-interest serve to moderate state behavior, as states realize they will have future interactions with the other actors involved.

Theory in Brief	
THE LIBERAL PERSPECTIVE ON THE INTERNATIONAL SYSTEM	
Characterization	Three liberal interpretations: interdependence among actors, international society, and anarchy
Actors	States, international governmental institutions, nongovernmental organizations, multinational corporations, substate actors
Constraints	None; ongoing interactions
Possibility of change	No need for radical change; constant shifting as actors are involved in new relationships

All liberals acknowledge and welcome change in the international system. Liberals see changes coming from several sources. First, changes in the international system occur as the result of exogenous technological developments—that is, progress occurring independently, or outside the control of actors in the system. For example, changes in communication and transportation are responsible for the increasing level of interdependence among states within the international system.

Second, change may occur because of changes in the relative importance of different issue areas. While realists give primacy to issues of national security, liberals identify the relative importance of other issue areas. Specifically in the last decades of the twentieth century, economic issues replaced national security issues as the topic of the international agenda, while in the twenty-first century, globalizing issues such as human rights and the environment may assume primacy. These represent fundamental changes in the international system, according to liberal thinking.

Third, change may occur as **new actors**, including multinational corporations, nongovernmental organizations, or other participants in global civil society, may augment or replace state actors. The various new actors may enter into new kinds of relationships and are apt to alter both international system and state behaviors. These types of changes are compatible with liberal thinking and are discussed by liberal writers. Yet, like their realist counterparts, liberal thinkers also acknowledge that change may occur in the overall power structure among the states. This is the view most compatible with realist thinking.

THE INTERNATIONAL SYSTEM ACCORDING TO REALISTS

Political realists have clear notions of the international system and its essential characteristics. All realists characterize the international system as anarchic. No authority exists above the state; the state is sovereign. This anarchical structure constrains the actions of decisionmakers and affects the distribution of capabilities among the various actors. Realists differ among themselves, however, about the degree of a state's autonomy in the international system. Traditional realists acknowledge that states act and shape the system, whereas neorealists believe that actors are constrained by the structure of the system. Yet for both, anarchy is the basic ordering principle and each state in the system must, therefore, look out for its own interests above all.

Realists differentiate the international system along the dimensions of polarity and stratification.

Polarity

System polarity simply refers to the number of blocs of states that exert power in the international system. Realists are particularly interested in polarity because of its focus on power. There are three types of system polarity: **unipolar**, **bipolar**, and **multipolar** (see Figure 4.1).

POLARITY IN THE INTERNATIONAL SYSTEM

Unipolar system: **The post–Cold War era**

Bipolar system: **The Cold War era**

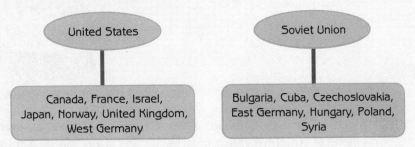

Multipolar system: **Nineteenth-century balance of power**

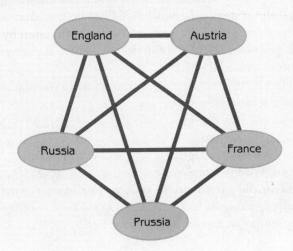

Is the system a unipolar one; that is, is there just one group or even one state that commands influence in the international system? Immediately at the end of the Gulf War in 1991, many states, including the United States closest allies and virtually all Third World states, grew concerned that the international system had become unipolar, with no effective counterweight to the power of the United States. During much of the Cold War era, particularly in the 1950s and 1960s, the international system was bipolar—the United States, its allies in the North Atlantic Treaty Organization (NATO), and Japan versus the Soviet Union and its Warsaw Pact allies. But over the course of the Cold War, the relative tightness or looseness of the bipolar system varied, as powerful states such as the People's Republic of China and France pursued independent paths.

If there are a number of influential actors in the international system, a balance-of-power, or a multipolar, system is formed. In classical balance of power, the actors are exclusively states, and there should be at least five of them. The nineteenth-century balance of power—between England, Russia, Prussia, France, and Austria—is the real-world antecedent discussed in Chapter 2. In multipolar systems, several states—at least three or more—enjoy relative power parity.

In a balance-of-power system, the essential norms of the system are clear to each of the state actors. The In Focus box at the left gives those basic norms of behavior. If an essential actor does not follow these norms, the balance-of-power system may become unstable. If the number of states declines to

IN FOCUS

BASIC NORMS OF THE BALANCE-OF-POWER SYSTEM

▶ Any actor or coalition that tries to assume dominance must be constrained.
▶ States want to increase their capabilities by acquiring territory, increasing their population, or developing economically.
▶ Negotiating is better than fighting.
▶ Fighting is better than failing to increase capabilities, because no one else will protect a weak state.
▶ Other states are viewed as potential allies.
▶ States seek their own national interests defined in terms of power.

three, stability is threatened, because coalitions between any two are possible, leaving the third alone and weak. When alliances are formed in balance-of-power systems, they are specific, have short duration, and shift according to advantage rather than ideology. Any wars that do break out are probably limited in nature, designed to preserve the balance of power.

In bipolar systems, the essential norms are different. Each bloc tries to eliminate its rival. In the bipolar system of the Cold War, each of the blocs (NATO and the Warsaw Pact) sought to negotiate rather than fight, to fight minor wars rather than major ones, and to fight major wars rather than fail to eliminate the rival bloc, although the Cold War never erupted into a "hot" war. In the bipolar system, alliances tend to be long term, based on relatively permanent, not shifting, interests. In a tight bipolar system, international organizations either do not develop or are completely ineffective, as the United Nations was during the height of the Cold War. In a looser bipolar system, international organizations may develop primarily to mediate between the two blocs, and individual states within the looser coalitions may try to use the international organizations for their own advantage.

Polarity is also an important characteristic of the realist international system because of its relationship to system management and stability. Are certain polarities more manageable and hence more stable than others? Are wars more likely to occur in bipolar systems, multipolar systems, or unipolar systems? These questions have dominated much of the discussion among realists, but the studies of these relationships are inconclusive.

Bipolar systems are very difficult to regulate formally, since neither uncommitted states nor international organizations are able to direct the behavior of either of the two blocs. Informal regulation may be easier. If either of the blocs is engaged in disruptive behavior, its consequences are immediately seen, especially if, as a result, one of the blocs gains in strength or position. Thus, Kenneth Waltz, for one, argues that the bipolar international system is the most stable structure in the long run: the two sides are "able both to moderate the other's use of violence and to absorb possibly destabilizing changes that emanate from uses of violence that they do not or cannot control."[4] In such a system, power is clearly differentiated between the two poles and the rest of the state actors. Because of the power disparity, each of the two sides is able to focus its activity on the other, and can anticipate the other's actions and accurately predict its response because of their history of persistent interactions. Each tries to preserve this balance of power in order to preserve itself and the bipolar system.

Pointing to the stability attained in the bipolar Cold War system, the University of Chicago's John Mearsheimer provoked controversy by suggesting that the world will miss the stability and predictability that the Cold War had forged. With the end of the Cold War bipolar system, Mearsheimer argues, more conflict pairs will develop, and hence more possibilities for war. He feels that deterrence will be more difficult and miscalculations more probable. He draws a clear policy implication: "The West has an interest in maintaining peace in Europe. It therefore has an interest in maintaining the Cold War order, and hence has an interest in the continuation of the Cold War confrontation; developments that threaten to end it are dangerous. The Cold War antagonism could be continued at lower levels of East-West tension than have prevailed in the past; hence the West is not insured by relaxing East-West tension, but a complete end to the Cold War would create more problems than it would solve."[5] Most analysts do not share this provocative conclusion, in part because factors other than polarity can affect system stability.

Theoretically, in multipolar and balance-of-power systems, the regulation of system stability ought to be easier than in bipolar systems. The whole purpose of the balancer role, such as that played by Great Britain in the nineteenth century, is to act as a regulator for the system, stepping in to correct a perceived imbalance—as when Great Britain intervened in the Crimean War of 1854–55, opposing Russia on behalf of Turkey. Under multipolarity, numerous interactions take place among all the various parties, and thus there is less opportunity to dwell on a specific relationship. Interaction by any one state actor with a variety of states leads to cross-cutting loyalties and alliances, and therefore moderates hostility or friendship with any one other state actor. States are less likely to respond to the arms buildup of just one party in the system, and so war becomes less likely.

Advocates of unipolarity claim that it is the most stable system. Hegemonic stability theorists claim that unipolarity, or dominance by a hegemon, leads to the most stable international system. Historian Paul Kennedy, in *The Rise and Fall of the Great Powers,* argues that it was the hegemony (though not unipolarity) of Britain in the nineteenth century and that of the United States in the immediate post–World War II era that led to the greatest stability.[6] Other proponents of this theory, such as Keohane, contend that hegemonic states are willing to pay the price and enforce norms unilaterally if necessary, in order to ensure the continuation of the system that benefits them. When the hegemon loses power and declines, then system stability is jeopardized.[7]

It is clear, then, that realists do not agree among themselves on how polarity matters. Individual and group efforts to test the relationship between polarity and stability have been inconclusive. The Correlates of War project (discussed in Chapter 1) did test two hypotheses flowing from the polarity-stability debate. Singer and Small hypothesized that the greater the number of alliance commitments in the system, the more war the system will experience. They also hypothesized that the closer the system is to bipolarity, the more war it will experience. On the basis of the data between 1815 and 1945, however, neither argument is proven valid across the whole time span. During the nineteenth century, alliance commitments prevented war, whereas in the twentieth century, proliferating alliances seemed to predict war.[8]

Behavioral evidence for hegemonic stability theory is explored by the political scientists Michael Webb and Stephen Krasner.[9] During the 1970s, the United States began to decline as a hegemon, according to most aggregate economic measures, although that decline is relative and has been stabilized. Yet through the period of the United States's decline, the international economic system remained relatively stable. These findings suggest that system stability may persist even when the hegemon is in relative decline. Thus system stability is not solely dependent on hegemonic power. The behavioral evidence drawn from realists themselves regarding the relationship between polarity and system stability is, therefore, inconclusive. One possible explanation for the failure to find a conclusive relationship is that determining a system's polarity may be a difficult task and that other factors may intervene, such as the degree of stratification found in the international system.

Stratification

The structure of the international system reflects stratification as well as polarity. Stratification refers to the uneven access to resources by different groups of states; the international system is stratified according to which states have vital resources, such as oil or military strength or economic power. While stratification is the key to understanding the radical notion of the international system (discussed later), it is also important to some realists.

Different international systems have had varying degrees of stratification. Indeed, in the 1990s, system stratification was strong. According to one set of measures, several of the world's powers (the United States, Japan, Germany, France, Britain, Russia, and China) accounted for about one-half of the world's total gross domestic product (GDP), while the other 180-plus states shared the other half (see Figure 4.2). From the stratification of control and resources comes the division between the haves, loosely characterized as the North, and the have-nots, states largely positioned in the South. This distinction is vital to the discussion of international political economy found in Chapter 8.

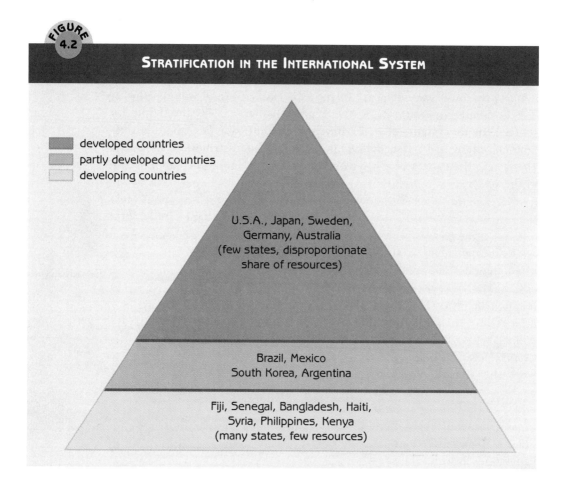

FIGURE 4.2

STRATIFICATION IN THE INTERNATIONAL SYSTEM

■ developed countries
■ partly developed countries
□ developing countries

U.S.A., Japan, Sweden,
Germany, Australia
(few states, disproportionate
share of resources)

Brazil, Mexico
South Korea, Argentina

Fiji, Senegal, Bangladesh, Haiti,
Syria, Philippines, Kenya
(many states, few resources)

Stratification of influence and resources has implications for the ability of a system to regulate itself, as well as for system stability. When the dominant powers are challenged by those states just beneath them in terms of access to resources, the system may become highly unstable. For example, Germany's and Japan's attempts to obtain and reclaim resources during the 1930s led to World War II. Such a group of second-tier powers has the potential to win a confrontation, whereas the real underdogs in a severely stratified system do not (although they can cause major disruptions). The rising powers, especially those who are acquiring resources, seek first-tier status and are willing to fight wars to get it. If the challenger does not begin a war, the top powers may do so to quell the threat of a power displacement.

How the International System Changes

Although realists value the continuity of systems, they recognize that international systems do change. For example, at the end of the nineteenth century the multipolar balance of power broke down and was replaced by a tight alliance system pitting the Triple Alliance against the Triple Entente. Why do systems change? Realists attribute system change to three factors: changes in the actors and hence the distribution of power, changes in the norms of the system, and changes emanating from outside of the system.

Changes in either the number of major actors or the relative power relationship among the actors may result in a fundamental change in the international system. Wars are usually responsible for such fundamental changes in power relationships. For example, the end of World War II brought the relative demise of Great Britain and France, even though they were the victors. The war also signaled the end not only of Germany's and Japan's imperial aspirations but of their basic national capabilities as well. Their re-

> **Theory in Brief**
>
> ### THE REALIST PERSPECTIVE ON THE INTERNATIONAL SYSTEM
>
> | | |
> |---|---|
> | **Characterization** | Anarchic |
> | **Actors** | State primary actor |
> | **Constraints** | Polarity; stratification |
> | **Possibility of change** | Slow change when the balance of power shifts |

spective militaries were soundly defeated; civil society was destroyed and infrastructure demolished. Two other powers emerged into dominant positions—the United States, now willing to assume the international role that it had shunned after World War I, and the Soviet Union, buoyed by its victory although economically weak. The international system had fundamentally changed; the multipolar world had been replaced by a bipolar one.

Robert Gilpin, in *War and Change in World Politics*, sees another form of system change where states act to preserve their own interests and thereby change the international system. Such changes can occur because states respond at different rates to political, economic, and technological developments. For example, the rapidly industrializing states in Asia— South Korea, Taiwan, and Hong Kong (though now part of China)—have responded to technological change the fastest. By responding rapidly and with single-mindedness, these states have been able to improve their relative positions in terms of system stratification. Thus, characteristics of the international system can be changed by the actions of a few.[10]

Changes in the social norms of a system can also lead to a fundamental shift in the system. Not all norm changes are system transforming, but some may be. The advent of nuclear technology in warfare, for example, resulted in what many scholars have labeled a fundamental change in rules. As the Cold War persisted without either of the superpowers exploding nuclear weapons, the norm of prohibition against their use strengthened and solidified. Decisionmakers in both the United States and the Soviet Union clearly saw the nuclear threshold to be a significant one. The longer the use of such weapons is forestalled, the more likely that the norm has changed. Indeed, in the 1990s, even open testing of these weapons, carried out by France in 1995 and the People's Republic of China in 1996, has been greeted with outrage in the international community; these countries are viewed as having violated the norms. These changes in norms had profound implications for the maintenance of the bipolar system. The superpowers, constrained by norms from directly fighting each other, fought through proxy, using conventional military technology and scrupulously avoiding breaching the nuclear threshold.

Exogenous changes may also lead to a shift in the international political system. Advances in technology—the instruments for oceanic navigation, the airplane for transoceanic crossings, or satellites and rockets for exploration of outer space—not only have expanded the boundaries of geographic space but also have brought about changes in the boundaries of the international political system. The Eurocentric system of the pre–World War II world has been expanded into a truly international system. With that change came a massive increase in the number of state actors, reflecting not only different political interests but also vastly different cultural traditions.

Thus, international systems can change, yet the inherent bias among the realist interpretations is for continuity. All realists agree that there are patterns of change in the system, although they may disagree on the appropriate time frame to study the changes. Efforts by realists to test many of the ideas coming from their notions about the international system have proven inconclusive.

THE INTERNATIONAL SYSTEM ACCORDING TO RADICALS

Whereas realists define the international system in terms of structure and the political power of interacting states, radicals seek to describe and explain the structure itself. The system that they see is totally different. In contrast to realists, who value system stability, radicals desire change and want to discover why change is so difficult to achieve.

Radicals are concerned primarily with stratification in the international system. Are influence and access to resources evenly distributed? Their answer is plainly no. Is there a group of major powers (the "top-dog" capitalists) who control a disproportionate percentage of the world's resources, and a large group of minor powers who have very little? The radical answer is unequivocally yes. The central question is: Why are some states economically advantaged, while others are permanently disadvantaged?

For Marxists, as well as most other radicals, crippling stratification in the international system is caused by capitalism. Capitalism structures the relationship between the advantaged and the disadvantaged, empowering the rich and disenfranchising the weak. Marxists assert that capitalism breeds its own instruments of domination, including international institutions whose rules are structured by capitalist states to facilitate capitalist processes, multinational corporations whose headquarters are in capitalist states but whose loci of activity are in dependent areas, and even individuals (often leaders) or classes (the national bourgeoisie) residing in weak states who are co-opted to participate in and perpetuate an economic system that places the masses in a permanently dependent position.

Theory in Brief

THE RADICAL PERSPECTIVE ON THE INTERNATIONAL SYSTEM

Characterization	Highly stratified
Actors	Capitalist states vs. developing states
Constraints	Capitalism; stratification
Possibility of change	Radical change desired but limited by the capitalist structure

Radicals believe that the greatest amount of resentment will be felt in systems where the stratification is most extreme. There, the poor are likely to be not only resentful but aggressive. They want change, but the rich have very little incentive to change their behavior. The call for the **New International Economic Order (NIEO)** in the 1970s was voiced by radicals and liberal reformers alike. The poorer, developing states of the South, the underdogs with a dearth of resources, sought fundamental changes, including debt forgiveness, international controls on multinational corporations, and major changes in how primary commodities were priced. They sought a greater share of the world's resources and an ability to exercise greater power. Other states of the South, including those which were further along in developing and their northern allies, sought a more reformist agenda, including debt refinancing (not forgiveness), more concessionary aid, and voluntary controls on multinational corporations.

In short, radicals find the explanation for great economic disparities built into the structure of the international system. All actions and interactions are constrained by this structure. Realists recognize this constraint as well, but for them it is a positive one, inhibiting aggressive actions. For Marxists, however, the constraint is profoundly negative, preventing economic change and development.

The world-system version of Marxism elucidated by Immanuel Wallerstein and others posits that the system structure *is* capitalism, which transcends geographic, political, or economic boundaries. Since the sixteenth century, capitalism has been the defining characteristic of the international system—shaping, constraining, and causing behavior.

World-system theorists, like other radicals, do see change within the capitalist system. Change is evident in the shuffling of the states at the core of the system: the Dutch were replaced by the British and the British by the Americans. Change may occur in the semiperiphery and periphery, as states change their relative positions vis-à-vis each other. And capitalism goes through cycles of growth and expansion, as occurred during the age of colonialism and imperialism, followed by periods of contraction and decline. So capitalism itself is a dynamic force.

But can the capitalist system itself be changed? In other words, is system transformation—like the change from the feudal to the capitalist system—possible? Here, the radicals differ among themselves. Wallerstein, for example, is quite pessimistic, claiming that any change that does occur is painfully slow. Others are more optimistic. Just as realists disagree among themselves about the critical dimension of the international system, radicals disagree about the likelihood that the system stratification that they all abhor will be altered.

ADVANTAGES AND DISADVANTAGES OF THE INTERNATIONAL SYSTEM AS A LEVEL OF ANALYSIS

For adherents of all three theoretical perspectives, there are clear advantages to using the international system as a level of analysis. The language of systems theory allows comparisons and contrasts across the system: the international system at one point in time may be compared with one at another point in time; international systems may be compared with their domestic counterparts; political systems may be contrasted with social or even biological systems. How these various systems interact is the focus of the social and natural sciences.

For all the sciences, the most significant advantage to this level of analysis lies in the comprehensiveness of systems theory. It enables a scholar to organize the seemingly disjointed parts into a whole; to hypothesize; and then to test how these various parts, actors, and rules are related and show how change in one part of the system results in changes in other parts. In this sense, the notion of a system is a significant research tool.

In short, systems theory is a holistic, or top-down, approach. Although it cannot provide descriptions of events at the micro level (such as why a particular individual acted a certain way), it does allow plausible explanations at the more general level. For the realists, generalizations derived

Theory in Brief

CONTENDING PERSPECTIVES ON THE INTERNATIONAL SYSTEM

	Liberalism	Realism	Radicalism
Characterization	Three liberal interpretations: interdependence among actors, international society, and anarchy	Anarchic	Highly stratified
Actors	States, international governmental institutions, nongovernmental organizations, substate actors	State primary actor	Capitalist states vs. developing states
Constraints	None; ongoing interactions	Polarity; stratification	Capitalism; stratification
Possibility of change	No need for radical change, but constant shifting as actors are involved in new relationships	Slow change when the balance of power shifts	Radical change desired but limited by the capitalist structure

from systems theory provide the fodder for prediction, the ultimate goal of all behavioral science. For liberals and radicals, these generalizations have definite normative implications; in the former case they affirm movement toward a positive system, and in the latter case they confirm pessimistic assessments about the place of states in the economically determined international system.

But systems theory also has some glaring weaknesses and inadequacies. The emphasis at the international system level means that the "stuff" of politics is often neglected, while the generalizations are broad and sometimes obvious. Who disputes that most states seek to maintain their relative capability or that most states prefer to negotiate rather than fight under all but a few circumstances? Who doubts that some states occupy a preeminent economic position that determines the status of all others?

Just as the theory has a number of weaknesses, so is the testing of the theory very difficult. In most cases, theorists are constrained by a lack of historical information. After all, few systems theorists, besides some radical and cyclical theorists, discuss systems predating 1648. In fact, most begin with the nineteenth century. Those using earlier time frames are constrained both by poor grounding in history and by glaring lapses in the historical record. Although these weaknesses are not fatal ones, they restrict the scholar's ability to test specific hypotheses over a long time period.

International system theorists have always been hampered by the problem of boundaries. If they use the notion of the international system, do they mean the international *political* system? What factors lie outside of the system? In fact, much realist theorizing systematically ignores this critical question by differentiating several different levels within the system, but only one international-system-level construct. Liberals do better, differentiating factors external to the system and even incorporating those factors into their expanded notion of an interdependent international system. Yet if you cannot clearly distinguish between what is inside and what is outside of the system, do you in fact have a system? And even more important, what shapes the system? What is the reciprocal relationship between international system constraints and unit (state) behavior? By way of contrast, constructivists do not acknowledge such boundaries. There is no relevant distinction between the international system and the state or between international system and the state or between international politics and domestic politics. There is no distinction between endogenous and exogenous sources of change.

IN SUM: FROM INTERNATIONAL SYSTEM TO STATE

Of the three theoretical approaches, realists and radicals pay the most attention to the international system level of analysis. For realists, the defining characteristic of the international system is polarity; for Marxists, it is stratification. To both, the international system constrains states, yet for realists the constraint is a positive one—preventing states from engaging in aggressive activity—while for the Marxists, the constraint is a negative one—preventing economically depressed states from achieving equity and justice. Preservation of the status quo is the goal of realists, whereas major system change is the goal of radicals. Liberals, by contrast, see the international system as a way to conceptualize various interactions above the level of the state. For liberals, the international system is seen in a positive light, as an arena and process for interaction.

Given the difficulties of determining boundaries and of assessing causation between the system and its parts, it is not surprising that many analysts prefer the state level of analysis, to which we turn in the next chapter.

NOTES

1. See especially Morton Kaplan, *System and Process in International Politics* (New York: Krieger, 1976).
2. Robert O. Keohane and Joseph S. Nye, *Power and Interdependence* (3rd ed.; New York: Longman, 2001).
3. Hedley Bull and Adam Watson, eds., *The Expansion of International Society* (Oxford, Eng.: Oxford University Press, 1984).
4. Kenneth Waltz, "International Structure, National Force, and the Balance of World Power," *Journal of International Affairs* 21:2 (1967), 229.
5. John J. Mearsheimer, "Back to the Future: Instability after the Cold War," *International Security* 15:1 (Summer 1990), 52.
6. Paul M. Kennedy, *The Rise and Fall of the Great Powers: Economic Change and Military Conflict from 1500 to 2000* (New York: Random House, 1987).
7. Robert O. Keohane, *After Hegemony: Cooperation and Discord in the World Political Economy* (Princeton, N.J.: Princeton University Press, 1984).
8. J. David Singer and Melvin Small, "Alliance Aggregation and the Onset of War," in *Quantitative International Politics*, ed. J. David Singer (New York: Free Press, 1968), 246–86.
9. Michael C. Webb and Stephen D. Krasner, "Hegemonic Stability Theory: An Empirical Assessment," *Review of International Studies* 15 (1989), 183–98.
10. Robert Gilpin, *War and Change in World Politics* (Cambridge, Eng.: Cambridge University Press, 1981).

THE STATE

5

- *What is the state, the major actor in international relations?*
- *What are the different views of the state held by the various theoretical perspectives?*
- *How is state power measured?*
- *What methods do states use to exercise power?*
- *What models help us explain how states make foreign-policy decisions?*
- *What are the major contemporary challenges to the state?*

In thinking about international relations, the state is central. We see the United States versus Russia, France and Germany as allies, and North and South Korea as enemies. Much of the history traced in Chapter 2 was the history of how the state developed, emerging from the post-Westphalian framework, and how the state, sovereignty, and the nation developed in tandem. Two of the theoretical perspectives—realism and liberalism—acknowledge the primacy of the state. Yet despite this emphasis on the state, it is inadequately conceptualized. As the scholar James Rosenau laments, "All too many studies posit the state as a symbol without content, as an actor whose nature, motives, and conduct are so self-evident as to obviate any need for precise conceptualizing. Often, in fact, the concept seems to be used as a residual category to explain that which is otherwise inexplicable in macro politics."[1] We need to do better.

THE STATE AND THE NATION

For an entity to be considered a **state,** four fundamental conditions must be met. First, a state must have a _territorial base_, a geographically defined boundary. Second, within its borders, a_stable population_ must reside. Third, there should be a _government_ to which this population owes allegiance. Finally, a state has to be _recognized diplomatically_ by other states.

These legal criteria are not absolute. Most states do have a territorial base, though the precise borders are often the subject of dispute. Until the Palestinian Authority was given a measure of control over the West Bank and Gaza, for instance, the state of the Palestinians was not territorially based. It was, however, given special observer status in international bodies and was viewed as a quasi-state. Most states have a stable population, but migrant communities and nomadic peoples cross borders, as the Masai peoples of Kenya and Tanzania do, undetected by state authorities. Most states have some type of institutional structure for governance, but whether the people are obedient to it can be unknown, because of lack of information, or problematic, because the institutional legitimacy of the government is constantly questioned. A state need not have a particular form of government, but most of its people must acknowledge the legitimacy of the government. In 1997, the peoples of Zaire (subsequently renamed the Democratic Republic of the Congo) told the rest of the international community that they no longer recognized the legitimacy of the government led by Mobutu Sese Seko, plunging the country into a civil war. Finally, other states must recognize the state diplomatically; but how many states does it take for this criterion to be fulfilled? The Republic of Transkei—a tiny piece of real estate carved out of South Africa—was recognized by just one state, South Africa. This proved insufficient to give Transkei status as a state, and the territory was soon reincorporated into South Africa. So while the legal conditions for statehood provide a yardstick, that measuring stick is not absolute. Some entities that do not fulfill all the legal criteria are still states.

The definition of a state differs from that of a **nation.** The nation refers to the characteristics of the people. Do a people share a common history and heritage, a common language and customs, or similar lifestyles? If so, then the people are a nation. It was this feeling of commonality, of people uniting together for a cause, that provided the foundation for the French Revolution and spread to the Americas and to central Europe. It was nationalism—the belief that nations should form their own states—that propelled the formation of a unified Italy and Germany in the nineteenth century. At the core of the concept of a nation is the notion that people having commonalities owe their allegiance to the nation and to its legal representative, the state. The recognition of commonalities among people (and hence of differences from other groups) spread with new technologies and education. When the printing press became widely used, the masses could read in their national languages; with improved methods of transportation, people could travel, witnessing firsthand similarities and differences among peoples. With better communications, elites could use the media to promote unity or sometimes to exploit differences.

Some nations, like France and Italy, formed their own states. This coincidence between state and nation, the **nation-state,** is the foundation for national self-determination. Peoples sharing nationhood have a right to determine how and under what conditions they should live. Other nations are spread among several states. For example, Germans resided and still live not only in a united Germany but in the far-off corners of eastern Europe; Kurds live in Iraq, Iran, and Turkey; Somalis live in Kenya, Ethiopia, and Djibouti as well as in Somalia. Still other states have within their borders several different nations—India, the United States, Canada, Russia, and South Africa are prominent examples. In the United States and Canada, a number of different Native American nations are a part of the state. In these cases, the state and the nation do not coincide. Some nations want to have states, as the Kurds have argued for decades and as some Quebecois seek for their province in Canada. Other nations, such as the Basques in Spain and France, desire adequate and fair representation within the existing state—special seats in representative bodies, concessions for language diversity, or even territory demarcated for special nationalities. Thus, the post-Westphalian state can be a nation-state, where there is a congruence between state and nation, or it may be a state, like the United States or Canada, where nationalities are diverse.

CONTENDING CONCEPTUALIZATIONS OF THE STATE

Just as the nation is more than a historic entity, the state is more than a legal entity. There are numerous competing conceptualizations of the state, many of which emphasize concepts absent from the legalistic approach.

The state is a normative order, a symbol for a particular society and the beliefs that bind the people living within its borders. It is also the entity that has a monopoly on the legitimate use of violence within a society. The state is a functional unit that takes on a number of important responsibilities, centralizing and unifying them.[2] Among these different conceptualizations, three perspectives of the state parallel the general theories discussed in Chapters 3 and 4. For two of these theoretical perspectives, the state is paramount.

The Liberal View of the State

In the liberal view, the state enjoys sovereignty but is not an autonomous actor. Just as the international system represents a process occurring among many actors, liberals see the state as a process whose function is to maintain the basic rules of the game. These rules ensure that various interests (both governmental and societal actors) compete fairly and effectively in the game of politics. There is no explicit or consistent national interest; there are many. These interests often compete against each other within a pluralistic framework. A state's national interests change, reflecting the interests and relative power positions of competing groups inside and sometimes outside of the state.

IN FOCUS

THE LIBERAL VIEW OF THE STATE

The state is:
▶ A process, involving contending interests
▶ A reflection of both governmental and societal interests
▶ The repository of multiple and changing national interests
▶ The possessor of fungible sources of power

The Realist View of the State

Realists generally hold a statist, or state-centric, view. They believe that the state is an autonomous actor constrained only by the structural anarchy of the international system. The state enjoys sovereignty; that is, the authority to govern matters that are within its own borders and affect its people, economy, security, and form of government. As a sovereign entity, the state has a consistent set of goals—that is, a national interest—defined in terms of power. Different kinds of power can

IN FOCUS

THE REALIST VIEW OF THE STATE

The state is:
▶ An autonomous actor
▶ Constrained only by the anarchy of the international system
▶ Sovereign
▶ Guided by a national interest that is defined in terms of power

be translated into military power. While power is of primary importance to realists, as we will see later in this chapter, ideas also matter; ideology, for example, can determine the nature of the state, as with the North Korean state under communism. But in international relations, once the state (with power and ideas) acts, according to the realists, it does so as an autonomous, unitary actor.

The Radical View of the State

Radicals offer two alternative views of the state, each emphasizing the role of capitalism and the capitalist class in the formation and functioning of the state. The *instrumental* Marxist view sees the state as the executing agent of the bourgeoisie. The bourgeoisie reacts to direct societal pressures, especially to pressures from the capitalist class. The *structural* Marxist view sees the state as operating within the structure of the capitalist system. Within that system, the state is driven to expand, not because of the direct pressure of the capitalists but because of the imperatives of the capitalist system. In neither view is there a national interest: state behavior reflects economic goals. In neither case is real sovereignty possible, as the state is continually reacting to external (and internal) capitalist pressures.

IN FOCUS

THE RADICAL VIEW OF THE STATE

The state is:
▶ The executing agent of the bourgeoisie
▶ Influenced by pressures from the capitalist class
▶ Constrained by the structure of the international capitalist system

Contrasting the Liberal, Realist, and Radical Views

The three conceptualizations of the state can be easily contrasted using the example of an important primary commodity—oil.[3] Liberals believe that multiple national interests influence state actions: consumer groups desire the oil at the lowest price possible; manufacturers, who depend on bulk supplies to run their factories, prefer stability of the supply of oil, otherwise they have no jobs; producers of oil, including domestic producers, want high prices, so they make profits and have incentives to reinvest in drilling. The state itself reflects no consistent viewpoint about the oil; its task is to ensure that the "playing field is level" and the procedural rules are the same for the various players in the market. The substantive outcome of the game—which group's interests predominate—changes depending on circumstances and is of little import to the state. When negotiations occur, the state assures that the various interests have a voice and provides a forum for the interactions. There is no single or consistent national interest: at times, it is defined in terms of low consumer prices; at other times, as stability of prices; and at still other times, as high prices in order to stimulate domestic production.

A realist interpretation, on the other hand, posits a uniform national interest that is articulated by the state. The state desires stability in the availability and prices of primary commodities. For example, the United States needs to be assured that there will be a safe and secure supply of oil and seeks to obtain it at relatively uniform prices. When the United States negotiates in international forums, with individual supplier states, or with multinational companies, the national interest of the state is the bottom line of the negotiations.

In the radical perspective, primary commodity policy reflects the interests of the capitalist class aligned with the bourgeoisie (in the instrumental Marxist view) and reflects the structure of the international capitalist system (in structural Marxist thinking). Both views would more than likely see the negotiating process as exploitative, where the weak (poor and dependent groups or states) are sacrificed for the advancement of strong capitalists or capitalist states. According to radical thinking, the international petroleum companies are the capitalists, aligned with hegemonic states. They are able to negotiate favorable prices to the detriment of poor, developing, oil-producing states like Mexico or Nigeria.

Thus, liberals, realists, and radicals hold different views about the state. These differences can be seen in four topic areas: the nature of state power (what is power? what are important sources of power?), the use of state power (the relative importance of different techniques of statecraft), how foreign policy is made (the statist vs. the bureaucratic or pluralist view of decisionmaking), and the determinants of foreign policy (the relative importance of domestic vs. international factors).

THE NATURE OF STATE POWER

States are critical actors because they have power, which is the ability not only to influence others but to control outcomes in a way that would not have occurred naturally. States have power vis-à-vis each other and with respect to those within the state. Yet power itself is a multidimensional relationship; there are different kinds of power. The outcome of the power relationship—whether and to what extent power is used or abused—is determined, in part, by the power potential of each of the parties involved.

All three theoretical perspectives acknowledge the importance of power. But to realists, power is the currency of international relations. It is the means by which international actors deal with each other. For this reason, we will pay particular attention to the realist view of power, then show how liberals, radicals, and constructivists see power differently.

Natural Sources of Power

Through the exercise of power, states have influence over others and can control the direction of policies and events. Whether power is effective at influencing outcomes depends, in part, on the **power potential** of each party. A state's power potential depends on its natural sources of power, each of which is critical to both realist and radical perspectives. The three most important natural sources of power are geographic size and position, natural resources, and population.

Geographic size and position are the natural sources recognized first by international relations theorists. A large geographic expanse gives a state automatic power (when one thinks of power, one thinks of large states—Russia, China, the United States, Australia, India, Canada, or Brazil, for instance). Long borders, however, may be a weakness: they must be defended, an expensive and often problematic task.

Two different views about the importance of geography in international relations emerged at the turn of the century within the realist tradition. In the late 1890s, the naval officer and historian Alfred T. Mahan (1840–1914) wrote of the importance of controlling the sea. He argued that the state that controls the ocean routes controls the world. To Mahan, sovereignty over land was not as critical as having access to and control over sea routes.[4] In 1904, the British geographer Sir Halford Mackinder (1861–1947) countered this view. To Mackinder, the state that has the most power is the one that controls the Eurasian geographic "heartland": "He who rules Eastern Europe commands the Heartland of Eurasia; who rules the Heartland commands the World Island of Europe, Asia, and Africa, and who rules the World Island commands the world."[5]

Both views have empirical validity. British power in the eighteenth and nineteenth centuries was determined largely by its dominance on the seas, a power that allowed Britain to colonialize distant places, including India, much of Africa, and North and Central America. Russia's lack of easy access to the sea and its resultant inability to wield naval power has been viewed as a persistent weakness in that country's power potential. Control of key oceanic choke points—the Straits of Malacca, Gibraltar, and Hormuz; the Dardanelles; the Persian Gulf; and the Suez and Panama Canals—is viewed as a positive indicator of power potential.

Yet geographic position in Mackinder's heartland of Eurasia has also proven to be a significant source of power potential. More than any other country Germany has acted to secure its power through its control of the heartland of Eurasia, acting very clearly according to Mackinder's dictum, as interpreted by the German geographer Karl Haushofer (1869–1946). Haushofer, who had served in both the Bavarian and the German armies, was disappointed by Germany's loss in World War I. Arguing that Germany could become a powerful state if it could capture the Eurasian heartland, he set out to make geopolitics a legitimate area for academic inquiry. He founded an institute and a journal, thrusting himself into a position as the leading supporter and proponent of Nazi expansion.

But geographic power potential is magnified or constrained by natural resources, a second source of natural power. Controlling a large geographic expanse is not a positive ingredient of power unless that expanse contains natural resources. The petroleum-exporting states (see Box 5.1), which are geographically small but have a crucial natural resource, have greater power potential than their sizes would suggest. States need oil and are ready to pay dearly for it, and will even go to war when access to it is denied. States that have such valuable natural resources, regardless of geographic size, wield power over states that do not. The United States, Russia, and South Africa exert vast power potential because of their diverse natural resources—oil, copper, bauxite, vanadium,

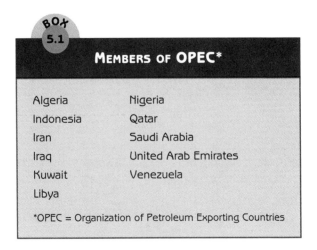

BOX 5.1

MEMBERS OF OPEC*

Algeria	Nigeria
Indonesia	Qatar
Iran	Saudi Arabia
Iraq	United Arab Emirates
Kuwait	Venezuela
Libya	

*OPEC = Organization of Petroleum Exporting Countries

gold, and silver. Of course, having a sought-after resource may prove a liability, making states targets for aggressive actions, as Kuwait soberly learned in 1990. The absence of natural resources does not mean that a state has no power potential, however; Japan is not rich in natural resources, but it has parlayed other ingredients into making itself an economic powerhouse.

Population is a third natural power ingredient. Sizable populations, like those found in China (1.2 billion people), India (960 million), the United States (281 million), and Russia (147 million), automatically give power potential, and often great power status, to a state.[6] Although a large population produces a variety of goods and services, characteristics of that population (poor educational levels, low level of social services) may serve as a constraint on state power. States with small, highly educated, skilled populations, like Switzerland, Norway, Austria, and Singapore, can nevertheless fill disproportionately large economic and political niches.

These natural power ingredients are modified by the use and organization of power into tangible and intangible sources. These sources are used to enhance, modify, or constrain power potential, as shown in Figure 5.1.

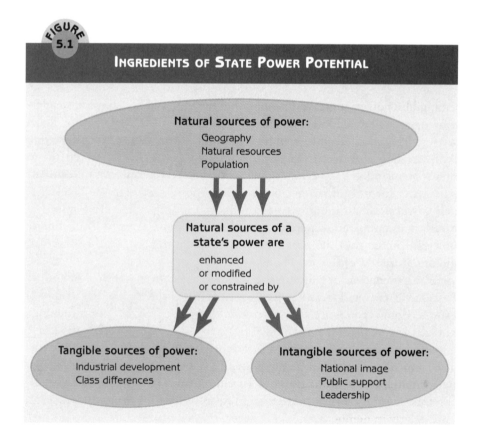

FIGURE 5.1

INGREDIENTS OF STATE POWER POTENTIAL

Natural sources of power:
Geography
Natural resources
Population

Natural sources of a state's power are
enhanced
or modified
or constrained by

Tangible sources of power:
Industrial development
Class differences

Intangible sources of power:
National image
Public support
Leadership

Tangible Sources of Power

Among the tangible elements, industrial development is among the most critical. With an advanced industrial capacity, the advantages and disadvantages of geography diminish. Air travel, for example, makes geographic expanse less a barrier to commerce, yet at the same time makes even large states militarily vulnerable. With industrialization, the importance of population is modified, too. Large but poorly equipped armies are no match for small armies with advanced equipment. Industrialized states generally have higher educational levels, more-advanced technology, and more efficient use of capital, all of which add to their tangible power potential.

Like realists, radicals acknowledge the importance of power ingredients and power potential. But where realists organize power around the state, radicals see power ingredients in class terms. According to radicals, differences over who has the power ingredients lead to the creation of different classes, some more powerful (the capitalist class that owns the means of production) than others (the workers). These classes transcend state and national borders.

Intangible Sources of Power

Intangible power ingredients—national image, public support, leadership—may be as important as the tangible elements. People within states have images of their state's power potential—images that translate into an intangible power ingredient. Canadians have typically viewed themselves as internationally responsible and eager to participate in multilateral peacekeeping missions, to provide generous foreign aid packages, and to respond unselfishly to international emergencies. The state has acted on and, indeed, helped to shape that image, making Canada a more powerful actor than its small population (30 million) would otherwise dictate.

The perception of public support and cohesion is another intangible element of power. China's power was magnified during the leadership of Mao Zedong (1893–1976), when there appeared to be unprecedented public support for the communist leadership and a high degree of societal cohesion. And Israel's successful campaigns in the Middle East in the 1967 and 1973 wars can be attributed in large part to strong public support, including the willingness of Israeli citizens to pay the cost and die for their country when necessary. When that public support is absent, particularly in democracies, the power potential of the state is diminished.

Witness the U.S. loss in the Vietnam War, when challenges to and disagreement with the war effort undermined military effectiveness. Loss of public support may also inhibit authoritarian systems. Remember the Iraqi soldiers haplessly surrendering to coalition troops on the deserts of Kuwait? Saddam Hussein's support from his own troops was woefully inadequate; they were not ready to die for the Iraqi regime.

Leadership is another intangible power ingredient. Visionaries and charismatic leaders such as India's Mohandas Gandhi, France's Charles de Gaulle, the United States's Franklin Roosevelt, Germany's Otto von Bismarck, and Britain's Winston Churchill were able to augment the power potential of their states by taking bold initiatives. Poor leaders, those who squander public resources and abuse the public trust, such as Libya's Muammar Qaddafi, Zaire's Mobutu Sese Seko, and Iraq's Saddam Hussein, diminish the state's power capability and its capacity to exert power over the long term. Liberals, in particular, pay attention to leadership: good leaders can avoid resorting to war; bad leaders may not be able to prevent it.

Clearly, when coupled with the tangible, intangible power ingredients either augment a state's capacity or diminish its power. Liberals, who have a more expansive notion of power, would more than likely place greater importance on these intangible ingredients, since several are characteristics of domestic processes. Yet different combinations of the sources of power may lead to varying outcomes. The victory by the NATO alliance over Milosevic's Yugoslavian forces in 1999 can be explained by the alliance's overwhelming natural sources of power coupled with its strong tangible sources of power. But how can Afghanistan's victory over the Soviet Union in the early 1980s be explained, or the North Vietnamese victory over the United States in the 1970s, or the Algerian victory over France in the early 1950s? In those cases, countries with limited natural and tangible sources of power were able to prevail over those with strong natural and tangible power resources. In these cases, the intangible sources of power, including the willingness of the populations to continue to fight against overwhelming odds, explains victory by the objectively weaker side.[7] Success in using various forms of state power clearly depends on the specific context.

Constructivists, by way of contrast, offer a unique perspective on power. They argue that power includes not only the tangible and intangible sources. In addition, power includes the power of ideas and language—as distinguished from ideology, which fueled the unlikely victory of the objectively weaker side. It is through the power of ideas and language that state identities are forged and changed.

USING STATE POWER

In all theoretical perspectives, power is not just to be possessed, it is to be used. Using state power is a difficult task.

States use a variety of techniques to translate power potential into effective power. All states use the techniques of statecraft shown in Figure 5.2: diplomacy, economic statecraft, and force. In a particular situation, a state may begin with one approach and then try a number of others to influence the intended target. In other cases, several different techniques may be utilized simultaneously. Which techniques political scientists think states emphasize varies across the theoretical perspectives.

The Art of Diplomacy

Traditional **diplomacy** entails states trying to influence the behavior of others by negotiating, by taking a specific action or refraining from such an action, or by conducting public diplomacy. In using diplomacy to project power, a state might engage in the following activities:

- Express to the target state, either publicly or privately, unhappiness with its policy choice.
- Suggest that a better relationship would follow if the target state's actions change in a specific way.

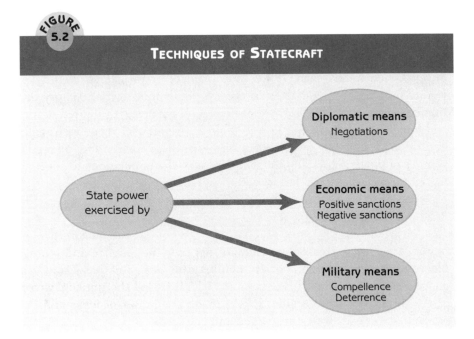

FIGURE 5.2

TECHNIQUES OF STATECRAFT

State power exercised by

Diplomatic means
Negotiations

Economic means
Positive sanctions
Negative sanctions

Military means
Compellence
Deterrence

- Threaten that negative consequences will follow if the target state continues to move in a specific direction.
- Turn to an international body to seek multilateral legitimization for its position, thus enlisting the support of other states on its behalf.
- Give the target state what it wants (diplomatic recognition, foreign aid) in return for desired actions.
- Remove what the target state wants (reduce foreign aid, withdraw diplomats, sever diplomatic ties) when it takes undesirable actions.

Diplomacy usually begins with bargaining, through direct or indirect communication, in an attempt to reach agreement on an issue. This bargaining may be conducted tacitly among the parties, each of whom recognizes that a move in one direction leads to a response by the other. The bargaining may be conducted openly in formal negotiations, where one side offers a formal proposal and the other responds in kind; this is repeated many times until a compromise is reached. In either case, reciprocity usually occurs, wherein each side responds to the other's moves in kind.

States seldom enter diplomatic bargaining or negotiations as power equals. Each has knowledge of its own and its opponent's power potential, as well as information about its own goals. Thus, although the outcome of the bargaining is almost always mutually beneficial (if not, why bother?), the outcome is not likely to please each of the parties equally.

Bargaining and negotiations are complex processes, complicated by at least two critical factors. First, most states carry out two levels of bargaining simultaneously: international bargaining between and among states, and the bargaining that must occur between the state's negotiators and its various domestic constituencies, both to arrive at a negotiating position and to ratify the agreement reached by the two states. Political scientist Robert Putnam refers to this as the "two-level game."[8] International trade negotiations within the World Trade Organization are such a two-level game. For example, Japan and South Korea bargain with the United States over the liberalization of rice markets. The United States supports liberalization in order to improve the balance of trade between it and the respective Asian powers; by advocating this position, the United States supports its own domestic rice producers, located in the key electoral states of California and Texas. Japan and South Korea have powerful domestic interests opposing liberalization, including rice farmers strategically located in virtually all voting constituencies. Thus, in each case, the United States and Japan or Korea are each conducting two sets of negotiations: one with the foreign state and the other within the domestic political arena. What makes the game unusually complex is that "moves that are rational for one player at one board . . . may be impolitic for that same player at the other board."[9] The negotiator is the formal link between the two levels of negotiation. Realists see the two-level game as constrained primarily by the structure of the international system, whereas liberals more readily acknowledge domestic pressures and incentives.

Second, bargaining and negotiating are, in part, a culture-bound activity. Approaches to bargaining vary across cultures—a view accepted among liberals, who place importance on state differences. At least two approaches to negotiations have been identified.[10] The two different styles may lead to contrasting outcomes.

In the negotiations during the 1970s for the New International Economic Order (NIEO), for example, culture influenced the negotiating style adopted by the South. Specifically, during bargaining on specific issues, the South argued in a deductive style—from general principles to particular applications. The task that the South saw for itself, then, was for its states to agree among themselves on basic principles of the NIEO and leave the particular details to be worked out at a later date. This approach conveniently masked conflict over details until a later stage. The South's approach contrasted sharply with that preferred by many countries in the North, who favored discussion of concrete detail, eschewing grand philosophical debate. The United States and Great Britain, key actors in the North, both favored pragmatically addressing concrete problems and resolving specific issues before broader principles were crystallized. These differences in negotiating approaches led, in part, to a stalemate in negotiations and eventually the failure to achieve any meaningful concessions.[11]

The use of **public diplomacy** is an increasingly popular diplomatic technique in a communication-linked world. Public diplomacy involves trying to create an overall image that enhances a country's ability to achieve its diplomatic objectives. For instance, former First Lady Hillary Rodham Clinton's international travels highlighting the role of women were designed to project a humanitarian image of the United States, built around caring about people, including women and children, and promoting values, democracy, and human rights.

Economic Statecraft

States use more than words to exercise power. States may use economic statecraft—both positive and negative **sanctions**—to try to influence other states.[12] Positive sanctions involve offering a "carrot," enticing the target state to act in the desired way by rewarding moves in the desired direction. Negative sanctions, however, may be more the norm: threatening to act or actually taking actions that punish the target state for moves in the direction not desired. The goal of using the "stick" (negative sanctions) may be to punish or reprimand the target state for actions taken or may be to try to change the future behavior of the target state. Table 5.1 provides examples of positive and negative sanctions used in economic statecraft.

A state's ability to use these instruments of economic statecraft depends on its power potential. States with a variety of power sources have more instruments at their disposal. Clearly, only economically well-endowed countries can grant licenses, offer investment guarantees, afford to grant preferences to specific countries, house foreign assets, or boycott effectively. Radicals often point to this fact to illustrate the hegemony of the international capitalist system.

While radicals deny it, liberals argue that developing states do have some leverage in economic statecraft in special circumstances. If a state or group of states controls a key resource of which there is limited production, their power is strengthened. Among the primary commodities, only petroleum has this potential, and it gave the Arab members of the Organization of Petroleum Exporting Countries (OPEC) the ability to impose oil sanctions on the United States and the Netherlands when those two countries strongly supported Israel in the 1973 Arab-Israeli War.

Weak states may also use less coercive measures, trying to influence the domestic policy process of a stronger state and move it in a desired direction.[13] Weak states may attempt to sway top decisionmakers through intermediation, utilizing personal contacts and persuasion tactics, often circumventing normal governmental channels. For example, in the late 1980s, the South Korean government hired Michael Deaver, former deputy chief of staff at the White House, to introduce Korean trade negotiators to high-level officials in the United States. Alternatively, individuals from a weak state can use knowledge of procedural mechanisms or the legal system in the stronger target state to intervene administratively or initiate litigation in order to promote their state's agenda. Thus, South Korea pays more than one hundred U.S. lawyers to chart U.S. regulatory trends, find loopholes, and devise strategies to advance South Korean trade interests.

Weak states may also use broader approaches, such as forging linkages between issues, trying to penetrate social networks, and linking groups across national borders. Taiwan was able to circumvent U.S. investigation of unfair Taiwanese trading practices in the late 1980s by carefully buying

TABLE 5.1

Types of Sanctions in Economic Statecraft

Type	Sanction	Example
Positive	Give the target state the same trading privileges given to your best trading partner (most-favored-nation [MFN] status).	U.S. granted MFN status to China, in spite of that country's poor human rights record.
	Allow sensitive trade with target state, including militarily useful equipment, through licenses to import and export key products.	France and Germany export equipment to Iran, even though Iran's government is hostile to the West.
	Give corporations investment guarantees or tax incentives to invest in target state, which may otherwise be seen as too risky.	U.S. offered insurance to U.S. companies willing to invest in post-apartheid South Africa.
	Allow importation of target state's products into your country at tariff rates charged your best trading partner (General System of Preferences).	Industrialized states allow imports from developing countries at lower tariff rates.
Negative	Freeze target state's assets in your banking system.	U.S. froze Iranian bank deposits during 1979 hostage crisis.
	Blacklist target state.	Arab states blacklisted companies that conducted business in Israel.
	Boycott goods and services of target state.	South Africa was boycotted in the 1970s and 1980s in response to its racially discriminatory apartheid policy.
	Sanction one or all products of target state.	Iraq was forbidden to sell oil on the world market as punishment for the Gulf War in 1991.

U.S. goods for export to Taiwan from large companies located in key congressional districts. Representatives from those districts then became less concerned with investigating Taiwan's trade practices. In a limited number of cases, weak states may try to use grassroots mobilization—writing letters, making campaign contributions, and relying on social networks. Israel and the pro-Israel domestic constituencies in the United States masterfully employ this technique, funneling money to politicians who are supportive of Israel and writing editorials in local and national U.S. newspapers on behalf of Israel. These same strategies are equally relevant for more powerful states; the strong just have more options. Liberal theorists place special emphasis on the diplomatic, economic, and less coercive avenues of power, since they view power as a multidimensional relationship. Realist theorists believe it necessary to resort to the use of force on a more regular basis.

The Use of Force

Force (and the threat of force) is another critical instrument of statecraft and is central to realist thinking. Similar to economic statecraft, force or its threat may be used either to get a target state to do something or to undo something it has done—compellence—or to keep an adversary from doing something—deterrence.[14] Liberal theorists are more apt to advocate compellent strategies, moving cautiously to deterrence, whereas realists promote deterrence.

With **compellence** strategy, a state tries, by threatening to use force, to get another state to do something to undo an act that it has undertaken. The prelude to the Gulf War serves as an excellent example: The United States, the United Nations, and coalition members tried to get Saddam Hussein to change his actions with the compellent strategy of escalating threats. Iraq's invasion of Kuwait was initially widely condemned and then formal U.N. Security Council measures gave multilateral legitimacy to the condemnation. Next, Iraq's external economic assets were frozen and economic sanctions were imposed. Finally, U.S. and coalition military forces were mobilized and deployed, and specific deadlines were given for Iraq to withdraw from Kuwait. During each step of the compellent strategy of escalation, one message was communicated to Iraq: withdraw from Kuwait or more coercive actions will follow. Similarly, the western alliance sought to get Serbia to stop abusing the human rights of Kosovar Albanians and withdraw its military forces from the region. In both cases, of course, it was necessary to resort to an invasion because compellence via escalation of threats failed. Note that compellence ends once the use of force begins.

With deterrence strategy, states commit themselves to punish a target state if the target state takes an undesired action. Threats or actual war is used as an instrument of policy to dissuade a state from pursuing certain courses of action. If the target state does not take the undesired action, deterrence is successful and conflict is avoided. If it does choose to act despite the deterrent threat, then the first state will deliver an unacceptable blow.

Since the advent of nuclear weapons in 1945, deterrence has taken on a special meaning. Today if a state chooses to resort to violence, then nuclear weapons can be launched against the aggressor. The cost of the aggression will therefore be unacceptable, as the viability of both societies are at stake. Theoretically, therefore, states that recognize the destructive capability of nuclear weapons and know that others have **second-strike capability**—the ability to retaliate even after an attack has been launched by an opponent—will refrain from taking aggressive action. Deterrence is then successful.

For either compellence or deterrence to be effective, states have to lay the groundwork. They must clearly communicate their objectives, have the means to make their threats believable, and have the capability to follow through with their threats. In short, both compellence and deterrence depend on a state's credibility, as well as its power.

Compellence and deterrence can fail, however. If compellence and deterrence fail, states may go to war, but even during war, states have choices. They choose the type of weaponry (nuclear or nonnuclear, strategic or tactical, conventional or chemical and biological), the kind of targets (military or civilian, city or country), and the geographic locus (city, state, region) to be targeted. They may choose to respond in kind, to escalate, or to de-escalate. In war, both implicit and explicit negotiation takes place, over both how to fight the war and how to end it. We will return to this discussion of war in Chapter 7.

Game Theory

Force and economic instruments are the major techniques states have at their command to translate power potential into power. Economic and military-strategic theorists have developed ways to analyze more systematically the choices states make and the probable outcomes. This method is called game theory. Game theory assumes that each state is an autonomous decisionmaking unit and has a unique set of options and stipulated payoffs associated with each of the options. These assumptions of a unitary state with one national interest make game theory of particular relevance to realists.

Recall from Chapter 3 the discussion of the prisoner's dilemma. In that situation, two prisoners were each given the option of confessing to a particular crime but would not know the choice made by the other prisoner. The choices and outcomes in this situation are illustrated in the two-by-two matrix in Figure 5.3. The payoff numbers in the matrix are arbitrary, but they denote the magnitude of the potential gains or losses: the greater the number, the more favorable the payoff. The goal of each prisoner is to avoid the worst possible outcome, and neither prisoner knows which option the other will choose. Suppose you are prisoner 1: according to the matrix in Figure 5.3, your potential payoffs are (clockwise from the upper-left cell) -1, -10, -8, and 0. The worst possible payoff to you is -10, which you would get if you do not confess and prisoner 2 does. Thus to avoid this worst possible outcome, you decide to confess, limiting your potential payoffs to 0 or -8 but avoiding the worst possible, -10. The situation is exactly the same from the perspective of prisoner 2. The solution to the game, then, is that both prisoners confess—an outcome that is neither the best nor the worst for both players. This solution is a safer solution but not the optimum one where both individuals cooperate. In this game, there is a disincentive for the individual or the state to cooperate. Cooperation may occur over time, as the result of reciprocal interaction.

Not all games are prisoner's dilemmas. Game theory can also be used in situations where one player wins and the other loses, zero-sum games.

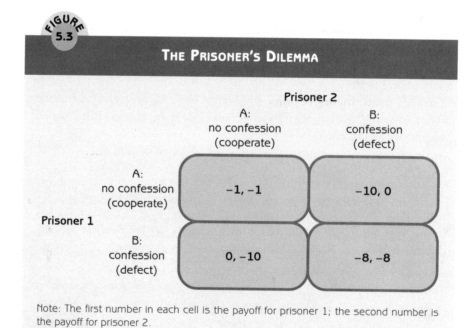

FIGURE 5.3

THE PRISONER'S DILEMMA

		Prisoner 2	
		A: no confession (cooperate)	B: confession (defect)
Prisoner 1	A: no confession (cooperate)	$-1, -1$	$-10, 0$
	B: confession (defect)	$0, -10$	$-8, -8$

Note: The first number in each cell is the payoff for prisoner 1; the second number is the payoff for prisoner 2.

In military confrontations, one side wins and the other loses, or in international crises, one state may win (power or prestige), while the other may lose (power or face). Games may also be non-zero sum with many players. In these situations, some of the parties may win, while others may lose. There are elements of both cooperation and conflict. In general, international relations is best conceptualized as a non-zero-sum game with many players, exercised over an extended time period.

There are advantages to using game theory as a simplification of the complex choices states make. Game theory forces both analysts and policymakers systematically to examine assumptions, helping to clarify the choices available and offering possibilities that may not have been explored. It helps the analyst and the policymaker to see not just their own state's position but also where the other state may stand.

Yet there are also clear limitations to game theory. Game theory makes some critical assumptions: it assumes a unitary state, in which internal factors play little role in determining a state's preferences. It assumes that the unitary state acts rationally, that states choose the best overall option available. It gives arbitrary payoff structures in advance, whereas in reality states do not know the relative values attached to their various choices or those of the other side. It assumes that the game occurs one time, although most realize that much of international relations is really an extended set of games between the same actors. Thus, the outcome of multiple iterations—in which knowing the choice at one point in time helps each side to predict the other's choice at a subsequent time period—may be quite different than the one-time encounter. All of these criticisms are key neoliberal points.

Indeed, game theory permits simplicity: choices are seen as interdependent, determined largely by the actions taken by others. But how are decisions within states taken? Given what we know about foreign-policy decisionmaking, is the notion of a unitary state actor a valid one?

MODELS OF FOREIGN-POLICY DECISIONMAKING

How are specific foreign-policy decisions actually made? Realists, liberals, and radicals view the decisionmaking process very differently.

The Rational Model

Realists and most policymakers begin with the rational model, in which foreign policy is conceived of as actions chosen by the national government that maximize its strategic goals and objectives. The state is assumed to be a unitary actor with established goals, a set of options, and an algorithm for deciding which option best meets its goals. The process is relatively straightforward, as shown in Figure 5.4. Taking as our case the 1996 incident in which China was testing missiles by launching

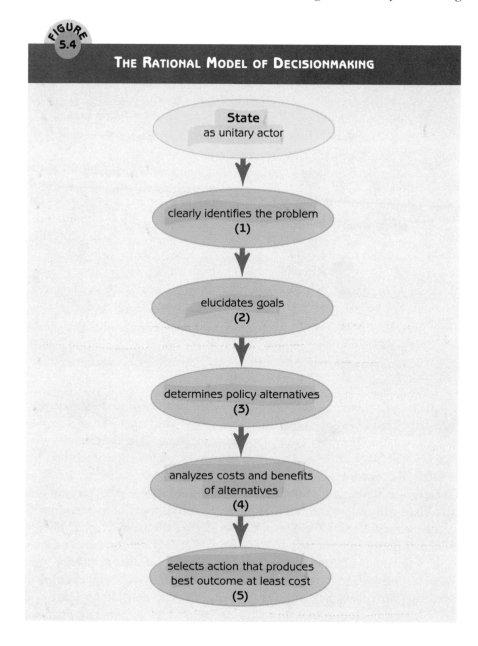

FIGURE 5.4

THE RATIONAL MODEL OF DECISIONMAKING

State
as unitary actor

↓

clearly identifies the problem
(1)

↓

elucidates goals
(2)

↓

determines policy alternatives
(3)

↓

analyzes costs and benefits
of alternatives
(4)

↓

selects action that produces
best outcome at least cost
(5)

them over Taiwan, a rational approach would view the situation in the following manner (the numbers correspond to the numbered steps in Figure 5.4):

1. The People's Republic of China is testing missiles over Taiwan, in direct threat to the latter's national security and just prior to Taiwan's first democratic election.
2. Both Taiwan and its major supporter, the United States, have as their goal to stop the firings immediately.
3. The Taiwanese have several options: do nothing; wait until the end of the Taiwanese elections, hoping that the Chinese will then stop; issue diplomatic protests; bring the issue to the U.N. Security Council; threaten or conduct military operations against China by bombing its missile sites or mounting a land invasion; or threaten or use economic statecraft (cutting trade, sanctions, embargoes).
4. The Taiwanese government analyzes the benefits and costs of these options. Mounting an invasion, for example, may eliminate the problem but will likely result in the destruction of Taiwan, an unacceptable side effect.
5. Taiwan, with U.S. support, chooses as a first step diplomatic protest, in the hope that the antagonistic firing will cease after the election. Doing nothing clearly would have suggested that the missile testing was acceptable, which it was not. Military action against China was too extreme, with possibly disastrous consequences.

In times of crisis, when decisionmakers are confronted by a surprising, threatening event and have only a short time to make a decision, then the rational model is an appropriate choice. If a state knows very little about the internal domestic processes of another state—as the United States did vis-à-vis mainland China during the era of Mao Zedong—then decisionmakers have little alternative but to assume that the state will follow the rational model. Indeed, most U.S. assessments of decisions taken by the Soviet Union during the Cold War, in the absence of better information, assumed a rational model: the Soviet Union had a goal, its alternatives were clearly laid out, and decisions were taken to maximize its achievement of its goal. Only since the opening of the Russian governmental archives following the end of the Cold War have historians found that, in fact, the Soviets had no concrete plans for

THE REALIST PERSPECTIVE ON STATE POWER AND POLICY

Nature of state power	Stress on power as key concept in international relations; geography, natural resources, population especially important
Using state power	Emphasis on coercive techniques of power; use of force acceptable
How foreign policy is made	Emphasis on rational model of decisionmaking; unitary state actor
Determinants of foreign policy	Largely external/international determinants

turning Poland, Hungary, Romania, or other East European states into communist dictatorships or socialist economies, as the United States believed. The Soviets appear to have been guided by events happening in the region, not by a specific rational plan or ideology.[15] The United States was incorrect in imputing the rational model for Soviet decisionmaking, but in the absence of information, this was the least-risky approach in the anarchy of the international system.

The Bureaucratic/Organizational Model

In the bureaucratic/organizational model, decisions are seen as products of either subnational governmental organizations, or bureaucracies (departments or ministries of government). **Organizational politics** emphasizes the standard operating procedures and processes of an organization. Decisions arising from organizational processes depend heavily on precedents; major changes in policy are unlikely. Conflicts can occur when different subgroups within the organization have different goals and procedures.

Bureaucratic politics, on the other hand, occurs among members of the bureaucracy representing different interests. Decisions determined by bureaucratic politics flow from the pull and haul, or tug-of-war, among these departments, groups, or individuals. In either political scenario, the ultimate decision depends on the relative strength of the individual bureaucratic players or the organizations they represent (see Figure 5.5).

Trade policy provides a ripe area to see the bureaucratic/organizational model of decisionmaking at work. For example, South Korean agricultural markets traditionally were closed to foreign imports. This closure was designed to protect Korean producers of major agricultural products, includ-

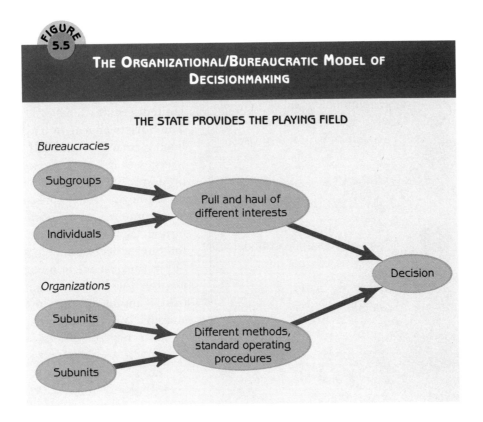

FIGURE 5.5

THE ORGANIZATIONAL/BUREAUCRATIC MODEL OF DECISIONMAKING

THE STATE PROVIDES THE PLAYING FIELD

Bureaucracies

Subgroups

Individuals

Pull and haul of different interests

Decision

Organizations

Subunits

Subunits

Different methods, standard operating procedures

ing rice, beef, and tobacco. In the 1980s, pressure from the United States grew for opening these markets. The South Korean Ministry of Agriculture, Forestry, and Fisheries strongly opposed the opening of agricultural markets, arguing that Korean farmers would be put out of work. But the Ministry of Finance and the Ministry of Trade and Industry were concerned about retaliatory measures that the United States might take against Korean manufacturers entering the U.S. market. Policy change resulted from the pull and haul among these various ministries. The Ministry of Agriculture capitulated on tobacco, opening the market to full liberalization, but for rice, whose producers were the strongest and the best organized politically, movement toward liberalization was very slow.

Noncrisis situations, like the Korean foreign-trade policy issue just described, are apt to reflect the bureaucratic/organizational model. When time is no real constraint, informal bureaucratic groups and departments have time to mobilize. They hold meetings, hammering out positions that satisfy all the contending interests. The decisions arrived at are not always the most rational ones; rather they are the decisions that "satisfice"—satisfy the most different constituents without ostracizing any.

Liberals especially can identify with this model of decisionmaking behavior, since for them the state itself is only the playing field; the actors are the competing interests in bureaucracies and organizations. The model is most relevant in large, democratic countries, which usually have highly differentiated institutional structures for foreign-policy decisionmaking and where responsibility and jurisdiction are divided among a number of different units. For example, most foreign-trade decisions made by the United States, Japan, or the governments of European Union countries closely approximate the bureaucratic/organizational model. But to invoke this model in policy circles and to analyze decisions for scholarly purposes, detailed knowledge of a country's foreign-policy structures and bureaucracies must be obtained. In the absence of such information, the rational model is the only alternative.

Theory in Brief

THE LIBERAL PERSPECTIVE ON STATE POWER AND POLICY

Nature of state power	Multiple power sources; tangible and intangible sources
Using state power	Broad range of power techniques; preference for noncoercive alternatives
How foreign policy is made	Organizational/bureaucratic and pluralist models of decisionmaking
Determinants of foreign policy	Largely domestic determinants

The Pluralist Model

The **pluralist model,** in contrast to the other two alternatives, attributes decisions to bargaining conducted among domestic sources—public opinion, interest groups, and multinational corporations (see Figure 5.6). In noncrisis situations and on particular issues, especially economic ones, societal groups may play very important roles. No one doubts the power of the rice farmer lobbies in both Japan and South Korea in preventing the importation of cheap, U.S.-grown rice. No one disputes the success of French wine growers in preventing the importation of cheap Greek or Spanish wines by publicly dumping their product for media attention. No

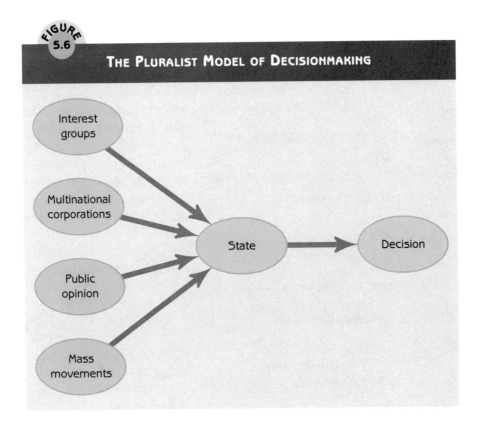

FIGURE 5.6

THE PLURALIST MODEL OF DECISIONMAKING

one denies the power of U.S. shoe manufacturers in supporting restrictions on the importation of Brazilian-made shoes into the United States, despite U.S. governmental initiatives to allow imports of products from developing countries.

Societal groups have a variety of ways of forcing decisions in their favor or constraining decisions. They can mobilize the media and public opinion, lobby the government agencies responsible for making the decision, influence the appropriate representative bodies (the U.S. Congress, the French National Assembly, the Japanese Diet), organize transnational networks of people with comparable interests, and, for high-profile heads of multinational corporations, make direct contacts with the highest governmental officials. The decision made will reflect these diverse societal interests and strategies—a result that is particularly compatible with liberal thinking. The movement to ban land mines in the 1990s is an example of a societally based pluralist foreign-policy decision.

Whereas realists accept the rational model of foreign-policy decision-making, and liberals the organizational/bureaucratic and pluralist models, most radicals do not believe that state decisionmakers have real choices. In the radical view, capitalist states' interests are determined by the structure of the international system and their decisions are dictated by the economic imperatives of the dominant class. To the extent that decisions reflect the interests of dominant social classes, there is a pluralist model, but since the dominant classes are confronted by no viable opposition, there are no contentious issues.

Each alternative model offers a simplification of the foreign-policy decision-making process. Each provides a window on how groups (both governmental and nongovernmental) influence the foreign-policy process. But these models do not provide answers to other critical issues. They do not tell us the content of a specific decision or indicate the effectiveness with which the foreign policy was implemented.

Theory in Brief

THE RADICAL PERSPECTIVE ON STATE POWER AND POLICY

Nature of state power	Economic power organized around classes
Using state power	Weak having few instruments of power
How foreign policy is made	States having no real choices; decisions dictated by economic capitalist elites
Determinants of foreign policy	Largely external determinants; co-opted internal elements

CHALLENGES TO THE STATE

The state, despite its centrality, is facing challenges on several fronts. In the words of Jessica Matthews, there has been a power shift. "The steady concentration of power in the hands of states that began in 1648 with the Peace of Westphalia is over, at least for a while."[16] Externally, the state is buffeted by **globalization** forces—the increasing internationalization of culture and economics—that potentially undermine traditional state sovereignty. For example, the internationalization of human rights and of environmental norms increasingly interferes with the state's exercise of sovereignty over its own natural resources. New and intrusive technologies—CNN, direct satellite broadcasting, fax machines, e-mail—increasingly undermine the state's control over communication. Countries such as Iran and the Gulf states have fought losing battles in trying to "protect" their populations from crass Western values transmitted through the modern media. Multinational corporations and the internationalization of production and consumption make it increasingly difficult for states to regulate their own economic policies. Globalization of financial markets has left states less powerful.

States are also confronted with strong transnational movements, including Islamic fundamentalism. This has led one well-known political scientist and astute observer, Samuel Huntington, to predict a "clash of civilizations," arising from underlying differences between Western liberal democracy and Islamic fundamentalism.[17]

Faced with globalization, transnational ideologies, and its weakened capacity to address those problems, the state's major task is still to provide security. But while the military threats from other states may have diminished and economic threats are more diffuse from the forces of globalization, nontraditional threats to security have escalated. Drug trafficking, organized crime, and terrorism undermine both state security and individual security.

One of the most severe challenges to the state and to individuals is found in ethnonational movements, often centered in the state. More than 900 million people belong to 233 increasingly demanding national subgroups around the world. These ethnonationalist movements identify more with a particular culture than with a state. Having experienced discrimination or persecution, many of these groups are now taking collective action in support of national self-determination. "Who is to tell the Bosnians, the Palestinians, Kurds, Druze, Scots, Basques, Quebecois and Bretons that they are not a people and are not entitled to self-determination?"[18]

Yet not all ethnonationalists want the same thing. A few seek separation from the state, preferring to forge their own destiny in a new, independent state. Some prefer irredentism—not just breaking away from an established state but joining with fellow ethnonationalists and creating another state, or joining with another state. Others seek solutions in federal arrangements, hoping to win guarantees of autonomy within an established state, and still others seek not much more than official recognition of their unique status, including the right to use their national language and practice their own religion.

TABLE 5.2	Ethnonational Challengers
State	**Ethnonational groups**
Indonesia	Timorese, Papuans, Moluccans
Malaysia	Sarawak, Sabah
Spain	Basques
People's Republic of China	Tibetans
Nigeria	Yoruba, Ibo
Burundi, Rwanda	Hutu, Tutsi
Syria, Iraq, Iran, Turkey	Kurds
Moldova	Romanians
Serbia, Macedonia	Albanians
Lebanon	Maronites, Palestinians
Mexico, Guatemala	Mayan, Zapotec, Mixe
Burma, Thailand	Karens
Canada	Quebecois
India	Kashmiris

Some of these ethnonational challenges lead to civil conflict and even war, particularly in states that are democratizing. Political scientist Jack Snyder has identified the causal mechanism whereby ethnic nationalists challenge the state on the basis of legitimacy of language, culture, or religion. Elites within these ethnonational movements, particularly when countervailing institutions are weak, may be able to incite the masses to war.[19] Table 5.2 lists some of the ethnonational challengers in the world today.

In Sum: The State and Challenges Beyond

The centrality of the state in international politics cannot be disputed. In this chapter, the state has been conceptualized according to the three contending theoretical perspectives. We have looked inside the state to describe the various forms of state power. We have discussed the ways that states are able to use power through the diplomatic, economic, and coercive instruments of statecraft. We have disaggregated the subnational

Theory in Brief

CONTENDING PERSPECTIVES ON STATE POWER AND POLICY

	Liberalism/ Neoliberal Institutionalism	Realism/ Neorealism	Radical/ Dependency
Nature of state power	Multiple power sources; tangible and intangible sources	Stress on power as key concept in international relations; geography, natural resources, population especially important	Economic power organized around classes
Using state power	Broad range of power techniques; preference for noncoercive alternatives	Emphasis on coercive techniques of power; use of force acceptable	Weak having few instruments of power
How foreign policy is made	Organizational/ bureaucratic and societal models of decisionmaking	Emphasis on rational model; unitary state actor	States having no real choices; decisions dictated by economic capitalist elites
Determinants of foreign policy	Largely domestic determinants	Largely external/ international determinants	Largely external determinants; co-opted internal elements

actors within the state to identify different models of foreign-policy decisionmaking. And we have examined the ways in which globalization, transnational ideologies, and ethnonationalist movements pose threats to state sovereignty and to the stability of the international system. Such movements, however, depend on individuals; it is individuals who lead the challenge. Some are elites who are charismatic and powerful leaders in their own right. Some are part of a mass movement. It is these individuals to whom we now turn.

NOTES

1. James N. Rosenau, *Turbulence in World Politics: A Theory of Change and Continuity* (Princeton, N.J.: Princeton University Press, 1990), 117–18.
2. Yale H. Ferguson and Richard W. Mansbach, *The Elusive Quest: Theory and International Politics* (Columbia, S.C.: University of South Carolina Press, 1988).
3. Stephen D. Krasner, *Defending the National Interest: Raw Materials Investments and U.S. Foreign Policy* (Princeton, N.J.: Princeton University Press, 1978).
4. Alfred T. Mahan, *The Influence of Seapower upon History 1660–1783* (Boston: Little, Brown, 1897).
5. Halford Mackinder, "The Geographical Pivot of History," *Geographical Journal* 23 (April 1904), 434.
6. John W. Wright, ed., *The New York Times 1998 Almanac* (New York: Penguin, 1997), 483. Updated.
7. Andrew Mack, "Why Big Nations Lose Small Wars: The Politics of Asymmetric Conflict," *World Politics* 27:2 (January 1975), 175–200.
8. Robert D. Putnam, "Diplomacy and Domestic Politics: The Logic of 2-Level Games," *International Organization* 42:3 (Summer 1988), 427–69.
9. Ibid., 434.
10. Raymond Cohen, *Negotiating across Cultures: Communication Obstacles in International Diplomacy* (2nd ed., Washington, D.C.: U.S. Institute of Peace, 1997).
11. Karen A. Mingst and Craig P. Warkentin, "What Difference Does Culture Make in Multilateral Negotiations?" *Global Governance* 2:2 (May 1996), 169–88.
12. David A. Baldwin, *Economic Statecraft* (Princeton, N.J.: Princeton University Press, 1985).
13. Chung-In Moon, "Complex Interdependence and Transnational Lobbying: South Korea in the United States," *International Studies Quarterly* 32:1 (March 1988), 67–89.
14. Thomas C. Schelling, *Arms and Influence* (New Haven, Conn.: Yale University Press, 1966).
15. Norman M. Naimark, *The Russians in Germany: A History of the Soviet Zone of Occupation, 1945–1949* (Cambridge, Mass.: Harvard University Press, 1995).
16. Jessica Matthews, "Power Shift," *Foreign Affairs* 76:1 (January–February 1997): 50.
17. Samuel P. Huntington, *The Clash of Civilizations and the Remaking of World Order* (New York: Simon and Schuster, 1996).
18. Nicholas Kittrie, "Absolutist vs. Pluralist Legitimacy: The New Cold War," *New Perspectives Quarterly* 13:1 (Winter 1996), 57.
19. Jack Snyder, *From Voting to Violence, Democratization and Nationalist Conflict* (New York: Norton, 2000).

THE INDIVIDUAL

6

- *Which individuals matter in international relations?*
- *What psychological factors have an impact on elites making foreign-policy decisions?*
- *What roles do other private individuals play in international relations?*
- *What roles do mass publics play in foreign policy?*
- *According to the various theoretical perspectives, how much do individuals matter?*

International relations certainly affects the lives of individuals, as discussed in Chapter 1. But individuals are not merely passive agents for actions taken by the state or for events emerging out of the structure of the international system. Individuals are actors, too, and as such represent the third level of analysis. Individuals head governments, multinational corporations, and international bodies. Individuals fight wars and make the daily decisions that shape the international political economy.

Recall the possible explanations given in Chapter 3 for why Iraq invaded Kuwait. One group of explanations focused on Saddam Hussein, his personal characteristics and those of his advisers. Clearly, one group of individuals that makes a difference is leaders. But individuals holding more informal roles can also have significant influence, as can the mass public.

FOREIGN-POLICY ELITES: INDIVIDUALS WHO MATTER

Do individuals matter in making foreign policy? <u>Liberals are particularly adamant that leaders do make a difference</u>. Whenever there is a leadership change in a major power, like the United States or Russia, speculation always arises about possible changes in the country's foreign policy. This reflects the general belief that individual leaders and their personal characteristics do make a difference in foreign policy, and hence in international relations. Ample empirical proof has been offered for this position. For instance, in March 1965 Nicolae Ceausescu became the new leader of the Communist party of Romania. During his twenty-two years as Romania's head of state, the course of Romanian security policy changed significantly, reflecting the preferences and skills of Ceausescu himself. Romania's security policy became more independent of the Soviet Union, often in defiance of that larger and more powerful neighbor. Much to the Soviets' disdain, Romania maintained diplomatic relations with Israel following the Arab-Israeli War of 1967. That same year, Romania established diplomatic relations with West Germany before the Soviet Union agreed to reconciliation with the West. Ceausescu strongly denounced the Warsaw Pact invasion of Czechoslovakia in 1968, and soon thereafter he strengthened ties to another maverick Eastern European state, Yugoslavia. Romania's voting pattern in the U.N. General Assembly increasingly deviated from that of the Soviet Union as Romania moved closer to countries in the nonaligned movement (those states purposely unallied with either the United States or the Soviet Union). Ceausescu maintained close ties to China despite the latter's increasingly hostile relations with the Soviet Union. In short, Ceausescu, a strong leader, significantly changed Romania's foreign policy, moving it in a direction that deviated from the preferences of its closest ally.

The example of the Soviet leader Mikhail Gorbachev also illustrates the fact that leaders can cause real change. Soon after coming to power in 1985, Gorbachev asked penetrating questions about the failures of the Soviet Union in Afghanistan and examined the reasons for the dismal performance of the Soviet economy. He began to frame the problems of the Soviet Union differently, identifying the Soviet security problem as part of the larger problem of weakness in the Soviet economy. Through a process of trial and error, and by living through and then studying failures, Gorbachev came to a new conceptualization of the Soviet security problem. He determined that the economic system had to be reformed in order to improve the country's security. In initiating that policy change, he needed to decide when and how change would happen, and how far it would go. Gorbachev's leadership made a difference in starting and sustaining broad economic reform in the Soviet Union, although he eventually lost power.

Individual elites are also important in constructivist thinking. Constructivists attribute the change to the Soviet Union's "New Thinking" not only to the change in calculations made by Gorbachev himself but more subtly to the change caused by the policy entrepreneurs, the networks of Western-oriented reformists and international affairs specialists who promoted new ideas. To constructivists like Robert Hermann, this is the relevant explanation for the monumental changes in the Soviet Union.[1]

According to realists and radicals, the structure of the international system is more important than individuals. They argue that individual leaders do not make much of a difference in foreign policy. Yet foreign policy is not always the same: *glasnost* and *perestroika* were introduced in the Soviet Union beginning in 1986, Romania did carve a foreign policy niche independent of the Soviet Union during the 1970s, and Cuba and the United States, once allies, did become mortal enemies in the 1960s. What caused these changes? Were individuals responsible for them or did individual leaders just happen to be the right (or wrong) person at the time? Given the same situation, would different individuals have made different decisions, thus charting a different course through international relations?

Two questions are most pertinent to determining the role of individuals in international relations: When are the actions of individuals likely to have a greater or lesser effect on the course of events? And under what circumstances do different actors (in terms of their personal characteristics) behave differently?

The Impact of Elites: External Conditions

An individual's actions affect the course of events when at least one of several factors is present (see Figure 6.1). When political institutions are unstable, young, in crisis, or collapsed, leaders are able to provide powerful influences. Founding fathers, be they the United States's George Washington, Kenya's Jomo Kenyatta, India's Mohandas Gandhi, Russia's Vladimir Lenin or the Czech Republic's Vaclav Havel, have a great impact

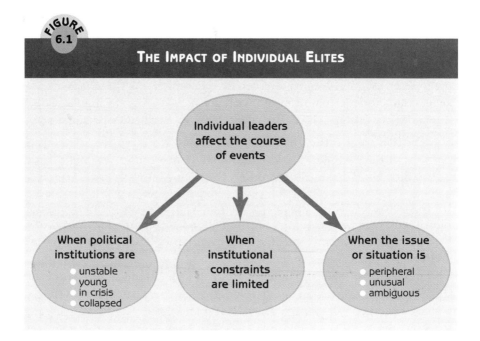

FIGURE 6.1

THE IMPACT OF INDIVIDUAL ELITES

Individual leaders affect the course of events

When political institutions are
- unstable
- young
- in crisis
- collapsed

When institutional constraints are limited

When the issue or situation is
- peripheral
- unusual
- ambiguous

because they lead in the early years of their nation's lives, when institutions and practices are being established. Adolf Hitler, Franklin Roosevelt, and Mikhail Gorbachev had more influence precisely because their states were in economic crises when they were in power.

Individuals also affect the course of events when they have few institutional constraints. In dictatorial regimes, top leaders are relatively free from domestic constraints such as societal inputs and political opposition, and thus are able to chart courses and implement foreign policy relatively unfettered. In democratic regimes, when decisionmakers are of high rank within the governmental structure, the role of constraints is muted, and organizational constraints are fewer. For example, U.S. president Richard Nixon in 1972 was able to engineer a complete foreign-policy reversal in relations with the People's Republic of China, secretly sending his top foreign-policy adviser, Henry Kissinger, for several meetings with Chinese premier Chou En-lai and his advisers. These moves were an unexpected change, given Nixon's Republican party affiliation and prior anticommunist record. Bureaucratic and societal constraints mattered little, even in such a relatively open democracy.

The specifics of a situation also determine the extent to which individuals matter. Decisionmakers' personal characteristics have more influence on outcomes when the issue is peripheral rather than central if the issue is not routine—that is, standard operating procedures are not available—or in ambiguous situations when information is unclear. Crisis situations, in particular, where information is in short supply and standard operating procedures inapplicable, create scenarios in which a decisionmaker's personal characteristics count most. Such a scenario arose during the Cuban missile crisis during which President John F. Kennedy's personal openness to alternatives and attention to group dynamics paid off.

The Impact of Elites: The Personality Factor

Even among elite leaders working amid similar external conditions, some individuals seem to have a greater impact on foreign policy than others; this leads us to examine both the personal characteristics that matter and the thought processes of individuals.

Political psychologist Margaret Hermann has found a number of personality characteristics that affect foreign-policy behaviors. Since top leaders do not take personality tests, Hermann used a different research strategy. She systematically collected spontaneous interviews and press conferences with eighty heads of state holding office in thirty-eight countries between 1959 and 1968. From this data, she found key personality characteristics that she felt influence a leader's orientation toward policy.[2] Those characteristics are listed in the top section of Figure 6.2.

These personality characteristics orient an individual's view of foreign affairs. Two orientations emerge from the personality traits. One group, leaders with high levels of nationalism, a strong belief in their own ability to control events, a strong need for power, low levels of conceptual complexity, and high levels of distrust for others, tend to develop an independent orientation to foreign affairs. The other group, leaders with a high need for affiliation, low levels of distrust of others, low levels of nationalism, and little belief in their ability to control events, tended toward a participatory orientation in foreign affairs. (The bottom of Figure 6.2 illustrates these orientations.) Then Hermann tested whether these personal characteristics and their respective orientations related to the foreign-policy behavior of the leaders. She found that they did.

University of South Carolina professor Betty Glad has developed a profile of former president Jimmy Carter that suggests how his personality characteristics played a key role in influencing the course of U.S. policy during the 1979–81 hostage crisis, which began when Iranian militants kidnapped more than sixty Americans and held them for more

FIGURE 6.2

PERSONALITY CHARACTERISTICS OF INDIVIDUAL LEADERS

Personality Characteristics of Leaders

1. *Nationalism:* strong emotional ties to nation; emphasis on national honor and dignity

2. *Perception of control:* belief in one's ability to control events: high degree of control over situations; governments can influence state and nation

3. *Need for power:* need to establish, maintain, and project one's power or influence over others

4. *Need for affiliation:* concern for establishing and maintaining friendly relationships with others

5. *Conceptual complexity:* ability to discuss with other people, places, policies, ideas in a discerning way

6. *Self-confidence:* individuals' sense of self-importance or image of their ability to deal adequately with environment

Foreign Policy Orientations

Independent leader:......... high in nationalism

high in perception of control

high in need for power

low in conceptual complexity

high in distrust of others

Participatory leader:......... low in nationalism

low in perception of control

high in need for affiliation

high in conceptual complexity

low in distrust of others

SOURCE: Margaret G. Hermann, "Explaining Foreign Policy Behavior Using the Personal Characteristics of Political Leaders," *International Studies Quarterly* 24:1 (March 1980), 7–46.

than a year. Box 6.1 provides some key quotes voiced by Carter about that ordeal. A perusal of these words shows clearly how Carter personalized the hostage taking. He was humiliated, obsessed, wanting above all to have *his* decisions vindicated. After an attempted helicopter rescue mission failed, he rationalized the failure as a "worthy effort," feeling that some action was better than nothing. In the last passage, when Carter is describing meeting with the families of those who were killed in the rescue operation, he personalizes the event, saying "their concern was about me."

BOX 6.1

PRESIDENT JIMMY CARTER AND THE HOSTAGE CRISIS: A PSYCHOLOGICAL PROFILE IN HIS OWN WORDS

"Our purpose is to get the hostages home and get them safe. That's my total commitment."[1]

"We must never lose sight of our basic goals in this crisis—the safety of our fellow-citizens and the protection of the long-term interests of the United Nations."[2]

"There is a deeper failure than that of incomplete success. That is the failure to attempt a worthy effort—a failure to try."[3]

"I may have to sit here and bite my lip and show restraint and look impotent, but I am not going to have those bastards humiliating our country in front of the White House!"[4]

"The release of the American hostages had almost become an obsession with me. Of course, their lives, safety, and freedom were the paramount considerations, but there was more to it. I wanted to have my decisions vindicated."[5]

"I have a lot of problems on my shoulders, but, strangely enough, I feel better as they pile up. My main concern is propping up the people around me who tend to panic (and who might possibly have a better picture of the situation than I do)."[6]

"They reached their arms out for me and we embraced each other, and I could feel that their concern was about me, not about them."[7]

SOURCES: 1. *Department of State Bulletin*, February 1980, 55.   2. *Department of State Bulletin*, February 1980, 55.   3. News Conference, April 29, 1980.   4. Jimmy Carter, *Keeping Faith: Memoirs of a President* (New York: Bantam Books, 1982), 40.   5. Ibid., 594.   6. Ibid., 524.   7. Ibid., 521.

Glad poignantly summarizes the case, drawing attention to the importance of Carter's own personality characteristics:

> Carter's problems in managing the hostage crisis . . . were not the result of his being too idealistic, too rigid, too cautious, or too pacific, as many have perceived him as being. On the contrary, he was a flexible, risk-taking, aggressive leader.
>
> His mistakes were more subtle. In mobilizing American emotions against the enemy, he unleashed psychodynamic forces that led the United States to participate in its own victimization. In making the hostages so important to the American people, Carter gave the clerics in Iran a psychological hold over the United States they would not have had if the issue had been dealt with in a less public way.
>
> . . . Carter's subsequent difficulty in admitting that he made mistakes in this situation was based on his more general need to be right. He had always had difficulty in learning from his mistakes. In this instance the psychic costs to the United States of its impotence in a crisis upon which the entire people and government focused for several months, as well as the political price Carter had to pay for that fixation, would make it particularly difficult for him to see where he had gone wrong.[3]

Personality characteristics, then, partly determine what decisions individual leaders make. But those decisions also reflect the fact that all decisionmakers are confronted with the task of putting divergent information in an organized form.

Individual Decisionmaking

The rational model of decisionmaking that we discussed earlier suggests that the individual possesses all the relevant information, stipulates a goal, examines the relevant choices, and makes a decision that best achieves the goal. In actuality, however, individuals are not rational decisionmakers. Confronted by information that is neither perfect nor complete, and often overwhelmed by a plethora of information and conditioned by personal experience, the decisionmaker selects, organizes, and evaluates incoming information about the surrounding world.

A variety of psychological techniques are used by individuals to process and evaluate information. In perceiving and interpreting new and often-times contradictory information, individuals rely on existing perceptions, often based on prior experiences. Such perceptions are the "screens" that enable individuals to process information selectively; these perceptions have an integrating function, permitting the elite to synthesize and interpret the information. And they serve an orienting function, providing guidance about future expectations and expediting planning for future contingencies. If those perceptions form a relatively integrated set of images, then they are called a **belief system**.

International relations scholars have devised suitable methods to test the existence of elite images, although research has not been conducted on many individuals, for reasons made obvious below. Duke University professor Ole Hosti systematically analyzed all of the publicly available statements of Secretary of State John Foster Dulles concerning the Soviet Union during the years 1953–54. From the 434 documents surveyed, Hosti singled out 3,584 of Dulles's assertions about the Soviet Union. His research showed convincingly that Dulles held a strong image of the Soviet Union, one focused on atheism, totalitarianism, and communism. To Dulles, the Soviet people were good, but their leaders were bad; the state was good, the Communist party bad. This image was unvarying; the character of the Soviet Union in Dulles's mind did not change. Whether this image gleaned from Dulles's statements affected U.S. decisions during the period cannot be stated with certainty. He was, after all, only one among a group of top leaders. Yet a plethora of decisions taken during that time are consistent with the image.[4]

Political scientists Harvey Starr and Stephen Walker both completed similar empirical research on Henry Kissinger.[5] Elucidating Kissinger's operational code (the rules he operated by) from his scholarly writings, Walker found that the Vietnam War, orchestrated in large part by Kissinger between 1969 and 1973, was congruent with the premises of his operational code and his conception of mutually acceptable outcomes. He wanted to negotiate a mutual withdrawal of external forces and to avoid negotiating about the internal structure of South Vietnam. He used enough force, applied in combination with generous peace terms, so that North Vietnam was faced with an attractive peace settlement versus unpalatable alternatives—stalemate or escalation.

These elite mindset studies were possible because the particular elites left behind an extensive written record, from before, during, and after they held key policymaking positions. Since few leaders leave such a record, however, our ability to empirically reconstruct an image, perception, or operational code is limited, as is our inability to state with certainty its influence on a specific decision.

Information-Processing Mechanisms

One's image and perception of the world are continually bombarded by new, sometimes overwhelming, and often discordant information. Images and belief systems, however, are not generally changed, and almost never are they radically altered. Thus, individual elites utilize, usually unconsciously, a number of psychological mechanisms to process the information that forms their general perceptions of the world. These mechanisms are summarized in Table 6.1.

First, individuals strive to be **cognitively consistent,** ensuring that images hang together consistently within their belief systems. For example, individuals like to believe that the enemy of an enemy is a friend, and the enemy of a friend is an enemy. Because of the tendency to be cognitively consistent, individuals select or amplify information that supports existing images and ignore or downplay contradictory information. For example, because both Great Britain and Argentina were friends of the United States prior to their war over the Falkland/Malvinas Islands in 1982, U.S. decisionmakers denied the seriousness of the conflict at the outset. The United States did not think that its friend, the "peaceful" Britain, would go to war with Argentina over a group of barren islands thousands of miles from Britain's shores. The United States underestimated the strength of public support for military action in Britain, as well as misunderstood the precarious domestic position of the Argentinian generals trying to bolster their power by diverting attention to a popular external conflict.

Elites in power also perceive and evaluate the world according to what they are concerned with at the moment. They look for those details of a present episode that look like a past one, perhaps ignoring the important differences. This is often referred to as the **evoked set.** During the 1956 Suez crisis, for instance, British prime minister Anthony Eden saw Egyptian president Gamal Abdel Nasser as another Hitler. Eden recalled Prime Minister Neville Chamberlain's failed effort to appease Hitler with the Munich agreement in 1938 and thus believed that Nasser, likewise, could not be appeased.

Individual perceptions are often shaped in terms of **mirror images:** while considering one's own action good, moral, and just, the enemy is automatically found to be evil, immoral, and unjust. Mirror imaging often exacerbates conflicts, making it all the more difficult to resolve a contentious issue.

These psychological mechanisms that we have discussed so far affect the functioning of individuals and of small groups. But small groups them-

TABLE 6.1

Psychological Techniques Used to Process Information

Technique	Explanation	Example
Cognitive consistency	Tendency to accept information that is compatible with what has previously been accepted, often ignoring inconsistent information. Desire to be consistent in attitude.	Just prior to the Japanese attack on Pearl Harbor, military spotters saw unmarked planes approaching the island. Not believing the evidence, they discounted the intrusions.
Evoked set	Tendency to look for details in a present situation that are similar to information previously obtained. Leads one to conclusions that are similar to those of the past.	U.S. decisionmakers during the Vietnam War saw the Korean War as a precedent, although there were critical differences.
Mirror image	Tendency of individuals and groups to see in one's opponent the opposite of characteristics seen in oneself. Opponent is viewed as hostile and uncompromising, while one's self is viewed as friendly and compromising.	During the Cold War, both U.S. elites and masses viewed the Soviet Union in terms of their own mirror image: the United States was friendly, the Soviet Union hostile.
Satisficing	Tendency for groups to search for a "good enough" solution, rather than an optimal one.	Decision of NATO to bomb and occupy Kosovo in 1999 in an attempt to stop the ethnic cleansing against the Albanian Kosovars.
Groupthink	Tendency for small groups to form a consensus and resist criticism of that core position, often disregarding contradictory information.	During the U.S. planning for the Bay of Pigs operation against Cuba in 1961, opponents were ostracized from the planning group.

selves also have psychologically based dynamics that undermine the rational model. The psychologist Irving Janis called this dynamic **groupthink**. Groupthink, according to Janis, is "a mode of thinking that people engage in when they are deeply involved in a cohesive in-group, when members' strivings for unanimity override their motivation to realistically appraise alternative courses of action."[6] The dynamics of the group, which include the illusion of invulnerability and unanimity, excessive optimism, the belief in their own morality and the enemy's evil, and the pressure placed on dissenters to change their views, leads to groupthink. During the Vietnam War, for example, a top group of U.S. decisionmakers, unified by bonds of friendship and loyalty, met in what they called the Tuesday lunch group. In the aftermath of President Lyndon Johnson's overwhelming electoral win in 1964, the group basked in self-confidence and optimism, rejecting out of hand the pessimistic information about North Vietnam's military buildup. When information mounted about the increasing casualties suffered by the South Vietnamese and the Americans, the group pulled even more tightly together; as the external stress intensified, the group further closed ranks, its members' taking solace in the security of the group. New information was inserted only into old perceptions; individuals not sharing the groupthink were both informally and formally removed from the group, as their contradictory advice fell on deaf ears.

Participants in small groups, then, are apt to employ the same psychological techniques, like the evoked set and the mirror image, to process new incoming information at the individual level. But additional distorting tendencies affect small groups, such as the pressure for group conformity and solidarity. Larger groups seeking accommodation look for what is possible within the bounds of their situation, search for a "good enough" solution, rather than an optimal one. Herbert Simon has labeled this trait satisficing.[7] These tendencies confirm again that the rational model of decisionmaking imperfectly describes reality. Yet top leaders—with their various personality characteristics and however inaccurate their perceptions—do influence foreign policy. It is not just the tyrants (Germany's Adolf Hitler, Uganda's Idi Amin, the Central African Republic's Jean Bokassa, or Cambodia's Pol Pot) but also the visionaries (Tanzania's Julius Nyerere, India's Mohandas Gandhi, South Africa's Nelson Mandela) and the political pragmatists (Great Britain's Margaret Thatcher, the Philippines's Corazon Aquino) who make a difference on the basis of their roles and positions.

A few of the top leaders who make a difference represent the international community rather than the state. The seven individuals who have served as secretary-general of the United Nations are one such group. Their personalities and interpretations of the U.N. Charter, as well as world events, have combined to increase the power, resources, and importance of the position and of the United Nations. Yet how they have used the position has depended largely on the individual characteristics of the officeholder.

While those individuals holding formal positions have more opportunity not only to participate in but to shape international relations, private individuals can and do play key roles.

PRIVATE INDIVIDUALS

Private individuals, independent of any official role, may by virtue of circumstances, skills, or resources carry out independent actions in international relations. Less bound by the rules of the game or by institutional norms, such individuals engage in activities in which official representatives are either unable or unwilling to participate. The $21 billion donation by Microsoft founder, Bill Gates, to the World Health Organization for international vaccination and immunization programs is one such example.

In the area of conflict resolution, for instance, private individuals increasingly play a role in so-called **track-two diplomacy.** Track-two diplomacy utilizes individuals outside of governments to carry out the task of conflict resolution. High-level track-two diplomacy has met with some success. In the spring of 1992, for example, Eritrea signed a declaration of independence, seceding from Ethiopia after years of both low- and high-intensity conflict. The foundation for the agreement was negotiated in numerous informal meetings in Atlanta, Georgia, and elsewhere between the affected parties and former president Jimmy Carter, acting through the Carter Center's International Negotiation Network at Emory University. In the fall of 1993, the startling framework for reconciliation between Israel and the Palestine Liberation Organization was negotiated through track-two informal and formal techniques initiated by Terje Larsen, a Norwegian sociologist, and Yossi Beilin of the opposition Labor Party in Israel. A series of preparatory negotiations was conducted over a five-month period in total secrecy. Beginning unofficially, the talks gradually evolved into official negotiations, building up trust in an informal atmosphere and setting the stage for an eventual agreement.[8]

Such high-level track-two diplomatic efforts are not always well received. For example, Jimmy Carter's eleventh-hour dash in 1994 to meet with North Korea's Kim Il Sung to discuss the latter's nuclear buildup was met by a barrage of probing questions. Was the U.S. government being preempted? For whom did Carter speak? Could the understandings serve as the basis of a formal intergovernmental agreement?

Other types of track-two diplomacy involve a more lengthy process. In some cases, unofficial individuals from different international groups are brought together in small problem-solving workshops in order to develop personal relationships and understandings of the problems from the perspective of others. It is hoped that these individuals will then seek to influence public opinion in their respective states, trying to reshape, and often rehumanize, the image of the opponent. This approach has been used to address the conflict between Protestants and Catholics in Northern Ireland and the Arab-Israeli dispute. In the latter case, more than twenty problem-solving workshops have been conducted over two decades. Sometimes the process is extended into establishing cooperative activities. For example, Co-operation North, between the Republic of Ireland and Northern Ireland, brings together business, youth, and educational leaders and sponsors joint small-business development. It is hoped that such activities will lead to a safer climate for formal negotiations.

Other private individuals have played linkage roles between different countries. Armand Hammer, a U.S. corporate executive, was for years a private go-between for the Soviet Union and the United States. His long-standing business interests in the Soviet Union and his carefully nurtured friendships with both Soviet economic and political leaders and U.S. officials provided a channel of communication at a time when few informal contacts existed between the two countries. In the immediate aftermath of the 1986 Chernobyl nuclear plant explosion, Hammer convinced Gorbachev to accept U.S. medical personnel and expertise. Similarly, during the Vietnam War, Ross Perot, a private citizen and entrepreneur, organized rescue efforts on behalf of U.S. prisoners of war.

Sometimes individuals are propelled into the international arena by virtue of their actions: the youthful West German pilot Mathias Rust, who in 1987 landed an airplane in Moscow's Red Square, a prank that called into question the invincibility of Soviet air defenses; the actress Jane Fonda, who illegally visited North Vietnam during the 1960s and questioned the morality of the United States's war against Vietnam; Olympic athletes who defect from their countries, thus calling attention to the abuses of repressive regimes; Elizabeth O'Kelly, who works to call attention to the nature of rural women's work, establishing the Corn Mill Societies in the Cameroon and women's cooperatives in Asia; Aziza Hussein, whose tireless efforts to change family law in Egypt later propelled her to the presidency of the International Planned Parenthood Federation; financier George Soros, who uses his private fortune to support democratization initiatives in the states of the former Soviet Union.[9]

Individuals, acting alone, can make a difference; they can significantly influence international relations. Yet more often than not, these individual stories are not what we typically have in mind when we think of international diplomacy.

Alternative critical and postmodernist approaches are attempting to draw mainstream theorists' attention to these other stories, because they, too, are part of the fabric of international relations. Feminist writers in particular have sought to bring attention to the role of private individuals and especially women. Political scientist Cynthia Enloe, in *Bananas, Beaches, and Bases,* shows strikingly how "the personal is international" by documenting the many ways that women influence international relations. She points to women in economic roles participating in the international division of labor, as seamstresses, light-industry "girls," nannies, Benetton models. She also identifies women more directly involved in foreign policy—the women living around military bases, diplomatic wives, domestic servants, and women in international organizations.[10] Theirs are the untold stories of marginalized groups that critical theorists, postmodernists, and constructivists are increasingly bringing to light.

MASS PUBLICS

Mass publics have the same psychological tendencies as elite individuals and small groups. They think in terms of perceptions and images, they see mirror images, and they use similar information-processing strategies. For example, following the seizure of the U.S. embassy in Iran in November 1979, public-opinion surveys showed the prevalence of mirror images. The majority of U.S. respondents attributed favorable qualities to the United States and its leader, and unfavorable ones to Iran and its leader. The United States was strong and brave; Iran, weak and cowardly. The United States was deliberate and decisive; Iran, impulsive and indecisive. President Carter was safe; the Ayatollah Khomeini, dangerous; Carter, humane; Khomeini, ruthless. In a relatively short period of time, under crisis conditions, the public's perception of Iran had crystallized. Yet whether this had an impact on top decisionmakers is unclear.[11] We have seen that President Carter focused almost exclusively on the hostages, becoming obsessed with his mission of freeing them. But was this because of the public attention being paid to the hostages? Or did Carter's personality characteristics predispose him to focus so exclusively and so passionately on the hostages, as Glad would have us believe?[12]

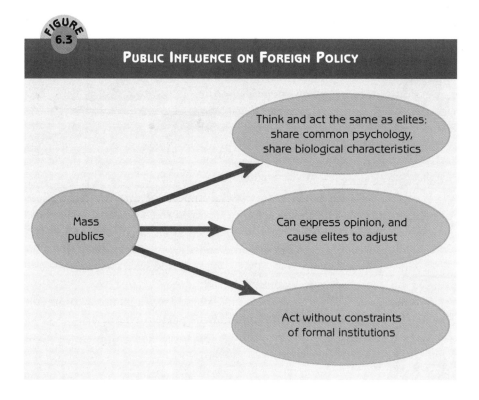

FIGURE 6.3

PUBLIC INFLUENCE ON FOREIGN POLICY

Mass publics

Think and act the same as elites: share common psychology, share biological characteristics

Can express opinion, and cause elites to adjust

Act without constraints of formal institutions

The influence that mass publics do have on foreign policy can be explained in three ways. First, it can be argued that elites and masses act the same because they share common psychological and biological characteristics. Second, the masses have opinions and attitudes about foreign policy and international relations, both general and specific, that are different from those of the elites. If these differences are captured by public-opinion polls, will elites listen to these opinions? Will policy made by elites reflect the public's attitudes? The third possibility is that the masses, uncontrolled by formal institutions, may occasionally act in ways that have a profound impact on international relations, regardless of anything that elites do. These three possibilities are illustrated in Figure 6.3.

Elites and Masses: Common Traits

Some scholars argue that there are psychological and biological traits common to every man, woman, and child and that societies reflect those characteristics. For example, individuals, like animals, are said to have an innate drive to gain, protect, and defend territory—the "territorial imperative." This, according to some, explains the preoccupation with defending territorial boundaries, such as Britain's determination in 1982 to defend its position on the Falkland Islands, a desolate archipelago 8,000 miles from Britain's shores. Individuals and societies also share the frustration-aggression syndrome: when societies become frustrated, just as with individuals, they become aggressive. Frustration, of course, can arise from a number of different sources—economic shocks such as those Germany suffered after World War I or those Russia experienced in the 1990s; or failure to possess what is felt to be rightfully one's own, as with the Palestinian claim to territory of the Israeli state.

The problem with both the territorial imperative and the frustration-aggression notion is that even if all individuals and societies share these innate biological predispositions, all leaders and all peoples do not act on these predispositions. So general predispositions of all societies or the similarities in predispositions between elites and masses do not explain the extreme variation in individual behavior.

Another possibility is that elites and masses share common traits differentiated by gender. Male elites and masses possess characteristics common to each other, while female elites and masses share traits different from the males'. These differences can explain political behavior. While there is considerable interest in this possibility, the research is sketchy. One much-discussed difference is that males, both elites and masses, are power seeking, whereas women are consensus builders. At the mass level, this difference holds up, as women are less likely to support war than men. But since there are fewer examples of women decisionmakers than men, it is impossible to demonstrate differences exclusively to gender. If there are differences in male and female attitudes and behavior, are these differences rooted in biology or are they learned from the culture? Most feminists, particularly the constructivists, contend that these differences are socially constructed products of culture and can thus be reconstructed over time. Yet, once again, these general predispositions, whatever their origin, cannot explain extreme variation in individual or elite behavior.

The Impact of Public Opinion on Elites

Publics do have general foreign-policy orientations and specific attitudes about issues that can be revealed by public-opinion polls. Sometimes, these attitudes reflect a perceived general mood of the population that leaders can detect. President Johnson probably accurately gauged the mood of the U.S. people toward the Vietnam War when he chose not to run for reelection in 1968. President George Bush was able to capitalize internationally on the positive public mood in the aftermath of victory in the war against Iraq, although the domestic effect was short lived; he did not win reelection. Even leaders of authoritarian regimes pay attention to dominant moods, since these leaders also depend on a degree of legitimacy.

More often than not, however, publics do not express one dominant mood; top leaders are usually confronted with an array of public attitudes. These opinions are registered in elections, but elections are an imperfect measure of public opinion since they select individuals for office—individuals who share voters' attitudes on some issues but not on others.

Occasionally and quite extraordinarily, the masses may vote directly on an issue with foreign-policy significance. For example, following the negotiation of the 1992 Maastricht Treaty, which detailed closer political cooperation among members of the European Union (EU), some states used popular referendums to ratify the treaty. At first, the Danish population defeated the referendum, thus choosing not to join the EU, despite the fact that the measure had support from most societal groups. Subsequently, the referendum was approved. The Norwegian public chose by a referendum to remain outside of the EU, in a rather rare instance of direct public input on a foreign-policy decision.

In most democratic regimes, public-opinion polling, a vast and growing industry, provides information about public attitudes. The European Union, for example, conducts the Eurobarometer, a scientific survey of public attitudes on a wide range of issues in EU countries. Because the same questions are asked during different polls over time, both top leaders in member states and the top leadership of the EU have sophisticated data concerning public attitudes. But do they make policy with these attitudes in mind? Do elites change policy to reflect the preferences of the public?

Evidence from the United States suggests that elites do care about the preferences of the public, although they do not always directly mirror those attitudes. Presidents care about their popularity because it affects their ability to work; a president's popularity is enhanced if he or she follows the general mood of the masses or fights for policies that are generally popular. Such popularity gives the president more leeway to set a national agenda. But mass attitudes may not always be directly translated into policy. For example, opinion polls suggest that U.S. elites, including top decisionmakers, are more supportive of an activist international agenda and of free trade, and less supportive of economic protectionism, than the mass public is. Thus, elite-made policy is not a direct reflection of public attitudes.

Public opinion does, however, act as a constraint on the elite in the United States. The masses often act as a brake on policy change. For many years, the effects of the "Vietnam syndrome"—a fear of getting involved in a military confrontation that could not be won—served to constrain U.S. decisionmakers from getting involved in potentially similar conflicts, whether in Angola, Nicaragua, or Bosnia. On a few occasions, the masses do have attitudes and desire actions that the elites are not ready to support. For example, Steven Kull and I. M. Destler's 1999 study of U.S. public opinion shows that Americans have not turned isolationist as the elite often claims. Americans by a two-to-one margin want the United States to play an active role in world affairs, particularly in multilateral and cooperative efforts, and there is mass support for foreign aid and humanitarian causes.[13] But the mass public may not have strong support for these views, and when confronted with specific choices, its preferences may change. So the relationship between elite and mass public opinion is, indeed, a complex one.

Mass Actions by a Leaderless Public

The mass public does not always have articulated opinions, nor is it always able to vote at the polls. Nor are groups of elites always able to control events. At times, the masses, essentially leaderless, take collective actions that have significant effects on the course of world politics.

Individuals act to improve their own political and economic welfare. An individual alone making such decisions usually will not impact international relations. However, when hundreds or even thousands of individuals act, the repercussions can be dramatic. It was the individual acts of thousands fleeing East Germany that led to the construction of the Berlin Wall in 1961. Twenty-eight years later, it was the spontaneous exodus of thousands of East Germans through Hungary and Austria that led to the tearing down of the wall in 1989. The spontaneous movement of "boat people" fleeing Vietnam and the ragged ships leaving Cuba and Haiti for the U.S. coast resulted in changes in U.S. immigration policy. The spontaneous mass uprising against Philippine president Ferdinand Marcos in 1986 signaled the demise of his regime. The "Velvet Revolution" of the masses in Czechoslovakia in the 1990s brought the end of the communist regime in that country.

The scenario of dramatic changes initiated by the masses is vividly illustrated by the "people's putsch" during October 2000 against Yugoslavian leader Slobodan Milosevic. After thirteen years of rule, people from all walks of Serbian life joined seven thousand striking miners, crippled the economic system, blocked transportation routes, and descended on Belgrade, the capital. Aided by new technology such as the cell phone, they were able to mobilize citizens from all over the country, driving tractors into the city, attacking the parliament, and crippling Milosevic's radio and TV stations. As *Time* reported, "Years of pent-up frustration under Milosevic's blighting misrule had finally erupted in a tumultuous showdown, as each new success taught Serbs to see they had the power to change their future. The revolution ran at cyberspeed from the disputed election two weeks ago, ending victoriously in the dizzying events of one day. Just like that, the Serbs took back their country and belatedly joined the democratic tide that swept away the rest of Eastern Europe's communist tyrants a decade ago."[14]

IN SUM: HOW MUCH DO INDIVIDUALS MATTER?

For liberals, the actions of individuals matter immensely. Individual elites can make a difference: they have choices in the kind of foreign policy they pursue and therefore can affect the course of events. Thus, we need to pay attention to personality characteristics and understand how individuals make decisions, how they use various techniques to process information, and how these processes impact on individual and group behavior. Mass publics matter to liberals because they help formulate the state's interests. Private individuals also matter, although they are clearly of secondary importance even in liberal thinking. Only in more recent postmodernist and constructivist scholarship, especially in feminist scholarship, have private individuals' stories found saliency.

Realists and radicals do not recognize the importance of individuals as independent actors in international relations. They see individuals as primarily constrained by the international system and by the state. To realists, individuals are constrained by an anarchic international system and by a state seeking to project power consonant with its national interest. Similarly, radicals see individuals within the confines of the international capitalist system and within a state driven by economic imperatives. In neither case are individuals sufficiently unconstrained to be considered a level of analysis on the same plane as either the international system or the state.

This debate over the relative importance of individuals as a level of analysis and indeed the debate over the relationship among the levels of analysis permeates the discussion of issues in international relations. Two of those major issues—war and strife, and international political economy—are the topics of our next two chapters.

NOTES

1. Robert G. Hermann, "Identity, Norms, and National Security: The Soviet Foreign Policy Revolution and the End of the Cold War," in *The Culture of National Security: Norms and Identity in World Politics,* ed. P.J. Katzenstein, (New York: Columbia University Press, 1996), 271–316.

2 Margaret G. Hermann, "Explaining Foreign Policy Behavior Using the Personal Characteristics of Political Leaders," *International Studies Quarterly* 24:1 (March 1980), 7–46.

3. Betty Glad, "Personality, Political and Group Process Variables in Foreign Policy Decision Making: Jimmy Carter's Handling of the Iranian Hostage Crisis," *International Political Science Review* 10 (1989), 58.

4. Ole Holsti, "The Belief System and National Images: A Case Study," *Journal of Conflict Resolution* 6 (1962), 244–52.

5. Harvey Starr, *Henry Kissinger: Perceptions of International Politics* (Lexington, Ky.: University Press of Kentucky, 1984); and Stephen Walker, "The Interface between Beliefs and Behavior: Henry Kissinger's Operational Code and the Vietnam War," *Journal of Conflict Resolution* 21:1 (March 1977), 129–68.

6. Irving L. Janis, *Victims of Groupthink: A Psychological Study of Foreign-Policy Decisions and Fiascoes* (Boston: Houghton Mifflin, 1972), 9.

7. Herbert Simon, "A Behavioral Model of Rational Choice," in *Models of Man: Social and Rational,* ed. Herbert Simon (New York: John Wiley, 1957).

8. David Makovsky, *Making Peace with the PLO: The Rabin Government's Road to the Oslo Accord* (Boulder, Colo.: Westview, 1996).

9. Marion Fennelly Levy, *Each in Her Own Way: Five Women Leaders of the Developing World* (Boulder, Colo.: Lynne Rienner, 1988); and Francine D'Amico and Peter R. Beckman, eds., *Women in World Politics: An Introduction* (Westport, Conn.: Bergin and Garvey, 1995).

10. Cynthia H. Enloe, *Bananas, Beaches and Bases: Making Feminist Sense of International Politics* (Berkeley: University of California Press, 1990).

11. Pamela Johnston Conover, Karen A. Mingst, and Lee Sigelman, "Mirror Images in Americans' Perceptions of Nations and Leaders during the Iranian Hostage Crisis," *Journal of Peace Research* 17:4 (1980), 325–37.

12. Betty Glad, "Personality, Political and Group Process Variables in Foreign Policy Decision Making."

13. Steven Kull and I. M. Destler, *Misreading the Public: The Myth of New Isolationism.* (Washington, D.C.: Brookings Institution, 1999).

14. Johanna McGeary, "The End of Milosevic," *Time,* October 16, 2000, 60.

WAR AND STRIFE

7

- *Why is the security dilemma an ironic fact of international life?*
- *How is insecurity managed in the world of the liberals?*
- *How are the approaches of realists trying to manage insecurity different from those of the liberals?*
- *What role does peacekeeping play in managing insecurity?*
- *Why is there war?*
- *By examining the Yugoslavian conflict, what can we learn about the causes of war?*
- *What are the new threats to international security?*

Among the numerous issues engaging the actors in international relations, security issues are the most salient, the most prevalent, and indeed the most intractable. States exist in an anarchic world. While there may be formal and informal rules that give rise to a type of international system structure, there is no international supreme authority, no centralized government empowered to manage or control the actions of individual elites, sovereign states, or even international intergovernmental organizations. Within states, individuals have recourse to governments and have protection under governments. States themselves have some avenues of recourse—international law and international organizations—but these avenues are weak.

In ancient Greece, when Melos was physically surrounded by the fleet of its archenemy Athens, Melos had few alternatives. It could appeal to a distant ally—another city-state, whose interests may have been fundamentally different from those of Melos—or it could rely on its own resources—its military strength and the men and women of Melos. Just as Melos was ultimately responsible for its own security, so, too, are states in an anarchic system. This is similar to the position of each prisoner in the prisoner's dilemma game described in Chapters 3 and 5; fearing the worst possible outcome, each player confesses to ensure himself a better outcome. There is no incentive to cooperate. Likewise, states, fearing the worst possible outcome—other states' amassing more and better armaments than they—choose to arm. The people of Melos, each prisoner, and states all rely on self-help.

Yet ironically, if a state prepares to protect itself, if it takes self-help measures—building a strong industrial base, constructing armaments, mobilizing a military—then other states become less secure. Their response is to engage in similar activities, increasing their own level of protection but leading to greater insecurity on the part of others. This situation is known as the **security dilemma: in the absence of centralized authority, one state's becoming more secure diminishes another state's security.** As political scientist John Herz describes, "Striving to attain security from attack, [states] are driven to acquire more and more power in order to escape the power of others. This, in turn, renders the others more insecure and compels them to prepare for the worst. Since none can ever feel entirely secure in such a world of competing units, power competition ensues, and the vicious circle of security and power accumulation is on."[1] The security dilemma, then, results in a permanent condition of tension and power conflicts among states. Thus, it is imperative to examine the ways that the security dilemma has been managed (short of war) over the decades.

APPROACHES TO MANAGING INSECURITY

There are five approaches to managing insecurity for states. Each approach recognizes the power disparity between states and is cognizant of the anarchic international environment. Two of these approaches fall under the liberal theoretical perspective and thus focus largely on multilateral responses by groups of states acting to coordinate their policies. Two other approaches are realist, requiring states themselves to maintain an adequate power potential. The final approach we will consider

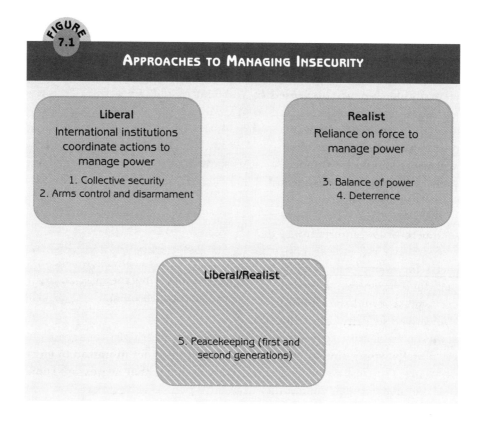

FIGURE 7.1

APPROACHES TO MANAGING INSECURITY

Liberal
International institutions coordinate actions to manage power

1. Collective security
2. Arms control and disarmament

Realist
Reliance on force to manage power

3. Balance of power
4. Deterrence

Liberal/Realist

5. Peacekeeping (first and second generations)

combines elements of the liberal and realist perspectives. These five approaches are illustrated in Figure 7.1.

Liberal Approaches

Liberal approaches to managing the security dilemma call on the international community or international institutions to coordinate actions in order to manage power.

The Collective Security Ideal   Collective security is captured in the old adage "one for all and all for one." Based on the proposition that aggressive and unlawful use of force by any state against another must be stopped, collective security posits that such unlawful aggression will be met by united action: all (or many) other states will join together against the aggressor. Potential aggressors will know this fact ahead of time, and thus will choose not to act.

Collective security makes a number of fundamental assumptions.[2] One assumption is that although wars can occur, they should be prevented, and they are prevented by restraint of military action. In other words, wars will not occur if all parties exercise restraint. Another assumption is that aggressors should be stopped. This assumption presumes that the aggressor can be identified easily by other members of the international community. (In some conflicts, for example, it is difficult to differentiate between the aggressor and the victim.) Collective security also assumes moral clarity: the aggressor is morally wrong because all aggressors are morally wrong, and all those who are right must act in unison to meet the aggression. Finally, collective security assumes that aggressors know that the international community will act to punish an aggressor.

> ### IN FOCUS
>
> ## ASSUMPTIONS OF COLLECTIVE SECURITY THEORY
>
> ▶ Wars are prevented by restraint of military action.
> ▶ Aggressors must be stopped.
> ▶ The aggressor is easily identified.
> ▶ The aggressor is always wrong.
> ▶ Aggressors know the international community will act against them.

Of course, the underlying hope of collective security proponents is compatible with the logic of deterrence (a realist strategy). If all countries know that aggression will be punished by the international community, then would-be aggressors will refrain from engaging in aggressive activity. Hence, states will be more secure with the belief that would-be aggressors will be deterred through the united action of the international community.

Collective security does not always work. In the period between the two world wars, Japan invaded Manchuria and Italy overran Ethiopia. In neither case did other states act as if it were in their collective interest to respond. Were Manchuria and Ethiopia really worth a war? In this instance, collective security did not work because of a lack of commitment on the part of other states and an unwillingness of the international community to act in concert. In the post–World War II era, collective security could not work because of fundamental differences in both state interests and ideologies. Agreement among the most powerful states was virtually impossible. And a collective security response against one of the Big Five powers themselves—the United States, the Soviet Union, Great Britain, France, or China—was impossible due to the veto power that each held in the U.N. Security Council. Two major alliance systems—the North Atlantic Treaty Organization (NATO) and the Warsaw Pact—arrayed states into two separate camps. States dared not engage in action against an ally or a foe, even if that state was an aggressor, for fear of embarking on another world war.

Collective security is also likely to be unworkable because of the problematic nature of its assumptions. Can the aggressor always be easily identified? Clearly not. In 1967 Israel launched an armed attack against Egypt: this was an act of aggression. The week before, however, Egypt had blocked Israeli access to the Red Sea. Clearly that, too, was an act of aggression. Twenty years earlier the state of Israel had been carved out of Arab real estate. That, too, was an act of aggression. Many centuries before, Arabs had ousted Jews from the territory they inhabited, also an aggressive action. So who is the aggressor? Furthermore, even if an aggressor can be identified, is that party always morally wrong? Collective security theorists argue, by definition, yes. Yet trying to right a previous wrong is not necessarily wrong; trying to make just a prior injustice is not unjust. Like the balance of power, collective security in practice supports the status quo at a specific point in time.

Arms Control and Disarmament **Arms control** and general **disarmament** schemes have been the hope of many liberals over the years. The logic of this approach to security is straightforward: fewer weapons means greater security. By regulating the upward spiral of armaments (arms control) and by reducing the amount of arms and the types of weapons employed (disarmament), the costs of the security dilemma are reduced.

During the Cold War, many arms control agreements were negotiated. For example, in the 1972 Treaty on the Limitation of Antiballistic Missile Systems (ABM treaty), both the United States and the Soviet Union agreed not to use a ballistic missile defense as a shield against a **first strike** by the other. The Strategic Arms Limitations Talks in 1972 and 1979 (SALT I and SALT II, respectively) put ceilings on the growth of both Soviet and U.S. strategic weapons. However, due to the Soviet invasion of Afghanistan in 1979, the second SALT treaty was never ratified by the U.S. Senate. The Treaty on the Nonproliferation of Nuclear Weapons (NPT) was negotiated in 1968 at the United Nations in response to the Cuban missile crisis.

Table 7.1 lists some of the important arms control agreements negotiated to date. Most of these treaties, be they bilateral or multilateral, call for individual states to reduce either the number or the type of armaments already deployed. A few are designed to halt the spread of particular weapons to states that do not yet have them. At least one major treaty has utilized formal, multilateral processes to verify whether the terms of the treaty are being met. Nevertheless, virtually all arms control treaties are fraught with difficulties.

The NPT provides both a positive and a negative example of the impact of such treaties. The NPT spells out the rules of **nuclear proliferation** since 1970. In the treaty, signatory countries without nuclear weapons agree not to acquire or develop them, while states with nuclear weapons promise not to transfer the technology to nonnuclear states. Like many of the arms control treaties, however, a number of key nuclear states and threshold nonnuclear states (i.e., states that probably have or could quickly assemble nuclear weapons) remain outside the treaty, including India, Israel, Pakistan, and Brazil. The International Atomic Energy Agency (IAEA), a U.N.-based agency established in 1957 to disseminate knowledge about nuclear energy and promote its peaceful uses, is designated guardian of the treaty. The IAEA created a system of *safeguards,* including inspection teams that visit nuclear facilities and report on any movement of nuclear material, in an attempt to keep nuclear material from being diverted to nonpeaceful purposes and to ensure that states that signed the NPT are complying. Inspectors for IAEA visited Iraqi sites after the Persian Gulf War, and North Korean sites in the mid-1990s. Their purpose in the first case was to verify that illegal materials had been destroyed and, in the second case, to confirm the existence of nuclear materials in that country.

The end of the Cold War and the dismemberment of the Soviet Union have resulted in major new arms control agreements, as Table 7.1 shows. More arms control agreements between the United States and Russia and its successor states are likely, as the latter are forced by economic imperatives to reduce their military expenditures. Yet the logic of arms control agreements is not impeccable. Arms control does not eliminate the security dilemma. You can still feel insecure if your enemy has a bigger or better rock than you do.

Complete disarmament schemes as envisioned by utopian liberal thinkers are unlikely, given how risky such a scheme would be. Unilateral disarmament would place the state involved in a highly insecure position. But incremental disarmament, such as represented by the Chemical

TABLE 7.1

Major Arms Control Agreements since 1959

Agreement	Signed by	Provisions	Year
Antarctic Treaty	43 states	Prohibits all military activity in Antarctic area.	1959
Partial Nuclear Test Ban Treaty	154 states	Prohibits nuclear explosions in the atmosphere, in outer space, and under water.	1963
Outer Space Treaty	127 states	Prohibits all military activity in outer space, including on the moon and other celestial bodies.	1967
Treaty of Tlatelolco	33 states	Prohibits nuclear weapons in Latin America.	1967
Nuclear Nonproliferation Treaty (NPT)	187 states	Prohibits acquisition of nuclear weapons by nonnuclear nations.	1968
Strategic Arms Limitation Treaty (SALT)	U.S., U.S.S.R.	Limits deployment of antiballistic missile systems to two sites in each country. Reduced to one site by 1974 agreement.	1972
SALT I: Interim Offensive Arms Agreement	U.S., U.S.S.R.	Provides for freeze on aggregate number of fixed, land-based ICBMs and SLBMs.*	1972
South Pacific Nuclear-Free Zone Treaty	18 states	Bans testing, manufacture, acquisition, stationing of nuclear weapons in the South Pacific.	1985
Confidence- and Security-Building Measures and Disarmament in Europe	54 states	Requires notification of military movements and maneuvers, observers, and inspection.	1986
Intermediate-Range Nuclear Forces (INF) Treaty	U.S., U.S.S.R.	Eliminates all missiles with range between 500 and 5,500 kilometers.	1987
Conventional Armed Forces in Europe (CFE) Treaty	30 states	Sets limits on NATO and Warsaw Pact tanks, other armored vehicles, artillery, combat helicopters, and aircraft. Updated in 1992.	1990

*ICBM = intercontinental ballistic missile; SLBM = submarine-launched ballistic missile

Major Arms Control Agreements since 1959 (continued)

Agreement	Signed by	Provisions	Year
Strategic Arms Reduction Treaty (START) I	U.S., U.S.S.R.	Reduces number of U.S. and former Soviet strategic nuclear warheads by approximately one-third; makes Russia, Belarus, Ukraine, and Kazakhstan responsible for carrying out former U.S.S.R. treaty obligations.	1991
Open Skies Treaty	27 states	Creates a regime for confidence-building and stability of arms control, by allowing observational flights by unarmed reconnaissance aircraft over signatory states.	1992
START II	U.S., Russia	Reduces the number of deployed U.S. and Russian strategic nuclear warheads by the year 2003; bans multiple-warhead land-based missiles.	1993
Chemical Weapons Convention (CWC)	169 states	Bans the use, production, development, and stockpiling of chemical weapons within 10–15 years of treaty's entry into force.	1993
U.N. Registration of Conventional Arms	97 states	Requires that states submit information on seven categories of major weapons exported or imported during prior year.	1993
Comprehensive Test Ban Treaty (CTBT)	156 states	Bans testing of nuclear weapons.	1996
Antipersonnel Landmines Treaty	135 states	Bans production and export of landmines.	1998

Weapons Convention (CWC), which bans the development, production, and stockpiling of chemical weapons, remains a realistic possibility. Liberals place their faith in international institutions like the IAEA to monitor adherence to such limited disarmament schemes.

Realist Approaches

As mentioned earlier, realist approaches to managing security place less faith in the international community and more faith in individual state power.

Balance of Power   In Chapter 4, we saw that a balance of power is a particular configuration of the international system. But theorists use the term in other ways as well. So *balance of power* may refer to an equilibrium between any two parties, and *balancing power* may describe an approach to managing power and insecurity. The latter usage is relevant here.

Balance-of-power theorists posit that, to manage insecurity, states make rational and calculated evaluations of the costs and benefits of particular policies that determine the state's role in a balance of power. Should we enlarge our power by seeking new allies? Is our enemy (or friend) altering the balance of power to our detriment? What can we do to make the balance of power shift in our favor? By either explicitly or implicitly asking and responding to such questions, states minimize their insecurity by protecting their own interests. All states in the system are continually making choices to increase their own capabilities and to undermine the capabilities of others, and thereby the balance of power is maintained. When that balance of power is jeopardized, insecurity leads states to pursue countervailing policies.[3]

Alliances represent the most important institutional tool for enhancing one's own power and meeting the perceived power potential of one's opponent. If a state is threatening to achieve a dominant position, the threatened state will join with others against the threat. This is *external balancing.* Formal and institutionalized military alliances play a key role in maintaining a balance of power, as the NATO and Warsaw Pact alliances did in the post–World War II world. States may also engage in *internal balancing*, increasing their own military and economic capabilities to counter potential threatening enemies.

A balance of power operates at both the international and regional levels. At the international level during the Cold War, for instance, a relative balance of power was maintained between the United States and the Soviet Union. If one of the superpowers augmented its power through the expansion of its alliances or through the acquisition of more deadly, more effective armaments, the other responded in kind. Absolute gains were not as critical as relative gains; no matter how much power accrued, neither state could afford to fall behind. Gaining allies in the uncommitted part of the Third World, through foreign aid or military and diplomatic intervention, was one way to ensure that the power was balanced. To not maintain the power balance was too risky a strategy; national survival was at stake.

Balances of power among states in specific geographic regions are also a way to manage insecurity. In South Asia, for example, a balance of power works to maintain peace between India and Pakistan, a peace made more forceful by the presence of nuclear weapons. In East Asia, Japan's alliance with the United States creates a balance of power vis-à-vis China. In the Middle East, the balance of power between Israel and its Arab neighbors continues. In some regions a complex set of other balances has developed: between the economically rich, oil-producing states of Saudi Arabia and the Persian Gulf and the economically poor states of the core Middle East; between Islamic militants (Iran, Libya), moderates (Egypt, Tunisia), and conservatives (Saudi Arabia). With the breakup of the Soviet Union, the newly independent states of central Asia are struggling for place and position within a newly emerging regional balance of power.

Realist theorists assert that the balance of power is the most important technique for managing insecurity. It is compatible with the nature of man and that of the state, which is to act to protect self-interest by maintaining one's power position relative to others. If a state seeks preponderance through military acquisitions or offensive actions, then war is acceptable under the balance-of-power system. But if all states act similarly, the balance can be preserved.

A major limitation of the balance-of-power approach, however, is its inability to manage security during periods of fundamental change. A balance-of-power approach supports the status quo. When change occurs, how should other states respond? Fundamental change occurred at the end of the Cold War, for example, with the dismemberment of the Soviet Union and the dissolution of the Warsaw Pact alliance. A balance-of-power strategy would have suggested that the United States also reduce its power potential, particularly its military capability, since the military of its rival had been impaired. Yet such a rational response is politically difficult to make. Fear of a resurgence of power from the opponent, fear of a return to the old order, and pressure from domestic constituencies to maintain defense spending and employment all make dramatic changes in policy difficult to accommodate.

One outcome of the change brought about by the end of the Cold War has been a reexamination of the role of NATO, the major Western alliance formed after World War II to counter the threat posed by the Soviet Union. With the disintegration of the Soviet Union as a state and the end of communist leadership in it and neighboring states, what role does NATO play now? Should NATO be expanded to include the states of eastern Europe and the former Soviet Union? Should Russia be asked to join? Poland, the Czech Republic, and Hungary have become members, and discussions with other countries continue. But if all states are included, what is the purpose of the alliance? Who is the enemy? What balance of power is being preserved or maintained? Realists see NATO expansion as an opportunity to expand Western influence during an era of Russian weakness. Liberals view the expansion as a way to support fledgling democracies and identities in eastern Europe and extend mechanisms for conflict management in the system. But the difficult questions posed by realists and liberals alike remain unanswered.

Deterrence: Balance of Power Revisited   The goal of deterrence theory, like that of the balance of power, is to prevent the outbreak of war. Deterrence theory posits that war can be prevented by the *threat* of the use of force.

The theory as initially developed is based on a number of key assumptions.[4] First and most important is the realist assumption of the rationality of decisionmakers. Rational decisionmakers are assumed to want to avoid resorting to war in those situations in which the anticipated cost of the aggression is greater than the gain expected. Second, it is assumed that nuclear weapons pose an unacceptable level of destruction, and thus that deci-

IN FOCUS

ASSUMPTIONS OF DETERRENCE THEORY

▶ Decisionmakers are rational.
▶ The threat of destruction from warfare is large.
▶ Alternatives to war are available.

sionmakers will not resort to armed aggression. Third, the theory assumes the existence of alternatives to war that are available to decisionmakers irrespective of the situation. Thus, under deterrence, war will not occur and insecurity is reduced, as long as rational decisionmakers are in charge, the threat is sufficiently large, and other nonmilitary options are available.

For deterrence to work, then, states must build up their arsenals in order to present a credible threat. Information regarding the threat must be conveyed to the opponent. Thus, knowing that an aggressive action will be countered by a damaging reaction, the opponent will decide, according to deterrence theorists, not to resort to force and destroy its own society.

The basic ideas of deterrence were developed with respect to conventional arms. The development and subsequent buildup of nuclear weapons in the second half of the twentieth century, however, has made deterrence an even more potent approach for managing power. With each superpower having second-strike capability—the ability to respond and hit the adversary even after the adversary has launched a first strike—then destruction of both sides is assured. According to deterrence, no rational decisionmaker will make the decision to start a nuclear war since his or her own society would be destroyed in the process. Decisionmakers thus turn to other alternatives to achieve their goals.

As logical as deterrence sounds and as effective as it has proved to be—after all, there was no nuclear war during the Cold War—the assumptions of the theory are troublesome. Are all top decisionmakers rational? Might not one individual or a group risk destruction? Might some states sacrifice a large number of people, as Adolf Hitler, Iran's Ayatollah Khomeini, and Iraq's Saddam Hussein were willing to do? How do states convey to a potential adversary information about their own capability? Why not choose to bluff or lie to feel more secure? For states without nuclear weapons, or nuclear-weapons states who are launching an attack against a nonnuclear state, the costs of war may not be that unacceptable: their own society may not be threatened with destruction. In such cases, deterrence will fail.

Both the balance of power and deterrence rely on the unilateral use of force or the threat of using force to manage power, whereas liberal approaches depend on collective efforts. Periodically, these approaches fail. In these situations, when conflict has already broken out, realists and liberals alike have turned to peacekeeping to manage insecurity.

Peacekeeping: The Stepchild of Liberals and Realists   During the Cold War, when collective security was an impossibility, peacekeeping evolved as a way to limit the scope of conflict and prevent it from escalating into a Cold War confrontation. Peacekeeping operations fall into two types, or generations. In **first-generation peacekeeping**, multilateral institutions such as the United Nations seek to contain conflicts between two states through third-party military forces. Ad hoc military units, drawn from the armed forces of nonpermanent members of the U.N. Security Council (often small, neutral members), have been used to prevent the escalation of conflicts and to keep the warring parties apart until the dispute can be settled. These troops operate under U.N. auspices, supervising armistices, trying to maintain cease-fires, and physically interposing themselves in a buffer zone between warring parties.

First-generation peacekeeping efforts are most effective under the following conditions:

- A clear and practicable *mandate* (purpose) for the operation
- Consent of the parties involved as to the mandate and composition of the force
- Strong financial and logistical support of members of the U.N. Security Council
- Acceptance by troop-contributing countries of the mandate and the risk that it may bring
- An understanding among peacekeepers to resort to the use of force only for self-defense

Table 7.2 lists some of the first-generation U.N. peacekeeping operations since they began in 1948. These operations served the limited purposes that were compatible with both realist and liberal thinking.

In the post–Cold War era, U.N. peacekeeping has expanded to address different types of conflicts and to take on new responsibilities. Whereas first-generation activities primarily address interstate conflict, **second-generation peacekeeping** activities respond to civil war and domestic unrest, much of it stemming from the rise of ethnonationalism, as described in Chapter 5. To deal with these new conflicts, second-generation peacekeepers have taken on a range of both military and nonmilitary functions. Militarily, they have aided in verification of troop withdrawal (Afghanistan) and have separated warring factions until the underlying issues could be settled (Bosnia). Sometimes resolving underlying issues has

TABLE 7.2

First-Generation Peacekeeping Operations

Operation	Location	Duration	Maximum strength
UNTSO (U.N. Truce Supervision Organization)	Egypt, Israel, Jordan, Syria, Lebanon	June 1948–present	572 military observers
UNEF I (First U.N. Emergency Force)	Suez Canal, Sinai peninsula	Nov. 1956–June 1967	3,378 troops
ONUC (U.N. Operation in the Congo)	Congo	June 1960–June 1964	19,828 troops
UNFICYP (U.N. Peacekeeping Force in Cyprus)	Cyprus	March 1964–present	6,411 military observers
UNEF II (Second U.N. Emergency Force)	Suez Canal, Sinai peninsula	Oct. 1973–July 1979	6,973 troops
UNDOF (U.N. Disengagement Observer Force)	Syrian Golan Heights	June 1974–present	1,450 military observers
UNMEE (U.N. Mission in Ethiopia and Eritrea)	Ethiopia/Eritrea border	Sept. 2000–present	4,200 troops

SOURCE: United Nations.

meant organizing and running national elections, such as in Cambodia and Namibia; sometimes it has involved implementing human rights agreements, such as in Central America. At other times U.N. peacekeepers have tried to maintain law and order in failing or disintegrating societies by aiding in civil administration, policing, and rehabilitating infrastructure, as in Somalia. And peacekeepers have provided humanitarian aid, supplying food, medicine, and a secure environment in part of an expanded version of human rights, as followed in several missions in Africa. Table 7.3 lists these second-generation peacekeeping operations. As the table clearly indicates, second-generation peacekeeping has vastly expanded in the post–Cold War period. This expansion has created difficulties for the international community, a topic we will explore further in Chapter 9.

TABLE 7.3

Second-Generation Peacekeeping Operations

Operation	Location	Duration	Maximum strength
UNTAG (U.N. Transition Assistance Group)	Namibia, Angola	April 1989– March 1990	4,493 troops, 1,500 civilian police, and 2,000 civilian election observers
UNPROFOR (U.N. Protection Force)	Former Yugoslavia: Croatia, Bosnia-Herzegovina, Macedonia	March 1992– Dec. 1995	30,500 troops and civilian staff
UNTAC (U.N. Transition Authority in Cambodia)	Cambodia	March 1992– Dec. 1993	15,900 troops, 3,600 police monitors, and 2,400 civilian staff
UNOSOM I, II (U.N. Operation in Somalia)	Somalia	Aug. 1992– March 1995	28,000 troops and 2,800 civilian staff
ONUMOZ (U.N. Operation in Mozambique)	Mozambique	Dec. 1992– Dec. 1994	7,000 military and civilian staff
UNIMIH (U.N. Mission in Haiti)	Haiti	Sept. 1993– June 1996	1,200 troops and 300 civilians
UNMIK (U.N. Mission in Kosovo)	Kosovo, Yugoslavia	June 1999– present	4,400 police
UNTAET (U.N. Transitional Administration in East Timor)	East Timor	Oct. 1999– present	9,229 total (7,700 military and 1,300 civilians)
MONUC (U.N. Mandate in Democratic Republic of Congo)	Congo	Nov. 1999– present	5,500 military and 500 civilian observers

SOURCE: United Nations.

THE CAUSES OF WAR

Although the techniques used to manage insecurity are many, sometimes the approaches fail and wars do break out. There have been approximately 14,500 armed struggles throughout history, with about 3.5 billion people dying either as a direct or indirect result.[5] In the contemporary era (since

1816), there have been between 224 and 559 international, internal, and colonialist wars, depending on how war is defined.

But while the security dilemma explains why states are insecure, it does not explain why war breaks out. An analysis of any war—Vietnam, Angola, Cambodia, World War II, or the Franco-Prussian War—would find a variety of reasons for the outbreak of violence. Kenneth Waltz in *Man, the State, and War* posits that the international system is the primary framework of international relations.[6] But that framework exists all the time, so to explain why sometimes wars occur and sometimes they do not, we also need to consider the other levels of analysis. Characteristics of individuals, both leaders and masses, and the internal structure of states are some of the forces that operate within the limitations of the international system. Waltz finds that all three different levels of analysis can be applied to explaining the causes of war.[7]

The Individual: Realist and Liberal Interpretations

Both the characteristics of individual leaders and the general attributes of people (discussed in Chapter 6) have been blamed for war. Some individual leaders are aggressive and bellicose; they use their leadership positions to further their causes. Thus, according to some realists and liberals, war occurs because of the personal characteristics of major leaders. It is impossible, however, to prove the veracity of this position. Would past wars have occurred had different leaders—perhaps more pacifist ones—been in power? We can only speculate.

If it is not the innate character flaws of individuals that cause war, is there a possibility that leaders, like all individuals, are subject to misperceptions? According to liberals, misperceptions by leaders—seeing aggressiveness where it may not be intended, imputing the actions of one person to a group—can lead to the outbreak of war. Historians have typically given a key role to misperceptions. There are several types of misperceptions that may lead to war. One of the most common is exaggerating the hostility of the adversary, believing that the adversary is more hostile than it may actually be or that the adversary has greater military or economic capability than it actually has. This miscalculation may lead a state to respond, that is, take actions like building up its own arms which, in turn, may be viewed as hostile activities by its adversary. Misperceptions thus spiral, potentially leading to war. Events leading to World War I are often viewed as a conflict spiral, caused by misperceived intentions and actions of the principal protagonists. We can only speculate.

If not because of the leaders, perhaps characteristics of the masses lead to the outbreak of war. Some realist thinkers—St. Augustine and Reinhold Niebuhr, for example—take this position. St. Augustine wrote that every act is an act of self-preservation on the part of individuals. For Niebuhr the link goes even deeper; the origin of war resides in the depths of the human psyche.[8] This approach is compatible with that of sociobiologists who study animal behavior. Aggressive behavior is adopted by virtually all species to ensure survival; it is biologically innate. Yet this view does not explain subtle differences among species; some do engage in cooperative behavior. And human beings are seen by many as an infinitely more complex species than animal species. If true, these presumptions lead to two possible alternative assessments, one pessimistic and the other optimistic. For pessimists, if war is the product of innate human characteristics or a flawed human nature, then there is no reprieve; wars will inevitably occur all the time. For optimists, if war, or aggression, is innate, the only hope of eliminating war resides in trying to fundamentally alter human nature.

Yet war does not, in fact, happen all the time; it is the *unusual* event, not the norm. So characteristics inherent in all individuals cannot be the only cause of war. Nor can the explanation be that human nature has, indeed, been fundamentally changed, since wars *do* occur. Most experiments aimed at changing mass behavior have failed miserably, and there is no visible proof that fundamental attitudes have been altered.

Thus the individual level of analysis is unlikely to provide the only cause of war, or even the primary one. Individuals, after all, are organized into societies and states.

State and Society: Liberal and Radical Explanations

A second level of explanation suggests that war occurs because of the internal structures of states. States vary in size, geography, ethnic homogeneity, and economic and political preferences. The question, then, is how do the characteristics of different states affect the possibility of war? Which state structures are most correlated with the propensity to go to war?

State and society explanations are among the oldest. Plato, for example, posited that war is less likely where the population is cohesive and enjoys a moderate level of prosperity. Since the population would be able to thwart an attack, an enemy is apt to refrain from coercive activity. Many thinkers during the Enlightenment, including Kant, believed that war was more likely in aristocratic states.

Drawing on the Kantian position, liberals posit that republican regimes (ones with representative government and separation of powers) are least likely to wage war; that is the basic position of the theory of the democratic peace. Democracies are pacific because democratic norms and culture inhibit the leadership from taking actions leading to war. Democratic leaders hear from multiple voices that tend to restrain decisionmakers and therefore lessen the chance of war. Such states provide outlets for individuals to voice opposing viewpoints, and structural mechanisms exist for replacing war-prone or aggressive rulers. To live in such a state, individuals learn the art of compromise. In the process, extreme behavior like waging war is curbed, engaged in only periodically and then only if necessary to make a state's own democracy safe.

Other liberal tenets hold that some types of economic systems are more war prone than others. Liberal states are also more apt to be capitalist states whose members enjoy relative wealth. Such societies feel no need to divert the attention of the dissatisfied masses into an external conflict; the wealthy masses are largely satisfied with the status quo. Furthermore, war interrupts trade, blocks profits, and causes inflation. Thus, liberal capitalist states are more apt to avoid war and to promote peace.

But not every theorist sees the liberal state as benign and peace loving. Indeed, radical theorists offer the most thorough critique of liberalism and its economic counterpart, capitalism. They argue that capitalist liberal modes of production inevitably lead to conflict between the two major social classes within the state, the bourgeoisie and the proletariat, for both economic dominance and political leadership. This struggle leads to war, both internally and externally, as the state dominated by the entrenched bourgeoisie is driven to expand the engine of capitalism at the expense of the proletariat and for the economic preservation of the bourgeoisie.

In this view, conflict and war are attributed to the internal dynamics of capitalist economic systems. Capitalist systems stagnate and slowly collapse in the absence of external stimulation. Three different explanations have been offered for what happens to capitalist states and why they must turn outward. First, the English economist John Hobson (1858–1940) claimed that the internal demand for goods will slow down in capitalist countries, leading to pressures for imperialist expansion to find external markets to sustain economic growth. Second, to Lenin and others, the problem is not one of underdemand but one of declining rates of return on capital. Capitalist states expand externally to increase the rates of return on capital investment. Third, Lenin and many twentieth-century radicals pointed to the need for raw materials to sustain capitalist expansion; external suppliers are needed to obtain such resources. So according to the radical view, capitalist states inevitably expand, but radical theorists disagree among themselves on precisely why expansion occurs.

While radical explanations are viable for colonialism and imperialism, the link to war is more tenuous. One possible link is that capitalist states spend not only for consumer goods but also for the military, leading inevitably to arms races and eventually war. Another link points to leaders who, in order to avert domestic economic crises, resort to external conflict. This is called scapegoating. Such behavior is likely to provide internal cohesion at least in the short run. For example, there is considerable evidence to support the notion that the Argentinian military used the Falkland/Malvinas conflict in 1982 to rally the population around the flag and draw attention away from the country's economic contraction. Still another link suggests that the masses may push a ruling elite toward war. This view is clearly at odds with the liberal belief that the masses are basically peace loving. Adherents point to the Spanish-American war of 1898 as an example where the public might have pushed the leaders into aggressive action.

Those who argue that contests over the structure of states are a basic cause of war have identified another explanation for the outbreak of some wars. Numerous civil wars have been fought over what groups, what ideologies, and which leaders should control the government of the state. The United States's own civil war (1861–65) between the North and the South, Russia's civil war (1917–19) between liberal and socialist forces, China's civil war (1927–49) between nationalist and communist forces, and the civil wars in Vietnam, Korea, the Sudan, and Chad—each pitting North versus South—are poignant illustrations. In many of these cases, the struggle among competing economic systems and among groups vying for scarce resources within the state illustrates further the proposition that internal structures are responsible for the outbreak of war. The United States's civil war was not just over which region should control policy but over a belief by those in the South that the government inequitably and unfairly allocated economic resources. China's civil war pitted a wealthy landed elite supportive of the nationalist cause against an exploited peasantry struggling, often unsuccessfully, for survival. And the ongoing Sudanese civil war pits an economically depressed south against a northern government that poured economic resources into the region of the capital. Yet in virtually every case, neither characteristics of the state nor the state structures were solely responsible for the outbreak of war. State structure is embedded in the characteristics of the international system.

The International System: Realist and Radical Interpretations

To realists, the anarchical international system is governed only by a weak overarching rule of law, which is easily dispensed with when states determine it is in their self-interest to do so. States themselves are the authority and ultimate arbiters of disputes; herein resides sovereignty. Such an anarchic system is often compared to a state of nature after Hobbes's characterization. The international system is equivalent to a state of war, where there are no enforcement instruments to make states cooperate. Thus, it is states that, when feeling threatened, decide to go to war against other, similarly situated states. And the inexorable logic of the security dilemma makes such perceptions of insecurity all the more likely. War breaks out, then, according to realists, because of the anarchical structure of the international system. This is the logical course of action to take. After all, states must protect themselves. A state's security is ensured only by accumulating military and economic power. One state's accumulation makes the others less secure, according to the logic of the security dilemma.

In an anarchical system, there may be few rules about how to decide among contending claims. One of the major categories of contested claims is territory. For thousands of years, the Jewish and Arab dispute has rested on competing territorial claims to Palestine; in the Horn of Africa, the territorial aspirations of the Somali people are disputed; and in the Andes, Ecuador and Peru have competing territorial claims. According to the international-system-level explanation, there are no authoritative and legitimized arbiters to such disputed territorial claims.

Neither is there an effective arbiter to competing claims on national self-determination. Who decides whether the Chechen, Bosnian, or Quebecois claims for independence are legitimate? Who decides whether Kurdish claims against Turkey and Iraq are worthy of consideration? Absent an internationally legitimized arbiter, authority is relegated to the states themselves, with the most powerful ones often becoming the decisive, interested arbiters.

In actuality, there are several realist variants attributing war to the anarchic nature of the international system. One alternative explanation for war, represented in the work of Kenneth Organski, is power transition theory. To Organski and his intellectual heirs, it is not just the inequality of capabilities that leads to war. It is the changes in state capabilities that lead to war. War occurs when a dissatisfied challenger state begins to attain the capabilities of the hegemon. The challenger will launch a war to solidify its position. Power transition theorists find that war can be explained by a challenger approaching the power of the dominant hegemon, as illustrated in the Franco-Prussian War (1870–71), the Russian-Japanese War (1904–5), and the two world wars.[9]

A variant derived from the power transition theory is that war is caused by the changing distribution of power that occurs because of uneven rates of economic development. George Modelski and William Thompson find regular cycles of power transitions since 1494. There are one hundred-year cycles between hegemonic wars, wars which fundamentally alter the structure of the international system. Hegemonic wars create a new hegemonic power; its power waxes and wanes, a struggle follows, and a new hegemon assumes dominance. The cycle begins once again.[10]

To radicals, as well, the international system structure is responsible for war. Dominant capitalist states within the international system need to expand economically, leading to wars with developing regions over control of natural resources and labor markets, or with other capitalist states over control of developing regions. The dynamic of expansion inherent in the international capitalist system, then, is the major cause of wars, according to radical thinking. Both the realist and radical attention to only one level of explanation may be overly simplistic. As we will see in the next section, wars are typically caused by the confluence of a number of factors from all three levels of analysis; a list of these various causes is given in Table 7.4.

TABLE
7.4

Causes of War by Level of Analysis	
Level	**Cause**
Individual	Aggressive characteristics of leaders
	Misperceptions by leaders
	Attributes of masses (innate behavior or flawed character, aggression)
	Communications failure
State/Society	Liberal capitalist states according to radicals
	Nonliberal/nondemocratic states according to liberals
	Domestic politics, scapegoating
	Struggle between groups for economic resources
	Ethnonational challengers
International	Anarchy
	Lack of an arbiter
	Prominence of long cycles of war and peace
	Power transitions
	Aggressiveness of the international capitalist class

The Case of Yugoslavia

All the specific causes of war can be neatly placed within the framework of the three levels of analysis. But in actuality, most wars are caused by the interaction between different levels of analysis and different explanatory factors. Yugoslavia is an excellent case through which to view the interaction of the three broad explanations for war. In Yugoslavia, the Cold War competition between East and West was played out, and centuries-old fault lines of ethnic, religious, political, cultural, and historical difference were frozen for half a century. The collapse of the Yugoslav Communist party in 1990 unleashed conflicts whose ferocity shocked those who thought that Europe was immune from such horrors. The issues raised by

The Former Yugoslavia, 1995

the unraveling of Yugoslavia go to the heart of the causes of war, touching on questions of self-determination, individual and group rights, the exercise and limits of sovereignty, and the lack of an arbiter in the international system. The conflict in Yugoslavia also goes to the heart of the problems of resolving and ending wars.

The civil war in Yugoslavia was brought about in part by the actions of individuals. After the communist collapse, the Serbian leadership attempted to maintain the country's unity in the face of strong separatist movements in Slovenia, Croatia, and Bosnia-Herzegovina. In particular, the rhetoric of Slobodan Milosevic galvanized the Serb cause; he was a dynamic speaker, stoking the fires of Serb nationalism and evoking memories of past injustices at the hands of the Croats, the Turks, the Albanians, and the Germans.

Milosevic was successful in promoting the Serb position, because in the face of ethnic divisions between Serb and Croat, Serb and Slovenian, Serb and Albanian, and Bosnian Serb and Croat, the Serbs felt that their economic development had been sacrificed as a result of federal government policies during the communist era under President Tito. After the fall of the Communist party, the question immediately arose as to what group, and specifically what individual, was going to control the state. From there, people moved quickly to the issue of the rights of the various republics to seek self-determination and become independent. Eventually the arguments degenerated into wars within each new state, particularly Bosnia, over which group would control the government and how each new state would reflect the ethnic diversity of its population.

States outside of Yugoslavia fueled the fire—Germany by prematurely recognizing the new states of Croatia and Slovenia, thus legitimizing the notion of a divided Yugoslavia; Russia and France by supporting old Serb allies; and Middle Eastern states by publicly siding with the Bosnian Muslims in their struggle against Christian Croat and Serb forces.

Many would-be international arbiters have tried to help settle the situation, but none of them has been effective or has been recognized as legitimate by all the contending parties. In 1991, members of the European Union (EU) and the Conference on Security and Cooperation in Europe (CSCE) sought to negotiate cease-fires among the warring ethnic groups. Although EU mediation was successful with respect to negotiating the independence of Slovenia, the Europeans could not agree on what their role should be with respect to the rest of disputed Yugoslavia. Prominent individuals such as Cyrus Vance, the personal envoy of the U.N. secretary-general, tried to assist with negotiations, as did the later U.N.

representative Yasushi Akashi. Vance's negotiations led to the establishment in 1992 of a U.N. peacekeeping operation, the U.N. Protection Force for Yugoslavia (UNPROFOR). The UNPROFOR was initially deployed in three U.N.-protected areas in Croatia, where 14,000 U.N. military and civilian personnel were expected to consolidate the cease-fire, disband and demilitarize the armed forces and local militias, oversee local policy and ensure protection of basic human rights, and assist humanitarian agencies in returning refugees to their homes.

Meanwhile fighting broke out among Bosnian Serbs, Bosnian Muslims, and Croats in Bosnia-Herzegovina. The Bosnian Serbs were aided militarily and diplomatically by the former Yugoslavia (the territories of Serbia and Montenegro). Bosnian Serb forces shelled the city of Sarajevo, closing its airport. There were reports of massacres and of large numbers of refugees being forced from their homes. In June 1992, with public pressure building for humanitarian assistance, the U.N. Security Council authorized the sending of peacekeepers to Sarajevo to reopen the airport and to support humanitarian relief efforts. The UNPROFOR mandate, however, precluded U.N. forces from intervening to halt the mass murders, assaults, and dislocations—called ethnic cleansing—by Serbian regular and irregular forces.

With the situation in Bosnia becoming increasingly desperate, the U.N. Security Council invoked Chapter VII of the U.N. Charter to "take all necessary measures" nationally or through regional organizations to facilitate the delivery of humanitarian aid. It authorized the establishment of U.N. safe areas in six Bosnian cities. Later, Chapter VII was also invoked to authorize enforcement of a ban on military aircraft (a no-fly zone) over Bosnia, an agreement to withdraw heavy weapons, bombing of Bosnian Serb forces who were attacking the safe areas, and economic sanctions against Serbia and Montenegro. Because UNPROFOR itself was authorized to use armed force only on a limited basis, however, implementation of these measures depended on action by individual member countries, especially the United States and members of the EU, through NATO. Thus began the first experiment in cooperation between U.N. peacekeepers and a military alliance.

The forces of the United Nations were replaced in 1995 by the NATO-led Implementation Force (IFOR), which has the authority and capability to implement the enforcement measures authorized by the United Nations. The IFOR is responsible for enforcing the zones of separation, allowing free movement of citizens, expelling foreign forces, negotiating a subregional arms control agreement, and cooperating with the International

Criminal Tribunal investigating war crimes in the region. In addition, IFOR has civil tasks: organizing elections, repatriating refugees, and establishing law and order. In a sense, IFOR has become the international arbiter.

Explanations for the outbreak of war in Yugoslavia can be seen at each level of analysis. *Individual leaders,* particularly Serbian leader Slobodan Milosevic, were able to stoke in the Serb masses an ultranationalism that threatened other groups in the Yugoslav federation. The masses were ripe for such action, in part because of a history of past injustices, including atrocities committed against the Serbs by the Croatians during World War II. *State and societal organization* exacerbated the situation. The Serbs felt themselves in an inferior economic position to their Croat and Slovenian neighbors to the north. And when those two provinces proclaimed independence—recognized by several European powers—the stage was set for an international conflict. Muslims in multiethnic Bosnia also felt that they were victims of centuries of economic discrimination, and they positioned themselves as an ethnonational challenger for control of the Bosnian state when it, too, declared independence. No effective international arbiter existed in the *international system* to settle these competing claims. In the face of this anarchy, both the European organizations (the EU and the CSCE) and the United Nations, and eventually NATO, inserted their multilateral presence.

Thus, each of the three levels of analysis helps us understand why war broke out in the former Yugoslavia. Waltz was perhaps correct that the characteristics of the international system—the lack of an accepted arbiter—provided the general explanation, but to understand the particulars, we need to delve into state and society and the individual level of analysis. For peace to break out, conditions at each of the levels of analysis must also be ripe.

TYPES OF WARFARE

Once the decision has been made to go to war, to aggress against a foe or to support an ally, decisionmakers are still faced with a variety of options for how to proceed. The nineteenth-century Prussian general Carl von Clausewitz, in *On War,* describes the political nature of these decisions: "War is not merely a political act, but also a political instrument, a continuation of political relations, a carrying out of the same by other means."[11]

The most significant decisions to be made are about what kind of war will be fought, a decision often dictated by long-range goals, and about what kind of weapons will be used.

International relations scholars have developed numerous classification schemes to categorize wars. These classifications include general war, limited war, civil war, and terrorism.

General War

General war, a twentieth-century phenomenon, is war to conquer and occupy enemy territory. To accomplish these goals, decisionmakers utilize all available weapons of warfare and target both civilian and military sites. The wars of the eighteenth and nineteenth centuries were more limited with regard to the goals to be achieved, the instruments utilized, and the targets under attack. World War I and World War II were critical turning points in making general war a policy option. And it was the invention of the atomic bomb, its use against Japan to end World War II, and the subsequent development of sophisticated nuclear weapons that made general war a less attractive and less rational option. Although nuclear war may now be obsolete, other forms reminiscent of earlier eras are not.

Limited War

Wars can be classified as limited wars on the basis of the goals to be pursued, the type of weapons to be used, and the targets. The Korean War, the Vietnam War, and the Gulf War are examples of wars fought in limited ways from the perspective of the United States. The United States and its allies decided that the enemy (North Korea and China, North Vietnam and its allies, and Iraq, respectively) were to be defeated in a specified territory. The capitals of the enemy were not occupied; lines were drawn across which the victorious forces would not pass. Equally as important, all available armaments were not unleashed. Conventional weapons of warfare were used—the tank, foot soldiers, aircraft, and missiles—but despite their availability, nuclear weapons were not deployed. Yet, from the viewpoint of the opposing forces in each of these cases— North Korea, North Vietnam, and Iraq—the war was not a limited one. Each country was under attack and responded using all the force that it had available.

Civil War

Civil war is war between factions within a state over control of territory or establishment of a government. Civil wars themselves can be general, as was the U.S. Civil War or the Russian Civil War, or they can be limited, as the intermittent civil wars in numerous African countries have been. Increasingly, civil wars have had international repercussions—refugees from civil conflict flow into neighboring states, funds are transferred out of the country, and weapons from uninvolved third parties flow in and out of the country. Thus, civil wars can be both domestic and international events.

Terrorism

Since the mid-1970s, international **terrorism,** sponsored both by states and by an ever-increasing number of nonstate actors, has evolved as an insidious form of warfare, often intended to selectively hurt civilian populations. Usually used by the powerless against the powerful, terrorism operates through surprise. Violence designed to instill fear in a population, a state, and the international community is the means that terrorists use to make a political statement.

In the 1970s, terrorists began to use aircraft hijackings to project their message. For example, in December 1973, Arab terrorists killed thirty-two people in Rome's airport during an attack on a U.S. aircraft. Hostages were taken in support of the hijackers' demand for the release of imprisoned Palestinians. In 1976 a French plane with mostly Israeli passengers was hijacked by a Middle Eastern organization and flown to Uganda, where the hijackers threatened to kill the hostages unless Arab prisoners in Israel were released. In the aftermath of a number of such high-profile cases, the international community responded by signing a series of international agreements designed to tighten airport security, sanction states that accepted hijackers, and condemn state-supported terrorism. The 1979 International Convention against the Taking of Hostages is a prominent example of such an agreement.

After a lull in the 1980s, terrorist activity escalated in the 1990s, with both the perpetrators and targets becoming more diverse. Much terrorist activity has its roots in the Middle East—in the Palestinians' quest for self-determination and their own internal conflicts over strategy, in the hostility among various Islamic groups, and in the resurgence of Islamic fundamentalism. The October 1994 killing of twenty Israeli commuters by the radical Palestine group Hamas is a relevant example. But other perpetrators are increasingly involved, such as the Irish Republican Army, which bombed London's financial district in April 1993; and the Muslim groups that killed 317 people in Bombay, India, in March 1993 in the aftermath of Hindu-Muslim riots. Targets, too, have become diverse; today they include buses, large buildings (New York's World Trade Center), and tenements (in India and Germany).

Responding to terrorist activity has become increasingly difficult, because most perpetrators have networks of supporters in the resident populations. Protecting populations from random acts of violence is an almost impossible task, given the availability of guns and bombs in the international marketplace and the necessity, at least in Western democratic states, of balancing civil and human rights with antiterrorist legislation. Pressure is very strong because people worry disproportionately about terrorism, even though it kills a relatively small number of people. Despite better devices for detection, committed individuals or groups of terrorists are difficult to deter. As the well-known phrase puts it, one person's terrorist is another person's freedom fighter.

New Threats to International Security

Prior to World War II, international security was conceptualized almost exclusively in terms of questions of war, peace, and armed conflict. National security involved protecting the nation and its territory from external attack or internal subversion. That is primarily the way the term *national security* has been used in this book.

At the same time, a broader definition of security has been elucidated—one that encompasses economic and social well-being, respect for human rights, literacy, adequate health care, and protection from diseases. Over much of the postwar period, this definition has been further broadened to include the security of a safe, nontoxic environment and the security of political and civil rights, as well as of social and economic rights. Human security is of paramount concern.

With the end of the Cold War, these difficult new security issues have jumped to the top of national and international agendas. How can both developed and developing countries be persuaded to use scarce resources for economic development and for assuring quality of life for their citizens rather than for the purchase of additional military hardware? What are the security and economic implications of AIDS (Acquired Immune Deficiency Syndrome), particularly for African countries whose young, middle-class populations are being decimated? How can the international community be assured that food relief, so vital to human security, is used to feed the hungry and not as an instrument of government control? Can the destructive international drug trade be eradicated without infringing on basic human rights and the right to earn a living? Will environmental degradation, cross-border water and air pollution, and toxic chemical waste-site problems be addressed? In the absence of Cold War security concerns, will funds be available and the political will generated to address these security questions? New and old, security issues will continue to dominate the list of problem areas in international relations.

IN SUM: INTERNATIONAL SECURITY, OLD AND NEW

In this chapter, we have explored issues of national security, beginning with the five approaches to managing insecurity, based on realist and liberal perspectives. We then examined why these approaches sometimes fail, leading to the age-old question of the causes of war. We found relevant explanations at the individual, state, and international system levels of analysis, depending on one's theoretical perspective. We studied the various types of war, and we introduced the newer issues of national security beyond war and peace that are increasingly salient in the post–Cold War world.

While these security issues remain prominent on the international agenda, they are not isolated. They are intimately related to economic issues, for military capability is, in part, a function of economic prowess. The state decides how much to spend on its military, what armaments to purchase, or how little it wishes to spend (Costa Rica, for example, does not spend anything). In addition, the domestic economic system and international economic trade are fueled, in part, by the demand for military and defense-related products. This is so evident that in 1967 a fictitious book was published called *Report from Iron Mountain on the Possibility and Desirability of Peace,* which predicted the economic collapse of societies should war be eliminated.[12] It is to economic issues that we now turn.

NOTES

1. John Herz, "Idealist Internationalism and the Security Dilemma," *World Politics* 2:57 (1949–50), 157.

2. For a very complete treatment, see Inis Claude, *Power and International Relations* (New York: Random House, 1962), 94–204.

3. Hans J. Morgenthau, *Politics among Nations: The Struggle for Power and Peace,* (4th ed.; New York: Knopf, 1967), 161–215.

4. See Glenn Snyder, *Deterrence and Defense* (Princeton, N.J.: Princeton University Press, 1961); and Alexander L. George and Richard Smoke, *Deterrence in American Foreign Policy: Theory and Practice* (New York: Columbia University Press, 1974).

5. Data on war frequency and number of deaths can be found in several, sometimes divergent, sources. These include Quincy Wright, *A Study of War*, 2 vols. (Chicago: University of Chicago Press, 1942; rev. ed., 1965); J. David Singer and Melvin Small, *The Wages of War, 1816–1965: Statistical Handbook* (New York: Wiley, 1972); Jack S. Levy, *War in the Modern Great Power System, 1495–1975* (Lexington, Ky.: University Press of Kentucky, 1983); and Ruth Leger Sivard, *World Military and Social Expenditures, 1996* (Washington, D.C.: World Priorities, 1996).

6. Kenneth Waltz, *Man, the State and War* (New York: Columbia University Press, 1954).

7. For a more comprehensive approach, see Jack S. Levy, "The Causes of War: A Review of Theories and Evidence," in *Behavior Society and Nuclear War,* vol. 1, eds. Philip E. Tetlock et al. (New York: Oxford University Press, 1989), 209–333.

8. St. Augustine, "Confessions" and "City of God," in *Great Books of the Western World,* vol. 18, ed. Robert Maynard Hutchins (Chicago: Encyclopedia Britannica, 1952, 1986); and Reinhold Niebuhr, *The Children of Light and Children of Darkness* (New York: Scribner, 1945).

9. A. F. K. Organski, *World Politics* (New York: Knopf, 1958), Chap. 12; and A. F. K. Organski and Jacek Kugler, *The War Ledger* (Chicago: University of Chicago Press, 1980).

10. George Modelski and William R. Thompson, "Long Cycles and Global War" in *Handbook of War Studies*, ed. Manus I. Midlarsky (Boston: Unwin Hyman, 1989).

11. Carl von Clausewitz, *On War,* trans. O. J. Mathias Jolles (New York: Random House, 1943).

12. Anonymous, *Report from Iron Mountain on the Possibility and Desirability of Peace* (New York: Dell, 1967).

INTERNATIONAL POLITICAL ECONOMY

8

- *Why is there increased attention to the international political economy?*
- *What is economic globalization?*
- *What theoretical perspectives guide the study of the international political economy?*
- *What are the major concepts of economic liberalism?*
- *What are the controversies in the debate over the New International Economic Order?*
- *How do trading blocs like the European Union and the North American Free Trade Agreement lead to controversies between economic liberals and statists?*
- *What roles have the major international economic institutions played in the post–World War II era?*
- *What roles have multinational corporations and nongovernmental organizations played in the international political economy?*

From World War II to the early 1960s, international relations centered on issues of war and peace, where the nation-state was the primary actor in an international political system. In the 1960s and 1970s, changes took place in the international system that led to a surge of interest in a second issue, the international political economy. International political economics is the study of the interrelationship between politics and economics—specifically, the political bargaining over economic issues.

The increasing importance of the international political economy is the result of several trends. First, transactions (trade, investment, lending) among national economies have been increasing dramatically. The number of interactions between nations has grown both in absolute terms and as a share of total economic activity. Second, there has been a rapid growth in national government responsibility for economic policies. Citizens increasingly expect their governments to formulate economic and social policy objectives in addition to political objectives. Third, as these economic issues become subject to public discussion, they become more visible to individuals and groups that are potentially affected by the decisions. Because of the increased visibility of economic issues, the policy outcomes are more politicized and more controversial.

With this increasing attention to issues of political economy, actors other than the state have become significant forces: state trading organizations, nongovernmental organizations such as multinational corporations (MNCs), and international organizations such as the World Bank, the International Monetary Fund (IMF), and the Organization of Petroleum Exporting Countries (OPEC). As a result, international relations has developed a new complexity. More actors are involved in the policy process, and policy decisions affect not only the nation-state, but all actors, including the individual citizen.

Many argue economic issues do not involve just interactions among states or even states and international organizations and multinational corporations. They suggest that in the twenty-first century, economic globalization has occurred. That is a process occurring beyond the control of states and of individuals themselves. With economic globalization, the state is less able to initiate actions but rather reacts to the largely unmanageable forces of globalization. Thinking about economic globalization has spawned a plethora of popular books, among them Thomas L. Friedman's *The Lexus and the Olive Tree: Understanding Globalization*. In this era of globalization, Friedman asserts, the power of the checkbook is not wielded by states but by the Electronic Herd. The Herd plays Monopoly, not chess. All the Herd—the Intels, Ciscos, Microsofts—care about is "how your country is wired inside, what level of operating system and software it's able to run and whether your government can protect private property."[1]

In this chapter, we will first examine the contending theoretical approaches to the international political economy (statism, economic liberalism, and radicalism). How states, groups, organizations, and people see their stake in the international political economy is in large part determined by their theoretical perspective. Next, we will introduce in more detail the concepts and terms of economic liberalism, because it is this perspective and these concepts that have been most influential. Third, we will analyze two issues in political economy: one pitting the wealthy North against the poorer South (the debate over the New International Economic Order) and the other pitting the North against the North in a battle over trading blocs, with specific reference to the European Union and the North American Free Trade Agreement. We will examine key international institutions (both intergovernmental and nongovernmental) to analyze the role they have played and will continue to play in the international political economy. Finally, we will return to the discussion spawned by economic globalization, whether economic processes are beyond the control of states, international organizations, and individuals.

CONTENDING THEORETICAL APPROACHES

Views concerning the international political economy are grounded in the economic variations of the three contending schools of thought: liberalism, realism (whose economic variation is termed *statism* or *mercantilism*), and radical Marxism. Like their theoretical political counterparts, these economic views differ from one another with regard to conceptions of basic human nature; the relationship between individuals, society, the state, and markets; and the relationship between domestic and international society. These contending views shape major debates on economic distribution and redistribution in international political economy.[2]

Realism: Statism or Mercantilism

The oldest approach to the international political economy is found in mercantilism, the economic interpretation of realism. Between the fifteenth and eighteenth centuries in Europe, powerful states were created, dedicated to the pursuit of economic power and wealth. Governments organized their then-limited capabilities to increase the wealth of the country: encouraging exports over imports and industrialization over agriculture, protecting domestic production against competition from imports, and intervening in trade to promote employment.

The early proponents of mercantilism were policymakers themselves. For example, Jean-Baptiste Colbert (1619–83), an adviser to Louis XIV, argued that states needed to accumulate gold and silver to guarantee power and wealth. That meant a strong central government was needed for efficient tax collection and maximization of exports, all geared to guaranteeing military prowess. The United States's first secretary of the treasury, Alexander Hamilton (1757–1804), advocated policies to protect the growth of the state's manufacturers. In his "Report on Manufactures" to Congress in 1791, he supported protectionist policies and investment in inventions. Likewise, Germany's political economist Friedrich List (1789–1846), writing in exile in the United States, advocated strong government intervention for economic development and government aid to technology, education, and, like Hamilton, to industry. Traditional mercantilists contend that a surplus balance of payments is critical to protect the national interest.

A modern version of mercantilism emphasizes the role of the state— hence the term *statism*—and the subordination of all economic activities to the goal of state building, which includes the maintenance of the state's security and military power. With economic policy subservient to the state and its interests, politics determines economics. Thus politics and the state are used to curb man's natural aggressiveness and conflictual tendencies and to make economic policies that enhance state power. This mercantilist-like thinking dominated explanations of the economic success of Japan and the newly industrializing countries of East Asia (South Korea, Taiwan, Thailand, and Singapore). States used their power to harness industrial growth. Consistent with mercantilist logic, states single out certain industries for special tax advantages; they promote exports over imports and encourage education and technological innovations to make their respective economies more competitive internationally.

Statists see the international economic system as anarchic, and therefore as inherently conflictual, just as their realist political counterparts see the international political system. Since all states cannot pursue simultaneously statist policies—all states cannot enjoy surpluses—significant economic

Theory in Brief

THE STATIST PERSPECTIVE ON THE INTERNATIONAL POLITICAL ECONOMY

Views of human nature	Humans are aggressive; conflictual tendencies.
Relationship between individuals, society, state, market	Goal is to increase state power, achieved by regulating economic life; economics is subordinate to state interests.
Relationship between domestic and international society	International economy is conflictual; insecurity of anarchy breeds competition; state defends itself.

competition and conflicts, such as massive trading wars, are likely to occur. Each state is continually trying to improve its own economic potential, acting defensively at the expense of other states. This view is similar to that of realists who seek to increase power in response to the security dilemma.

Economic Liberalism

Economic liberals, from the eighteenth-century British economist Adam Smith to contemporary thinkers, also share a set of assumptions about human beings and economic activities. They think that human beings act in rational ways to maximize their self-interest. When individuals act rationally, markets develop to produce, distribute, and consume goods. These markets enable individuals to carry out the necessary transactions to improve their own welfare. Market competition, when there are many competing buyers and sellers, ensures that prices will be as low as possible. Low prices result in increased consumer welfare. Thus, in maximizing economic welfare and stimulating individual (and therefore collective) economic growth, markets epitomize economic efficiency.

For markets to function most efficiently, economics and politics must be separated as much as possible; that is, markets must be free. Although government should provide basic order in society, its institutions are largely developed to facilitate the free flow of trade and to maximize economic intercourse, which in the long term guarantees both optimum prices

Theory in Brief	
THE LIBERAL PERSPECTIVE ON THE INTERNATIONAL POLITICAL ECONOMY	
Views of human nature	Individuals act in rational ways to maximize their self-interest.
Relationship between individuals, society, state, market	When individuals act rationally, markets are created to produce, distribute, and consume goods; markets function best when free of government interference.
Relationship between domestic and international society	International wealth is maximized with free exchange of goods and services; on the basis of comparative advantage, international economy gains.

(equilibrium) and economic stability. Thus, in contrast to the statist view that politics determines economics, liberals see economics as determining politics, though ideally the two should be kept separated as much as possible.

At the international level, if national governments and international institutions encourage the free flow of commerce and if they do not interfere in the efficient allocation of resources provided by markets, then increasing interdependence among economies will lead to greater economic development for all states involved. Multinational corporations play a key role as engines of this growth, as discussed in more detail later in this chapter.

Some economic liberals go further than extolling the economic benefits of liberalism; they see a positive relationship between the international liberal economy and war and peace. We saw one aspect of this view in our discussion of the democratic peace in Chapter 7. Norman Angell, recipient of the Nobel peace prize in 1933, argued in favor of stimulating free trade among liberal capitalist states, in the belief that enhanced trade would be in the economic self-interest of all states. But more than that, Angell argued that national differences would vanish with the formation of an international market. Interdependence would lead to economic well-being and eventually to world peace; war would become an anachronism.[3] While not all liberals agree with this formulation, economic liberalism does suggest desirable economic policies (open markets, free trade, free flow of goods and services) and a minimal role for political institutions. Under this formulation, international competition is viewed as healthy and desirable, though it may not inevitably lead to peaceful interactions.

Radicalism: Marxist and Dependency Alternatives

Radicalism and its various permutations from socialism to communism have clearly had worldwide influence since the mid-nineteenth century. Labor movements and political party competition have been influenced by Marxist ideas. Although interpretations of radicalism vary, a number of core beliefs unite the body of Marxist and neo-Marxist writing. First, while individuals may be naturally cooperative, when in society they act in conflictual ways. Second, the conflict emerges from the competition among groups of individuals, particularly between owners of wealth and workers over the distribution of scarce resources. Third, the state acts to support the owners of the means of production, placing the state and the workers in opposition to each other. Fourth, in such situations, in capitalist systems, the owners of capital are determined to expand and accumulate resources at the expense of developing regions. Thus, the international system is basically conflictual.

But the radical view does not end there. Marxists also take a normative position that resources must be more equitably distributed both within societies and between societies in the international system. In short, radicals seek system-level change. It is for that reason that radicals are also labeled structuralists. Structure conditions outcomes—the structure is both at the international and national level.

Because the former Soviet Union both embodied and championed one model of Marxist/socialist thinking on economics, that model was the major competitor of liberal economic thought during the interwar and Cold War periods. The Soviet model emphasized internationally a conflictual system and domestically a system based on central planning and the regulation of all economic activity by the state and on the development of heavy industry at the expense of agriculture and consumer goods.

The anticapitalism and anti-imperialism of Marxism (and of Soviet policies) has had a strong appeal among developing countries, as did the Soviet model of central planning and rapid industrialization. In the late 1950s a strand of thinking emerged in the writings of Latin American economists who had been influenced by Marxism. As discussed in Chapter 3, this strand is known as dependency theory. Dependency theorists assert that developing countries are in a permanent state of economic dependency on the capitalist states. Liberal economic policies, they believe, lead to greater inequality among states. For dependency theorists, multinational corporations are

---

Theory in Brief

THE RADICAL/MARXIST PERSPECTIVE ON THE INTERNATIONAL POLITICAL ECONOMY

Views of human nature	Naturally cooperative as individuals; conflictual in groups.
Relationship between individuals, society, state, market	Competition among groups, particularly between owners of wealth and laborers; conflictual and exploitative.
Relationship between domestic and international society	Conflictual relationships because of inherent expansion of capitalism; seek radical change in international economic system.

one of the culprits, exploiting the resources of the poor in favor of the rich, thus extending and perpetuating the dependency of the poor. The distribution of international and economic power must radically change, then, if the disadvantaged position of developing countries is to be altered. These views undergirded much of the thinking and the agenda of the developing countries in the 1960s and 1970s. The New International Economic Order, discussed later in this chapter, is one manifestation of such thinking.

The three theoretical schools of thought have shaped the policies of governments around the world toward international economic relations generally and international trade and economic development specifically.

Theory in Brief

CONTENDING PERSPECTIVES ON INTERNATIONAL POLITICAL ECONOMY

	Statists	Economic Liberals	Radicals / Marxists
Views of human nature	Humans aggressive; conflictual tendencies.	Individuals act in rational ways to maximize their self-interest.	Naturally cooperative as individuals; conflictual in groups.
Relationship between individuals, society, state, market	Goal is to increase state power, achieved by regulating economic life; economics is subordinate to state interests.	When individuals act rationally, markets are created to produce, distribute, and consume goods; markets function best when free of government interference.	Competition among groups, particularly between owners of wealth and laborers; conflictual and exploitative.
Relationship between domestic and international society	International economy conflictual; insecurity of anarchy breeds competition; state defends itself.	International wealth is maximized with free exchange of goods and services; on the basis of comparative advantage, international economy gains.	Conflictual relationships because of inherent expansion of capitalism; seek radical change in international economic system.

Liberal economics dominates the discourse, however, and thus it is critical to become acquainted with its key concepts and ideas.

KEY CONCEPTS IN LIBERAL ECONOMICS

Liberal economics is based on the recognition that states differ in their resource endowments (land, labor, and capital). Under these conditions, worldwide wealth is maximized if states engage in international trade. The British economist David Ricardo (1772–1823) developed a theory that states should engage in international trade according to their **comparative advantage.** That is, states should produce and export those products which they can produce most efficiently, relative to other states. Because each state differs in its ability to produce specific products—because of differences in the natural resource base, labor force characteristics, and land values—each state should produce and export that which it can produce relatively most efficiently and import goods that other states can produce more efficiently. Thus, gains from trade are maximized for all.

Consider the production of cars and trucks in the United States and Canada. The United States can produce both cars and trucks using fewer workers than Canada, making production less expensive in the United States. Under the principle of *absolute* advantage, the United States would manufacture both cars and trucks and export both to Canada. However, under *comparative* advantage, each country should specialize; the United States should produce the car where it has a relative advantage in production, and Canada, the truck. By trading cars for trucks, each country gains by specialization. Each state minimizes its opportunity cost. Each gives up something to get something else. The United States gives up the production of trucks for more car production; Canada gives up the production of cars in favor of more truck production. Liberal economics states that under comparative advantage, production is oriented toward an international market. Efficiency in production is increased, and worldwide wealth maximized.

The liberal ideal is not fully achieved in trade. Governments following more statist policies put restrictions on free trade in order to achieve objectives other than economic efficiency. For example, they impose tariffs or quotas on imported goods to create new revenue or to protect domestic producers from international competition. They restrict exports of strategic materials for national security reasons. They protect home industries from competition to lessen the effects of economic adjustment on individuals or groups such as laborers in a certain industry or producers of a specific agricultural crop. Such protectionist actions favor domestic groups over international efficiency and may serve other objectives, as well, such as establishing a positive balance of trade (a trade surplus), a goal that is compatible with statist thinking.

In liberal economic thinking, national currencies, like goods and services, should be bought and sold in a free market system. In such a system of *floating exchange rates*, the market—individuals and governments buying and selling currencies—determines the actual value of one currency as compared with other currencies. Just as for a tangible good, there is a supply and demand for each national currency, and the prices of each currency constantly adjust according to market supply and demand. According to liberal thinking, floating exchange rates will lead to market equilibrium, in which supply equals demand.

However, currency exchange rates have not always been allowed to float and are still not permitted to float in all regions all the time. After World War II, a system of fixed exchange rates was established, whereby many currencies were supported by government commitments to keep them at specific values. In other words, currencies were pegged at a fixed exchange rate. Governments also intervene in currency markets, by changing the interest rates that they pay, in order to regulate supply and demand. Governments themselves buy and sell currency to quell the effects of speculation by private investors. Or they may even form a "basket" of currencies whose exchange rates float together, as practiced in the early years of the European Union. Currently, the EU has adopted a single currency—the euro—to be fully operational in January 2002.

States having a radical economic perspective are also likely to interfere with the workings of liberal economic markets. Like statists, radicals want to protect domestic industries by restricting imports. They seek control of the export of precious commodities in order to drive up prices, as OPEC members did with oil beginning in the 1970s. And in order to reduce the deleterious impact of currency fluctuations, states in the Third World tend to link their exchange rates with one of the stronger "international" currencies, such as the U.S. dollar, the Japanese yen, the Swiss franc, the German mark, or the French franc. While achieving one goal, currency stability, however, such states often find themselves dependent on the same international capitalist system that they so disdain—a dilemma well known to radicals.

The clash among economic ideologies has led to major controversies of power, competition, and development in the international political economy. Liberals and radicals from the North and the South have faced off since the 1970s, creating deep divisions in the international economic system. And in the 1980s and 1990s, different interpretations of economic liberalism and statism have clashed in Europe, the United States, and the newly industrializing countries (NICs).

POWER, COMPETITION, AND DEVELOPMENT IN THE INTERNATIONAL POLITICAL ECONOMY

The New International Economic Order: Liberalism versus Radicalism

The division between the developed North and the developing South is more than geographic; it is punctuated by sharp economic and political differences. The economic distinction is clear: In 1998 the states of the North had a gross domestic product (GDP) per capita of $17,000, ranging from North America's $30,000 to Russia and East Europe's $4,000. The states in the South had a GDP per capita of $3,120, ranging from the Latin American states' $6,800 to Africa's $1,400. Aggregate data mask the stark contrasts: The North basks in relative wealth, consumptive habits, high levels of education, health services, social welfare nets; the South lies mired in relative poverty, struggling to meet basic caloric needs, with poor educational and health services and no welfare nets to meet the needs of the poorest of the poor. The quality-of-life statistics in Table 8.1 tell the story.

Given these wide economic disparities, it is not surprising that the South has sought dramatic changes in the international system. During the late 1960s, the newly named **Group of 77**, a coalition of countries of the South, adopted the Charter of Algiers, which advocated global economic change. The group brought their demands to a special session of the United Nations in May 1974, signaling their call for a New International Economic Order (NIEO). These demands and the responses by the North reflect strongly the theoretical split between liberalism and radicalism.

TABLE 8.1

Quality-of-Life Indicators, 1997

	Life expectancy at birth (in years)	Adult literacy rate (%)	Educational enrollments of school-age population (%)	Real GDP per capita (PPP$)	Human development index (HDI)*
All developing countries	64.4	71.4	59	3,240	.637
Least developed countries	51.7	50.7	37	992	.432
Sub-Saharan Africa	48.9	58.5	44	534	.463
Industrial countries	77.7	98.7	92	23,741	.919
World	66.7	78.0	63	6,332	.706

SOURCE: U.N. Development Programme (UNDP) *Human Development Report, 1999* (New York: Oxford University Press, 1999), 137.
*The HDI has three components: life expectancy at birth; educational attainment, comprising adult literacy, with two-thirds weight, and a combined primary, secondary, and tertiary enrollment ratio, with one-third weight; and income. The HDI value for each country indicates how far that country has to go to attain certain defined goals: an average life span of 85 years, access to education for all, and a decent level of income. The closer a country's HDI is to 1.0, the closer it is to attaining those goals.

The South sought changes in five major areas of international economic relations, as shown in Box 8.1. These proposals are unified by the belief that fundamental change in the international political economy is necessary and that the regulation of both markets (prices, exports) and institutions (donor states, multinational corporations, the World Bank, the IMF) is imperative. These demands are consistent with the radical theoretical perspective on the international political economy.

The success of the Organization of Petroleum Exporting Countries (OPEC) provided a model, in part, for the demands of the South. Recalling the success of Muammar Qaddafi's nationalization of the Libyan oil industry in 1973 and the dramatic increases of petroleum prices that followed, the oil exporters formed and strengthened the OPEC cartel. In 1974, the Arab members of OPEC used an embargo to withhold oil from states supporting Israel, causing a significant increase in oil prices (and hence revenues) and a substantial economic disruption in the United States and the Netherlands, both of which were embargoed. The exporters

BOX
8.1

DEMANDS OF THE SOUTH IN THE
NEW INTERNATIONAL ECONOMIC ORDER

1. *Change the terms of international trade.* Stabilize, then raise the price of exports from the South for primary commodities (coffee, cocoa, bauxite, tin, and sugar) to keep up with the price of capital goods and finished products (computers, automobiles, machinery) imported from the developed North. Index prices, establish price regulation, and establish commodity cartels and multilateral commodities agreements.

2. *Establish a Common Fund.* Link prices of commodities together in order to establish a joint fund to help countries whose economies have been adversely affected by price declines.

3. *Regulate multinational corporations.* Require technology transfer from the MNCs to the South.

4. *Relieve the debt burden of the South.* Restructure debt burdens, reduce interest rates, and/or cancel debt.

5. *Increase foreign aid to the South.* Improve the terms and conditions of aid; grants and untied aid are preferred.

6. *Change the structure of the World Bank and International Monetary Fund.* Modify the weighted voting system, so that the South can use these organizations more effectively.

of OPEC had been able to change the terms of trade by cooperating to substantially increase the price they received for commodity exports. Buoyed by OPEC's success, southern producers of other primary commodities joined the bandwagon, forming cartels in copper, tin, cocoa, coffee, and bananas. These cartels, however, met with little success. The South thus turned its attention to lobbying forcefully for the Common Fund of the NIEO, which was designed to link various commodity producers together through a multilateral fund that would help countries that were having major economic problems because of changing commodity prices.

The NIEO record is one of differential outcomes. The South won some concessions through the 1975 Lomé Convention, which gave countries of the South preferential access to European markets and more favorable terms for commodity price-stabilization plans. Some states of the South were able to reschedule their debts, in part through innovative refinancing plans. However, on most critical issues, the North refused to negotiate concessions. No Common Fund was established. No mandatory code to regulate multinational corporations was negotiated. No widespread debt cancellation was immediately undertaken. No major changes were made in the World Bank or IMF institutional structures. Of these issues only debt renegotiation and cancellation has remained on the international agenda in 2000. The European states and the United States agreed in 1999 to debt cancellation of almost $100 billion for a group of thirty three most-affected countries.

The NIEO set the economic agenda for almost two decades in various international forums. But the failure of the South to achieve the NIEO agenda led some countries to moderate their tone and approach; they concluded that a more restrained approach might achieve more favorable outcomes. Many countries have turned to other international organizations, including the Association of Southeast Asian Nations (ASEAN), the Organization of African States, the Arab League, and the U.N. Conference on Trade and Development (UNCTAD), to seek economic improvements. By the 1990s, most developing states had embraced economic liberalism, dropped their demands for the NIEO, and tempered their radical perspectives. In fact, at the eighth UNCTAD meeting, held at Cartagena, Colombia, in 1992, a broad consensus emerged on the viability of market-oriented economic policies and political pluralism as the foundation for economic development. In view of this ideological and policy change, the confrontational tactics of the past have been replaced by an emphasis on consensus building and developing appropriate domestic policies, rather than on imposing international regulations, which had been the cornerstone of the original NIEO proposals.

Competitive Trading Blocs: Liberalism versus Statism

Not all conflicts in the international political economy are between the North and South. Significant differences have arisen among the developed states over liberal principles and policies. This conflict is not surprising, given that many of the developed countries produce the same products: automobiles in the United States, Japan, France, and Germany; computers in the United States, Great Britain, Japan, Taiwan, and Germany; jet aircraft in the United States and Europe. In addition, each state has a different approach to achieving economic prosperity, as well as different ideas about the role that states and larger economic entities might play in the process.

Although virtually all developed states espouse the principles of economic liberalism, states have different conceptions of the role and responsibilities of government in ensuring liberalism. Should government be the umpire of the economic game, making sure that the game is played fairly? Or should government be an administrator, taking on a specific economic task and following a set of procedures? Or should government be an active player, using incentives or coercion in order to achieve its objectives? Differences in how liberalism is interpreted and administrated can be seen by comparing two important economic coalitions.

The European Union   The idea of a united Europe goes back centuries. Plans presented by Immanuel Kant and Jean-Jacques Rousseau were filled with ideas of how to unite Europe.[4] After World War I, theorists grew enamored of the idea that a united Europe could have forestalled the conflagration. World War II only intensified these sentiments. Hence, after that war, some theorists and political leaders began reviving discussion about a united Europe, initially in economic terms.

The Treaty of Rome, signed in 1957, established the framework for the European Economic Community (EEC), a common market among the six founding nations—Belgium, France, Italy, Luxembourg, the Netherlands, and West Germany. A common economic market is achieved when goods flow freely between member states without being taxed, while imposing uniform tariffs on goods from outside. Under the Rome Treaty, internal tariff barriers among the six members were gradually eliminated over a twelve- to fifteen-year transitional period. But the treaty also provided for free movement of workers, enterprises, capital, agriculture, and transportation.

According to liberal economic theory, the economic welfare of the member states would be enhanced with the establishment of the EEC. The larger economic market would permit economies of scale and benefits of specialization; opportunities for investment would be enhanced, and competition and innovation stimulated. Until the mid-1960s the internal program was achieved more quickly than anticipated.

Yet the establishment of a common external barrier is incompatible with economic liberalism, as is the practice of state subsidies to assure that certain products continue to be produced regardless of their economic viability. Products from outside parties are discriminated against, while products from within the union are given privileged, unfettered access, sometimes with state assistance in critical sectors. These aspects of the economic union are consistent with statist economic thinking—protection of the state against intrusion and use of state mechanisms to assure a privileged position. Only in the case of the EEC, the state was not one but a group of states.

Ironically, in the 1950s and early 1960s, much of the impetus for a united Europe came from the United States. The United States believed that Europe would become stronger both economically and politically if the barriers between countries were gradually reduced. But U.S.-based multinational corporations quickly realized that their products would be discriminated against unless they established facilities in Europe to avoid the external tariff barrier. Only later did U.S. agricultural interests, among others, realize that their products, too, would be discriminated against under one aspect of the EEC, the Common Agriculture Policy (CAP), which guaranteed high prices to ensure the viability of the community's agricultural sector. This policy has been one of the most virulent controversies between the liberal states of the EEC and the United States.

Between the mid-1960s and the mid-1980s, stagnation set in. Specific political actions were required to push integration and break the deadlock. (Table 8.2 lists the most significant of these events and actions.) One group of actions expanded the size of the community. The original six members were joined by Denmark, Great Britain, and the Republic of Ireland in 1973; by Greece in 1981; by Portugal and Spain in 1986; and by Austria, Finland, and Sweden in 1995. In 1979 the European Monetary System (EMS) was established and the European Parliament became directly elected; it was expected that elections of representatives would affix the loyalties of people behind the new Europe.

In 1986, a critical step was taken in the integration process. The passage of the Single European Act made some institutional changes to ensure more speedy decisions. New environmental and technological issues were addressed and the objective of a monetary union was outlined; three thousand specific measures needed to be taken in order to complete the single market.

In February 1992, leaders of the member states concluded the Maastricht Treaty, committing members to a closer political and economic unit by the year 2000. The treaty made it clear that political union was desired, including the establishment of common foreign and defense policies, a single currency, and a regional central bank. With this treaty, the EEC became known as the European Union (EU).

The Maastricht Treaty, however, met with stiff opposition during and after the negotiations. The United Kingdom was allowed to opt out of the monetary union and some social commitments. In a June 1992 referendum, the Danish public rejected the treaty; the French electorate approved it by only a slim margin later in the same year. (Danish citizens approved the treaty in a second referendum in 1993.) These referenda

TABLE 8.2

Significant Events in the European Union

Year	Event
1952	European Coal and Steel Community created by Belgium, France, Italy, Luxembourg, Netherlands, and West Germany.
1954	French National Assembly rejects proposal to form a European Defence Community.
1958	Treaties of Rome establish the European Economic Community (EEC) and the European Atomic Energy Community, comprising same six members.
1968	Customs union is completed; all internal customs, duties, and quotas are removed and common external tariff is established.
1973	EEC is joined by Denmark, Ireland, and the United Kingdom.
1975	Lomé Convention between the EEC and 46 developing countries in Africa, the Caribbean, and the Pacific signed.
1979	High-level negotiations on European Monetary System are completed; first direct elections to the European Parliament.
1981	Greece joins the EEC; European political cooperation is extended.
1986	Passage of the Single European Act designed to ensure faster decisions; more attention to environmental and technological issues; list of measures compiled that need to be taken before achieving single market in 1992; Spain and Portugal join the EEC.
1990	West and East Germany reunited after fall of Berlin Wall; larger Germany maintains EEC membership.
1992	Maastricht Treaty completed, committing members to political union, including the establishment of a common foreign and defense policy, a single currency, and a regional central bank; name changed to European Union (EU); controversial referendums held in several countries.
1995	Austria, Finland, and Sweden join EU.
1997	Treaty of Amsterdam extends competence on Justice and Home Affairs, defines European citizenship.
1999	Common monetary policy and single currency (the euro) launched.

signaled to the European leaders, who negotiated Maastricht with little public consultation, that while members of the European public support the idea of economic and political cooperation, they fear a diminution of national sovereignty—particularly losing their national currencies—and are reluctant to surrender their democratic rights by placing more power in the hands of bureaucrats and other nonelected elites.

The European Union is much more than a trading bloc as the Maastricht Treaty and Amsterdam Treaty have made abundantly clear. There are three pillars of the EU. The first is the economic union; although the

Expansion of the European Union, 1952–2000

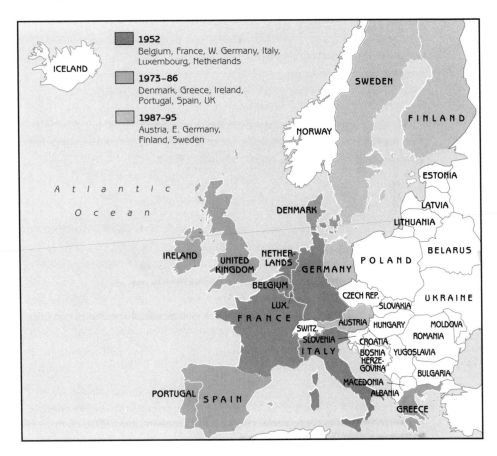

economic phase is still unfinished, Europe is even now more economically integrated than most had thought possible. The other two pillars are the Common Foreign and Security Policy and the Justice and Home Affairs Cooperation. Recent events in the EU have emphasized these two areas.

Some problems are far from being resolved. Should the European Union expand its membership to include others who want to join—Hungary, the Czech Republic, Turkey, Cyprus, Malta, Poland—and those who might—the Ukraine, the Baltic republics? Any such broadening would have far-reaching implications, as all applicants are not at the same level of economic and social development. Or should the European Union concentrate on deepening—integrating key policies to achieve better economic redistribution? Can the European Union continue on its path without causing trade wars with Japan, South Korea, and the United States, whose products are discriminated against in EU markets? In 2000, the European members have moved to revamp the EU's institutions as it brings in up to twelve new members during the next years. What should be the role of national governments and of the EU governing institutions? Currently, the EU institutions (see Figure 8.1) are not just umpires; they are administrators and players. Enhanced majority voting, reallocating votes among the members, and trimming the size of the commission are all on tap for the upcoming years.[5]

One response by other states to the economic power of the European Union has been to establish other trading blocs that give their members more favorable access than those from outside. The North American Free Trade Agreement (NAFTA) is but one example of such a free trade area that does not have political integration as its final goal.

The North American Free Trade Agreement   The free trade area negotiated by the United States, Canada, and Mexico in 1994 differs substantially from the European Union and other regional schemes. It comprises one dominant economy and two dependent ones: Mexico's and Canada's combined economic strength is one-tenth that of the United States. The driving force in NAFTA is not political elites but multinational corporations (MNCs) that seek larger market shares than their Japanese and European competition. The agreement phases out many restrictions on foreign investment and most tariff and nontariff barriers. This has allowed MNCs to shift production to low-wage labor centers in Mexico and to gain economically by creating bigger companies through mergers and acquisitions.

The social, political, and security dimensions we saw in the European Union are absent from NAFTA. Cooperation in trade and investment is not intended to lead to free movement of labor, as championed by the European Union. Quite the opposite: the United States expects that Mexican labor will *not* seek employment in the United States since economic development in Mexico will provide ample employment opportunities. And economic cooperation does not mean political integration in NAFTA. As public questioning of the Maastricht Treaty suggests, even Europe may not be ready for this final step in regional integration. With NAFTA, economic integration is to remain just that—confined to specific economic sectors.

The North American Free Trade Agreement supports the phased elimination over ten years of tariff and nontariff barriers. Specifically, tariffs on over nine thousand categories of goods produced in North America are to be eliminated by 2008. At the same time, NAFTA protects the property rights of those companies making investments in the three countries.

FIGURE 8.1

STRUCTURE OF THE EUROPEAN UNION

Members

Austria	Germany	Netherlands
Belgium	Greece	Portugal
Denmark	Ireland	Spain
Finland	Italy	Sweden
France	Luxembourg	United Kingdom

12 more in future

European Parliament

Function: Legislates, approves budget, supervises executive.

Members: 626, divided among member states; elected every 5 years by citizens of member states; projected to increase to 738 members.

Council of the European Union (or Council of Ministers)

Function: Legislates, sets political objectives, coordinates national policy, resolves differences. Decisions taken either by qualified majority or by unanimity.

Members: 15 ministers of the member states; will increase in size.

European Commission

Function: Initiates proposals for legislation; acts as "guardian" of the treaties; manages and executes EU policies and international trade relationships.

Members: 20, plus 15,000 support staff; will expand to 27 members.

Court of Justice

Function: Adjudicates disputes on matters covered by EU treaties, ensures uniform interpretation of EU laws.

Members: 15 judges and 9 advocates-general, appointed by member states for 6-year renewable terms.

Court of First Instance

Function: Established in 1989 to improve judicial protection of individual interests and enable Court of Justice to concentrate on fundamental task of ensuring uniform interpretation.

Members: 15 judges, appointed by member states for 6-year renewable terms.

SOURCE: http://europa.eu.int/en/comm/opoce/brocint/gb/.

Some domestic producers are given special protection, notably the Mexican oil and gas industry and the U.S. shipping industry. The agreement, a five-volume, 15-pound document, is clearly detailed and complex. By the year 2000, trade among the three countries doubled from 1990 levels.

Yet the economic controversies generated by NAFTA are profound, illustrating that the state is not a unitary actor. Labor unions in the United States estimate that between 150,000 to 500,000 workers lost their jobs to Mexico and that over one-third of those individuals will never receive comparable wages again. Environmental groups in the United States fear free trade with Mexico comes at the expense of the environment, as firms in the United States relocate to Mexico to skirt domestic environmental regulations. They point to the degraded environment of the border regions between the two countries. Radical Mexican economists argue that NAFTA is yet another example of U.S. expansionism and exploitation of the Mexican workforce. Canadian labor contends that manufacturing in that country is fast becoming a lost art and that the country is becoming too dependent on exports of natural resources. Others fear that Canadian sovereignty is threatened as economic decisions are taken out of the country, that its national identity is in jeopardy.

In 1994 an army of peasant guerrillas seized towns in the southern Mexican state of Chiapas to protest against an economic and political system that was viewed as biased against them. The date of the protest coincided with the beginning of NAFTA. Individuals, feeling that economic decisions were beyond their control, protested against the structures of the international market, the state, and globalization.

These two cases—the European Union and NAFTA—provide clear evidence that economic controversies are not confined to the North and South, where the economic gaps are so great and where differences in economic theory are so clear. Controversies are also found among liberal economies. Both governmental and nongovernmental institutions play key roles in the various policy debates in international political economy; often the institutions themselves are the subject of controversy.

THE ROLE OF INSTITUTIONS IN MANAGING POWER, COMPETITION, AND DEVELOPMENT

To liberals, institutions play a key role in developing and shaping policy debates, making commitments credible, reducing transaction costs, and ensuring reciprocity among participants. Radicals, on the other hand, generally see these same institutions as exploitative actors in the stratified international economy. As you might expect, then, adherents of these two theoretical perspectives disagree about the roles and usefulness of the three very different kinds of institutions involved in the policy debates over international economic issues: the intergovernmental organizations set up at the end of World War II, multinational corporations, and nongovernmental organizations.

The Bretton Woods Institutions

The World Bank, the International Monetary Fund (IMF), and to a lesser extent the General Agreement on Tariffs and Trade (GATT)—now the World Trade Organization (WTO)—have played and continue to play important roles in addressing international economic problems. All three were established as the embodiment of economic liberalism, based on the notion that economic stability and development are best achieved when trade and financial markets flow with as few restrictions as possible (see Figure 8.2). From their inception in Bretton Woods, New Hampshire, in 1944, the policies of these institutions have reflected this philosophy.

The World Bank—Stimulating Economies The **World Bank** was designed initially to facilitate reconstruction in post–World War II Europe, hence its formal name: the International Bank for Reconstruction and Development. During the 1950s, the World Bank shifted its primary emphasis from reconstruction to development. It generates capital funds from member-state contributions and from borrowing in international financial markets. Like all banks, its purpose is to loan these funds, with interest, to states for their economic development projects. Its lending is designed not to replace private capital but to facilitate the use of private capital. Over the years, a high proportion of the World Bank's funding has been used for infrastructure projects, including hydroelectric dams, basic transportation needs such as bridges and highways, and agribusiness ventures.

To aid in meeting the needs of developing countries, the International Finance Corporation (IFC) and the International Development Association (IDA) were created in 1956 and 1960, respectively. The IDA provides capital to the poorest countries, usually in the form of interest-free loans. Repayment schedules of fifty years theoretically allow the developing countries time to reach economic takeoff and sustain growth. Funds for the IDA need to be continually replenished by major donor countries. The IFC provides loans to promote the growth of private enterprises in

FIGURE 8.2

THE BRETTON WOODS INSTITUTIONS (REVISED)

World Bank
Loans funds to states proposing economic development projects

International Finance Corporation (IFC)
Provides loans to promote growth of private enterprises in developing countries

International Development Association (IDA)
Provides interest-free loans to the poorest countries

Multilateral Investment Guarantee Agency (MIGA)
Encourages the flow of private equity capital to less-developed countries

International Monetary Fund (IMF)
Original purpose was to guarantee exchange-rate stability. Purpose is as lender of last resort to keep debtor countries from collapsing

International Trade Organization
(was not formed)

At the Brenton Woods Conference in July 1944, world leaders agreed to create three institutions to facilitate worldwide economic coordination and development. Two of these institutions—the World Bank and the International Monetary Fund—were created shortly after the conference. Although the third institution proposed at Bretton Woods—the International Trade Organization—was never created, the principles behind it were later incorporated in the General Agreement on Tariffs and Trade, which recently evolved into the World Trade Organization.

General Agreement on Tariffs and Trade (GATT)
Series of multilateral trade negotiations designed to stimulate trade by lowering trade barriers

World Trade Organization (WTO)
Replaced GATT as forum for negotiating new trade agreements. Includes stronger dispute-settlement procedures

developing countries. In 1988 the Multilateral Investment Guarantee Agency (MIGA) was added to the World Bank group. This agency's goal— to augment the flow of private equity capital to developing countries—is met by insuring investments against losses. Such losses may result from expropriation, government currency restrictions, and civil war or ethnic conflict.

The World Bank has changed its orientation over time, moving from an emphasis on major infrastructure projects in the 1950s and 1960s to basic human needs and poverty reduction in the 1970s, to private- sector participation in the 1980s, to sustainable development in the 1990s, as pushed by the U.N. Conference on Environment and Development in Rio de Janeiro, Brazil. In **sustainable development,** economic development is to be coupled with a concern for renewable resources and the environment. Furthermore, World Bank–funded projects are carried out more frequently today by nongovernmental groups than in previous decades; involvement of such groups encourages popular local participation. These changes in the bank's orientation, however, are not always accepted or appreciated by the developing countries.

The IMF—Stabilizing Economies   From its establishment, the task of the **International Monetary Fund (IMF)** was different: to stabilize exchange rates by providing short-term loans for member states confronted by temporary balance-of-payments difficulties. Originally, the fund established a system of fixed exchange rates and, with the United States, guaranteed currency convertibility. From the 1940s to the 1970s, the United States guaranteed the stability of this system by fixing the value of the dollar against gold, at $35 an ounce. In 1971, however, this system collapsed, when the United States announced that it would no longer guarantee a system of fixed exchange rates; today the exchange rates float.

Since the early 1980s, the IMF has played an increasing role in developing countries plagued by persistent, high debts. Expanding its short-term loan function, the IMF provides longer-term loans and the "international stamp of approval" for other multilateral and bilateral lenders as well as private banks. In return for assistance, the IMF encourages **structural adjustment programs,** requiring countries to institute certain policies or to achieve certain conditions in order to receive IMF assistance (see Figure 8.3). These policies are consistent with economic liberalism.

With such programs initiated by the IMF, the distinction between the IMF and the World Bank has been blurred. Both play key roles in structural-adjustment lending, mutually reinforcing each other, bilateral

IMF STRUCTURAL ADJUSTMENT PROGRAMS

PROFILE

Profile of a Country in Need of Structural Adjustment
- Large balance-of-payments deficit
- Large external debt
- Overvalued currency
- Large public spending and fiscal deficit

GOALS

Typical Goals of Structural Adjustment Programs
- Restructure and diversify productive base of economy
- Achieve balance-of-payments and fiscal equilibrium
- Create a basis for noninflationary growth
- Improve public sector efficiency
- Stimulate growth potential of the private sector

TYPICAL STRUCTURAL ADJUSTMENT POLICIES

Economic Reforms
- Limit money and credit growth
- Devaluation of the currency
- Reform the financial sector
- Introduce revenue-generating measures
- Introduce user fees
- Introduce tax code reforms
- Eliminate subsidies, especially for food
- Introduce compensatory employment programs
- Create affordable services for the poor

Trade Liberalization Reforms
- Remove high tariffs and import quotas
- Rehabilitate export infrastructure
- Increase producers' prices

Government Reforms
- Cut bloated government payroll
- Eliminate redundant and inefficient agencies
- Privatize public enterprises
- Reform public administration and institutions

Private-Sector Policies
- Liberalize price controls
- End government monopolies

donors, and international banks. All have been the subject of intense criticism.

Radical economists and policymakers from the South see these institutions as following the ethically wrong and substantively incorrect economic philosophy of liberalism. For radicals like Cheryl Payer, the World Bank

> has deliberately and consciously used its financial power to promote the interests of private, international capital in its expansion to every corner of the "underdeveloped" world.

. . . The Bank is perhaps the most important instrument of the developed capitalist countries for prying state control of its Third World member countries out of the hands of nationalists and socialists who would regulate international capital's inroads.[6]

This occurs because under the weighted voting system used by the IMF (and the World Bank), donors (i.e., the North) are guaranteed voting power commensurate with their contributions. In addition, the World Bank and IMF bureaucracies are made up predominantly of economists trained in Western countries in the same liberal economic tradition in which the decisionmakers from the major donors have been trained.

Furthermore, critics argue, the IMF conditions or policies such as those listed in Figure 8.3 are too rigid. Critics claim that these policies are instituted without regard for the local situation. Such policies often disproportionately affect the disadvantaged sectors of the population: the unskilled, women, and the weak. Some structural adjustment policies have led to urban riots (Nepal in 1992, the Ivory Coast in 1990, Nigeria in 1988, Zambia in 1986) and are purportedly responsible for the fall of several governments.[7]

In the 1990s, just when some moderation began to appear in the views of many in the Third World regarding the NIEO, the World Bank and the IMF came under renewed attack. In 1994, fifty years after the Bretton Woods meetings that established the two institutions, the "Fifty years is enough" campaign was launched. This campaign united the critics who claimed that the World Bank's commitment to growth had to be replaced by an emphasis on poverty reduction and that its record of support for authoritarian regimes had to be replaced by a commitment to democracy. In the words of one critic, "The World Bank is an old temple of cold warriors; a highly centralized, secretive, undemocratic vestige of another time. Fifty years is enough."[8]

GATT and the WTO—Managing Trade   The third part of the liberal economic order is the **General Agreement on Tariffs and Trade (GATT)**. This treaty enshrined important liberal principles:

- Support of trade liberalization, since trade is the engine for growth and economic development
- Nondiscrimination in trade (i.e., most-favored-nation treatment), by which states agree to give the same treatment to all other GATT members as they give to their best (most-favored) trading partner
- Exclusive use of tariffs as devices for protecting home markets
- Preferential access in developed markets to products from the South in order to stimulate economic development in the South

Procedures have put these principles into practice. The GATT established a continual process of multilateral negotiations among those countries sharing major interests in the issue at hand (major producers and consumers of a product, for example); the agreements reached in these negotiations are then expanded to all GATT participants. Individual states can claim exemptions (called safeguards) to accommodate any domestic and balance-of-payments difficulties that may occur because of the resulting trade agreements.

Most of the work of GATT was carried out over the course of eight negotiating rounds—each round progressively cutting tariffs, giving better treatment to the developing countries, and addressing new problems (subsidies and countervailing duties). The final round, called the Uruguay Round, began in 1986. The Uruguay Round covered new items such as services (insurance), intellectual property rights (copyrights, patents, trademarks), and for the first time agriculture. Previously, agriculture was seen as too contentious an issue, complicated by both U.S. agricultural subsidies and the European Union's protectionist Common Agriculture Policy. Agreement was reached to begin to phase out agricultural subsidies. In late 1994, a four hundred–page agreement was finally reached, the most comprehensive trade agreement in history, covering paper clips to computer chips. Tariffs on manufactured goods were cut by an average of 37 percent among members. Analysts predicted that global wealth would increase by more than $200 billion per year by 2005 because of the Uruguay Round negotiations.

In 1995, GATT became a formal institution, renaming itself the **World Trade Organization (WTO).** The WTO incorporated the general areas of GATT's jurisdiction, as well as expanded jurisdiction in services and intellectual property. Regular ministerial meetings give WTO a political prominence that GATT lacked. Representing states that conduct over 90 percent of the world's trade, WTO's task is to implement the Uruguay Round, serve as a forum for trade negotiations, and provide a venue for trade review, dispute settlement, and enforcement.

Two important procedures were initiated in WTO. First is the Trade Policy Review Mechanism (TPRM), which conducts periodic surveillance of trade practices of member states. Under this procedure there is a forum where states can question each other about trade practices. Second is the Dispute Settlement Body, designed as an authoritative panel to hear and settle trade disputes. With the authority to impose sanctions against violators, the body is more powerful than other economic dispute resolution arrangements.

The WTO is serving as a lightning rod for domestic groups from many countries who feel that the organization, a symbol of economic globalization, is usurping the decisions of states, exploiting developing states, and degrading the welfare of individuals. Thus, in December 1999, at the WTO meeting in Seattle, Washington, the United States, there were massive citizen protests from individuals from around the world. This "battle of Seattle" became another focal point for antiglobalization forces, which oppose the intrusion of international rules in their daily lives.

The World Bank, the IMF, and the WTO are international intergovernmental institutions whose members are states. Another type of institution has played an important role in economic issues for a long time, and, for better or worse, its power is increasing: the multinational corporation.

Multinational Corporations: Stimulating Development or Instruments of Exploitation?

One of the most significant developments in the post–World War II era has been the growth of multinational corporations (MNCs). The institution itself is not new—the Greek, Phoenician, and Mesopotamian traders were its ancient forerunners, as were the British East India Company, the Hudson Bay Company, Levant Company, and the Dutch East India Company in the seventeenth and eighteenth centuries. But following World War II, the trend toward larger companies conducting business in different states accelerated. This trend was led by U.S.-based MNCs.

The MNCs take many different forms, ranging from companies that participate only in direct importing and exporting, to those making significant investments in a foreign country, to those buying and selling licenses in foreign markets, to others engaging in contract manufacturing (permitting a local manufacturer in a foreign country to produce their products) and to still others opening manufacturing facilities or assembly operations in foreign countries.

Whatever the specific form that their business takes, all MNCs choose to participate in international markets for a variety of reasons. They seek to avoid tariff and import barriers, as many U.S. firms did in the 1960s when they established manufacturing facilities in Europe to circumvent the external barriers of the newly established EEC. They may seek to reduce transportation costs by moving facilities closer to consumer markets. Some MNCs are able to obtain incentives like tax advantages or labor concessions from host governments; these incentives can cut production costs and increase profitability. Others go abroad in order to meet the competition and the customers, capitalizing on cheaper labor markets (e.g., U.S. firms operating in Mexico or Romania) or to obtain the services of foreign technical personnel (e.g., computer firms in India). Note that these reasons are based in economics. Political rationales may also play a role. The MNCs may move abroad to circumvent tough governmental regulations at home, be they banking rules, currency restrictions, or environmental regulations. In the process, MNCs become not only economic organizations but political ones, potentially influencing the policies of both home and host governments.

While there are over 45,000 MNCs, with over 280,000 foreign affiliates, MNCs are, in fact, concentrated. Just 1 percent of the MNCs own half the total of all existing foreign assets. Before World War II, most MNCs were in the minerals and extractive resource business (Exxon, Shell, British Petroleum). After World War II, MNCs were prominent in manufacturing (General Motors, Ford, Toyota, Sony, Siemens, Nestle, Bayer), and currently, they are in services (Citigroup, ICI, Bank of America, Deutsche Bank, Fuji Bank). Very little economic activity originates in the developing countries; most comes from the Western industrized countries and a handful of Asian and Latin American states, including China, Malaysia, Hong Kong, Korea, Singapore, Brazil, and Mexico. States through taxation, regulation, even nationalization, attempt to control MNCs. States and MNCs are involved in a complex bargaining relationship.

Three Perspectives on MNCs   To economic liberals, MNCs are the vanguard of the liberal order. They are "the embodiment par excellence of the liberal ideal of an interdependent world economy. [They have] taken the integration of national economies beyond trade and money to the internationalization of production. For the first time in history, production, marketing, and investment are being organized on a global scale rather than in terms of isolated national economies."[9] For liberals, MNCs represent a positive development: economic improvement is made through the most efficient mechanism. The MNCs invest in capital stock worldwide, they move money to the most efficient markets, and they finance projects that industrialize and improve agricultural output. The MNCs are the transmission belt for capital, ideas, and economic growth. In the liberal ideal, the MNCs should act independently of the states, perhaps replacing the states in the long term.

Statists see MNCs quite differently. Because of the importance they attach to pursuing the interests of nation-states, statists prioritize national economic and political objectives at the expense of the international economic efficiency so valued by the liberals and their instrument, the MNCs. The MNCs at the service of the state can be powerful allies, but when the MNCs act contrary to state political interests, they become dangerous agents to be controlled by both home and host states. The MNCs are, according to statists, an economic actor to be controlled.

The radical perspective offers a powerful critique of MNCs. Abhorring the notion that MNCs are positive instruments of economic development, radicals see them as an instrument of exploitation. The MNCs, particularly those from the developed world, perpetuate the dominance of the North and explain, in large part, the dependency of the South. So the interdependence that MNCs represent to liberals is interpreted by radicals as imperialism and exploitation. In that system, decisions are taken in the economic and financial centers of the world—Tokyo, Berlin, New York, Seoul—while the work of carrying out those decisions occurs in factories of the developing countries. According to radical theorists, MNCs embody the inherent inequality and unfairness of the international economic system.

Not surprisingly, each perspective has a position on what should be done about MNCs. To liberals, nothing should be done; MNCs police each other, and any unfair practices such as monopoly pricing will be eliminated through the competitive market. Statists clearly suggest imposing national controls on MNCs, including denying market entry, taxing, limiting repatriation of profits, imposing currency controls, even nationalizing industries. Such policies are not inevitable; the key goal for the statist is to ensure that MNCs make economic decisions that are in the home state's national interest. For radicals, MNCs are neither positive nor benign, so both state and international regulation is necessary. State regulation is problematic, however, because many host states in the Third World are highly economically dependent on the MNCs and their leaders. Leaders who have the authority to pass appropriate control measures are often co-opted by the very same MNCs to be regulated. Thus, radicals have fought for international regulations in many forums, including under the NIEO. Since these attempts at international regulation have been uniformly unsuccessful, MNCs remain for radicals the major inhibitors of economic development.

The MNCs remain dominant actors in the international political economy, especially in the economy dominated by liberal economic theory and practices. Yet new groups are becoming increasingly important actors in dealing with economic issues, especially nongovernmental not-for-profit organizations. They are consistent with liberal economic thinking—that private-sector involvement is critical—but many seek to try to mitigate some of the harsher effects of economic liberalism on individuals and marginalized groups.

Nongovernmental Organizations: New Actors in the International Political Economy

Nongovernmental organizations (NGOs) reflect the growth in popular social movements; they offer new channels of participation for states whose importance on economic issues has diminished. Thus, NGOs have become important actors in the international political economy. With respect to economic development, NGOs serve in a number of important capacities. Disillusioned with past trends in approaches to economic development, NGOs, working with the World Commission on Environment and Development headed by former Norwegian prime minister Gro Harlem Brundtland, helped to formulate the whole notion of sustainable development, which we discussed briefly in the preceding section.

Sustainable development is a concept that recognizes that the South cannot develop in the same way that Great Britain, the United States, Germany, and other industrialized nations did because humanity cannot survive another diminution of scarce global resources. Both pragmatic self-interest and moral arguments (as elucidated by southern proponents of the NIEO) dictate that the North should aid the Third World in finding new, more environmentally safe ways to foster development. The NGOs can provide the impetus for such joint efforts.

When a state is either weak or unwilling to aid in an economic development effort or when international assistance is absent, NGOs can be al-

IN FOCUS

OBJECTIVES OF SUSTAINABLE DEVELOPMENT

► Reorient the Bretton Woods system to focus on sustainable development.
► Reschedule debts in less-developed countries when they lead to overexploitation of natural resources.
► Create new sources of financing for the global commons, such as ocean fishing, Antarctica.
► Include environmental conditions in international commodity agreements and structural adjustment programs.
► Strengthen the U.N. Environmental Program and regional environmental institutions.

ternative channels for assistance. One particularly effective effort has been the Grameen Bank in Bangladesh. Created in 1983 by an academic turned banker, Muhammad Yunus, the bank provides small amounts of capital to people who cannot qualify for regular bank loans. Its founder was convinced that such individuals, particularly women, would benefit from small loans, enabling them to pull themselves out of poverty. Having eventually convinced the government of Bangladesh to provide the seed money, this independent bank began making small loans averaging $100, although many loans were as little as $10 to $20. A typical housing loan is $300. Initially, the client has to recruit five other coborrowers in order to generate local-level support. The terms are stiff; interest rates are relatively high and repayment times short.

The Grameen Bank has been a tremendous success. It now has more than one thousand branches, each run as a franchise by staff trained in other branches. Branches borrow money from headquarters at 12 percent interest and lend money at 20 percent, providing to the franchisees considerable opportunity for profit. The bank has provided loans to more than 1.6 million borrowers in 34,000 villages, lending about $30 million per month. Amazingly, its loan recovery rate is 97 percent! Clients for housing loans have a perfect repayment record. Over 47 percent of those borrowing have risen above the poverty line. The effects are more than economic: In Grameen families, "the nutrition level is better than in non-Grameen families, child mortality is lower and adoption of family-planning practices is higher. All studies confirm the visible empowerment of women."[10]

Other NGOs play a more direct role, organizing individuals at the grassroots level to carry out profitable locally based projects. Some of these NGOs have an international base. For example, during the Sahelian droughts in the 1970s, the World Church Service, among other NGOs, organized local food cooperatives, providing seeds and technical expertise to help women in Senegal grow food crops in depleted soils. These projects, small and scattered throughout the countryside, had the immediate function of providing food and the long-term function of providing income stability. Furthermore, indigenous NGOs are on the rise. The Asociacion de Mujeres Campesinas de la Huasteca, a local women's organization in Mexico, for example, provided loans for a facility to manufacture a water pump. The small plant not only hired women workers, giving them a livelihood, but also produced a technologically appropriate product that makes the average woman's life easier.

Some NGOs have emerged to lobby international organizations with regard to economic questions, often acting in concert with each other. The

Women's Environment and Development Organization (WEDO), for one, united 283 women's NGOs into a caucus at national and international levels. Members of such coalitions do not always agree, but their joint efforts add depth and multiple perspectives to the lobbying effort. For example, one group in WEDO focuses on the need to develop environmental programs aimed at assisting women and on the need to include women as environmental resource managers. Another group approaches the issue from an "ecofeminist" perspective, emphasizing women's unique tie to the forces in nature. The result of those groups' working together was greater activism for women's groups on sustainable development issues.

The NGOs are also strongly involved in financial and trade issues. Among those lobbying for debt relief and cancellation for the developing states is an umbrella NGO, Jubilee 2000. The group is devoted to spreading information about the need for such action, lobbying national legislatures, and working with international organizations charged with addressing debt relief. Like the WTO, the IMF has also spawned a plethora of NGO action, in many cases seeking reform of the institution and its practices. Among the opposition voices are the labor movement, most notably the International Confederation of Free Trade Unions.[11] The NGOs reflect positions all along the ideological spectrum.

IN SUM: ECONOMIC CONVERGENCE AND DIVERGENCE

In this chapter, differences in perspectives on the international political economy among economic liberals, statists, and economic radicals, rooted in eighteenth- and nineteenth-century thinking, have been explored. We illustrated how these different approaches to the international political economy influence power, competition, and development. Namely, the NIEO pits liberalism versus radicalism, and trading blocs pit liberalism versus statism. We explored the role of institutions in the policy debates, including the Bretton Woods institutions, multinational corporations, and nongovernmental organizations.

In the waning years of the twentieth century, beliefs about economic theory began to converge. The principles of economic liberalism proved more effective at raising the standard of living of people worldwide. The radical alternatives developed to foster economic development did not prove viable. Statist alternatives, however, remained attractive to many states.

Yet convergence in economic theory does not mean the absence of conflict over issues in the international political economy. While economic liberalism has raised the standard of living more than alternative approaches have, disparities within states and between the states of the North and those of the South remain significant. Some liberal economic theorists no longer speak of economic development but of sustainable development, focusing on programs to improve life in its multiple dimensions. They acknowledge the importance of programs of international governmental institutions—the World Bank and the IMF—that try to soften the effects of structural adjustment policies on individuals. Liberal economists call for MNCs to engage in more socially responsible practices. They laud the efforts of NGOs to reach groups and individuals who have been marginalized in the economic system. But not all liberals have moved in this direction. Some are less convinced of the soundness of sustainable development. They see the bureaucracy in the IMF and the World Bank as part of the problem. They believe that both MNCs and NGOs should continue to address their initial mandates. Policies continue to be controversial.

In the twenty-first century, divergence is also found in attitudes about economic globalization. The Asian crisis of the late 1990s brought to the attention of the international community the dangers of economic globalization. In a relatively short period of time, beginning in Thailand in 1997 and spreading to others in Asia and beyond, exchange rates plummeted to 50 percent of precrisis values, stock markets fell 80 percent, and real GDP dropped 4 to 8 percent. Individuals lost their jobs as companies went bankrupt or were forced to restructure. In Southeast Asian countries, Korea and Taiwan, and spreading to Brazil and Russia, economies which had previously depended on external trade, experienced an unparalleled sense of economic vulnerability. Fueled by instantaneous communication, global financial markets capable of moving $1.3 trillion daily, and the power of MNCs, traders, and financial entrepreneurs, the pitfalls of economic globalization quickly manifested themselves. The largely unregulated market had melted down and states and individuals appeared helpless. The repercussions of economic globalization were widely experienced.

Thus, theoretical convergence on economic issues and practical divergences brought out by such events as the Asian financial crisis have led to greater interest in how to organize international life more generally. Such discussions have gained new urgency as demands for global action reach historic levels. It is this quest for global governance that we now address.

NOTES

1. Thomas L. Friedman, *The Lexus and the Olive Tree. Understanding Globalization* (New York: Farrar Straus & Giroux, 1999), 257.

2. Robert Gilpin, "Three Models of the Future," *International Organization* 29:1 (Winter 1975), 37–60.

3. Sir Norman Angell, *The Great Illusion* (New York: Putnam, 1933).

4. Immanuel Kant, "Idea for a University History from a Cosmopolitan Point of View" (1784), reprinted in *Kant Selections,* ed. Lewis White Beck (New York: Macmillan Co., 1988); and Jean-Jacques Rousseau, "State of War," "Summary," and "Critique of Abbé Saint-Pierre's Project for Perpetual Peace," in *Reading Rousseau in the Nuclear Age,* ed. Grace G. Roosevelt (Philadelphia: Temple University Press, 1990), 185–229.

5. James A. Caporaso, *The European Union Dilemmas of European Integration* (Boulder Colo.: Westview, 2000).

6. Cheryl Payer, *The World Bank: A Critical Analysis* (New York: Monthly Review, 1982), 20.

7. John Walton and David Seddon, *Free Markets and Food Riots: The Politics of Global Adjustment* (Oxford, Eng.: Blackwell, 1994).

8. Kevin Danaher, ed., *50 Years Is Enough: The Case Against the World Bank and the International Monetary Fund* (Boston: South End Press, 1994).

9. Gilpin, "Three Models of the Future," 39.

10. Mohammed Yunus, quoted in Judy Mann, "An Economic Bridge out of Poverty: Grameen Bank in Bangladesh Loans Money to Poor Women Who Want to Start Business," *Washington Post,* October 14, 1994, E3.

11. Robert O'Brien, Ann Marie Goetz, Jan Aarte Scholte, and Marc Williams, *Contesting Global Governance Multilateral Economic Institutions and Global Social Networks* (Cambridge, Eng.: Cambridge University Press, 2000).

THE QUEST FOR GLOBAL GOVERNANCE

9

■ *What is the contribution of traditional international law to international order?*

■ *Why do international organizations form?*

■ *How have international organizations like the United Nations contributed to international order?*

■ *What is global governance?*

■ *What are the newer forms of global governance?*

■ *What arguments do those skeptical of the possibility of global governance make?*

In this book we have examined the contending theories of international relations and have seen how these theories help us describe and explain interactions according to the three major levels of analysis—the international system, the state, and the individual. Armed with these theoretical frameworks, we tackled two of the major issues of the twenty-first century—war and strife, and the international political economy. This exploration has led us to the fundamental dilemma of contemporary international relations: the increasing demands for global action in security and economics versus the weakness of states and contemporary international organizations.

Demands in the 1990s for new approaches to managing insecurity, for new breakthroughs in peacekeeping, for more creative approaches in second-generation peacekeeping activities, for addressing the new security issues of environmental degradation and protection of human rights, and for more effective programs to promote sustainable development test the capacity of states. The new states of central Europe and the former Soviet

Union, like many small, developing states, lack the resources to address these issues domestically. They may be unable to implement international rules dealing with environmental degradation or the terms of World Bank loans. They are obviously unable to provide resources for global solutions.

So, too, are traditional international organizations unable to meet new demands. The provisions within multilateral institutions for dealing with threats to international peace and security were not designed to address the escalation in civil conflicts. The institutions designed to cope with economic development issues are cumbersome in the fast-paced globalizing economy of the twenty-first century: hence the movement toward the nongovernmental sector that we saw in Chapter 8.

In this chapter, we first examine two traditional approaches for addressing these issues—international law and international organizations—approaches that are primarily compatible with the liberal tradition. We explore the strengths and weaknesses of these liberal approaches, and briefly look at realist and radical alternatives. Then we turn to a more expansive way of thinking about international order. Under the rubric of global governance, we explore newer pieces of the international relations puzzle that will be addressed in the twenty-first century. In the newer framework, various actors are able to address the issues arising from globalization.

TRADITIONAL LIBERAL APPROACHES

International Law

International law is largely a product of Western civilization. The man dubbed as the father of international law, the Dutch legal scholar Hugo Grotius (1583–1645), elucidated a number of fundamental principles that serve as the foundation for modern international law and international organization. For Grotius, all international relations are subject to the rule of law—that is, a law of nations and the law of nature, the latter serving as the ethical basis for the former. Grotian thinking rejects the idea that states can do whatever they wish and that war is the supreme right of states and the hallmark of their sovereignty. Grotius, a classic idealist, believed that states, like people, are basically rational and law abiding, capable of achieving cooperative goals.

The Grotian tradition argues that there is an order in international relations based on the rule of law. Although Grotius himself was not concerned with an organization for administering this rule of law, many subsequent theorists have seen an organizational structure as a vital component in realizing the principles of international order.

The Grotian tradition was challenged by the Westphalian tradition, which established the notion of state sovereignty within a territorial space, as discussed in Chapter 2. A persistent tension arose between the Westphalian tradition, with its emphasis on sovereignty, and the Grotian tradition, with its focus on law and order. Did affirmation of state sovereignty mean that international law was irrelevant? Could international law undermine or even threaten state sovereignty? Would states join an inter-national body that could challenge or even subvert their own sovereignty?

International Law and Its Functions   Law includes norms of permissible and impermissible behavior. It sets a body of expectations, provides order, protects the status quo, and legitimates the use of force by the government to maintain order. It provides a mechanism for settling disputes and protecting states against each other and against government. It serves ethical and moral functions, aiming in most cases to be fair and equitable, delineating what is socially and culturally desirable. These norms demand obedience and compel behavior.

At the state level, law is hierarchical. Established structures exist for both making law (legislatures and executives) and enforcing law (executives and judiciaries). Individuals and groups within the state are bound by law. Because of a general consensus within the state on the particulars of law, there is widespread compliance with the law. It is in the interest of everyone that order and predictability be maintained. But if law is violated, the state authorities can compel violators to judgment and use the instruments of state authority to punish wrongdoers.

At the international level, while the notion and functions of law are comparable with those at the state level, the characteristics of the system are different. In the international system, authoritative structures are absent. There is no international executive, no international legislature, and no judiciary with compulsory jurisdiction. For the realist, that is the fundamental point: the state of anarchy. Liberals, while admitting that law in the international system is different from that in domestic systems, see more order in the international system. To most liberals, international law not only exists, but it has an effect in daily life. As political scientist Louis Henkin explains,

> If one doubts the significance of this law, one need only imagine a world in which it were absent. . . . There would be no security of nations or stability of governments; territory and airspace would not be respected; vessels could nav-

igate only at their constant peril; property—within or without any given territory—would be subject to arbitrary seizure; persons would have no protection of law or diplomacy; agreements would not be made or observed; diplomatic relations would end; international trade would cease; international organizations and arrangements would disappear.[1]

We turn now to an assessment of the ways that international law is similar to and different from national law.

The Sources of International Law   International law, like domestic law, comes from a variety of sources (see Figure 9.1). Virtually all law emerges from custom. Either a hegemon or a group of states solves a problem in a particular way; these habits become ingrained as more states follow the same custom, and eventually the custom is codified into law. For example, Great Britain and later the United States were primarily responsible for developing the law of the sea. As great seafaring powers, each state adopted practices—rights of passage through straits, signaling other ships, conduct during war, and the like—that became the customary law of the sea and were eventually codified into law.

FIGURE 9.1

SOURCES OF INTERNATIONAL LAW

Custom

Treaties

International law

Authoritative bodies

Courts (international, national, and local)

But customary law is limited. For one thing, it develops slowly; British naval custom evolved into the law of the sea over several hundred years. Sometimes customs become outmoded. For example, the 3-mile territorial extension from shore was established because that was the distance a cannonball could fly. Eventually law caught up with changes in technology, and states were granted a 12-mile extension of territory into the ocean. Furthermore, not all states participate in the making of customary law, let alone give assent to the customs that have become law through European-centered practices. And the fact that customary law is initially uncodified leads to ambiguity in interpretation.

International law also comes from treaties, the dominant source of law today. Treaties, explicitly written agreements among states, number more than 25,000 since 1648 and cover all issues. Most judicial bodies, when deciding cases, look to treaty law first. Treaties are legally binding (*pacta sunt servanda*): only major changes in circumstances, or *force majeur,* gives states the right not to follow treaties they have ratified.

International law has also been formulated and codified by authoritative bodies. Among these bodies is the U.N. International Law Commission, composed of prominent international jurists. That commission has codified much customary law: the Law of the Sea (1958), the Vienna Convention of the Law of Treaties (1969), and the Vienna Conventions on Diplomatic Relations (1961) and on Consular Relations (1963). The commission also drafts new conventions for which there is no customary law. For example, laws on product liability and on the succession of states and governments have been formulated in this way, then submitted to states for ratification.

Courts are also sources of international law. Although the International Court of Justice (ICJ), with its fifteen judges located in the Hague, the Netherlands, has been responsible for some significant decisions, the ICJ is basically a weak institution, for several reasons. First, the court actually hears very few cases (between 1946 and 2000, it handed down seventy judgments and twenty-four advisory opinions—or about three decisions a year) because under the court's noncompulsory jurisdiction both parties must agree to the court's jurisdiction before a case is taken. This stands in stark contrast to domestic courts, which enjoy compulsory jurisdiction. Accused of a crime, you are compelled to judgment. No state is compelled to submit to the ICJ. Second, when cases are heard, they rarely deal with the major controversies of the day such as the war in Vietnam, the invasion of Afghanistan, or the unraveling of the Soviet Union or of Yugoslavia. Those controversies are political and outside of the court's reach. Third, only states may initiate proceedings; individuals and nongovernmental actors like multinational corporations cannot. Hence, with such a limited caseload concerning few fundamental issues, the court could never be a major source of law. In contrast, the European Court of Justice of the European Union is a significant source of European law. It has a heavy caseload, covering virtually every topic of European integration.

National and even local courts are also sources of international law. Such courts have broad jurisdiction; they may hear cases occurring on their territory in which international law is invoked or cases involving their own citizens who live elsewhere, and they may hear any case under the principle of universal jurisdiction. Under **universal jurisdiction,** states may claim jurisdiction if the conduct of a defendant is sufficiently heinous to violate the laws of all states. Several states claimed such jurisdiction as a result of the genocide in World War II and more recently for war crimes in Bosnia, Kosovo, and Rwanda. In the European Union, national and local courts are a vital source of law. A citizen of an EU country can ask a national court to invalidate any provision of domestic law found to be in conflict with provisions of the EU treaty. A citizen can also seek invalidation of a national law found to be in conflict with self-executing provisions of community directives issued by the EU's Council of Ministers. Thus, in the European system, national courts are both essential sources of community law and enforcers of that law.

Enforcement of International Law   In the absence of authority structures at the international level, why do most states obey international law most of the time? The liberal response is that states obey international law because it is right to do so. States want to do what is right and moral, and international law reflects what is right. To liberals, individual states benefit from doing what is right and moral, and all states benefit from living in an ordered world where there are general expectations about other states' behavior. States want to be looked on positively, according to liberal thinking. They want to be respected by world public opinion, and they fear being labeled as pariahs and losing face and prestige in the international system.

Should states choose not to obey international law, other members of the international system do have recourse. A number of the possibilities are self-help mechanisms that realists rely on:

- Issue diplomatic protests, particularly if the offense is a relatively minor one.

- Initiate reprisals, actions that are relatively short in duration and intended to right a previous wrong.
- Threaten to enforce economic boycotts, or impose embargoes, on both economic and military goods if trading partners are involved.
- Use military force, the ultimate self-help weapon.

But liberals contend, rightly in many cases, that self-help mechanisms of enforcement from one state are apt to be ineffective. A diplomatic protest from an enemy or a weak state is likely to be ignored, although a protest from a major ally or a hegemon may carry weight. Economic boycotts and sanctions by one state will be ineffective as long as the aggressor state has multiple trading partners. And war is both too costly and unlikely to lead to the desired outcome. In most cases, then, for the enforcement mechanism to be effective, several states have to participate. To be most effective, all states have to join together in collective action against the violator of international norms and law. For liberals, states find protection and solace in collective action and in collective security.

Many practices of international law are carried out in international organizations; such organizations are the sources and sometimes the interpreters of law. Yet the organizations themselves would not exist without law. Hence, liberals see the two as inextricably linked.

International Organizations

Contending Theories: Why International Organizations Are Created
Why have states chosen to organize themselves collectively? Responses to this question revolve around three major theories about the formation and development of international organizations: federalism, functionalism, and collective goods.

Federalism   Jean-Jacques Rousseau expanded on ideas of his predecessors in support of a united Europe. Whereas the Treaty of Westphalia acknowledged the principle of state sovereignty—the prerogative of leaders to act on the basis of their self-interest—Rousseau reasoned that if war is the product of this sovereign relationship among states, then war can be abolished by removing the attribute of state sovereignty. Peace can be attained if states give up their sovereignty and invest it in a higher, federal body. Thus, Rousseau, in his *Project towards a Perpetual Peace*, proposed that states establish "such a form of federal government as shall unite nations by bonds similar to those which already unite their individual members and place the one no less than the other under the authority of the law."[2] Federalism suggests that states join together with other states, each surrendering some pieces of sovereignty. A diminution of sovereignty, or a pooling of sovereignty to a higher unit, will help eliminate the root cause of war. That is the main intention of federalists in international relations.

Many of the specific schemes for federalism have focused on Europe. Indeed, one of the first proposals for European cooperation after World War II was that for the European Defense Community, which would have placed the military under community control, thus touching at the core of national sovereignty. This revolutionary proposal was defeated by the French Parliament, however, in 1954. Having been invaded by Germany twice in the twentieth century, the French were unwilling to place their security in the hands of an untested supranational body.

Functionalism   Functionalists believe that international organizations form for very different reasons. This viewpoint is best articulated by the scholar David Mitrany in *A Working Peace System*: "The problem of our time is not how to keep the nations peacefully apart but how to bring them actively together."[3] Thus, he proposed that units "bind together those interests which are common, where they are common, and to the extent to which they are common."[4] Like the federalists, the functionalists also want to eliminate war. However, they believe that the root cause of war is economic deprivation and disparity, not the fact that sovereign states each have military capability. Furthermore, functionalists believe that states are not suitable units to resolve these problems.

Functionalists promote building on and expanding the habits of cooperation nurtured by groups of technical experts, outside of formal state channels. Eventually, those habits spill over into cooperation in political and military affairs, as functional experts lose their close identification with the state and develop new sets of allegiances to like-minded individuals around the globe. Along the way, functionalists believe, the economic disparities will have been eliminated and war will therefore be less likely.

The route of the European Union was a functionalist one. Its architect, Jean Monnet, believed that the weakened forces of nationalism could in the long run be further undermined by the logic of economic integration. Beginning with the creation of the European Coal and Steel Community (the predecessor of the EEC), he proposed cooperative ventures in nonpolitical issue areas. Eventually, the process of integration was extended to other nonpolitical areas under an accelerated timetable. Tariffs and duties between members were progressively decreased during the 1960s and 1970s; restrictions on the movement of labor were progressively removed; and workers increasingly labored under community-wide standards for wages, benefits, and safety regulations. Where the functionalists fell short was in the prediction that these cooperative habits would spill over from the economic area to areas of national security. This has not occurred, although functionalists might reply that not enough time has passed.

IN FOCUS

FUNCTIONALISM

▶ War is caused by economic deprivation.

▶ Economic disparity cannot be solved in a system of independent states.

▶ Create new functional units to solve specific economic problems.

▶ People will develop habits of cooperation, spilling over from economic cooperation to political cooperation.

▶ In the long run, economic disparities will lessen and war will be eliminated.

At the core, functionalists, like federalists, are liberals in the idealist fashion. But whereas federalists place their faith in formal institutions to help curb states' appetites, functionalists believe that individuals can change and that habits of cooperation will develop if given sufficient time.

Collective Goods   The third theoretical perspective suggests that international organizations develop for quite different reasons. Biologist Garrett Hardin in "The Tragedy of the Commons" tells the story of a group of herders who share a common grazing area. Each herder finds it economically rational to increase the size of his own herd, allowing him to sell more in the market. Yet if all herders follow what is individually rational behavior, then the group loses: too many animals graze the land and the quality of the pasture deteriorates, which leads to decreased output for all. As each person rationally attempts to maximize his own gain, the collectivity suffers, and eventually all individuals suffer.[5]

What Hardin describes—the common grazing area—is a **collective good.** The grazing area is available to all members of the group, regardless of individual contribution. The use of collective goods involves activities and choices that are interdependent. Decisions by one state have effects for other states; that is, states can suffer unanticipated negative consequences as a result of the actions of others. In the international case, the decision by wealthy countries to continue the production and sale of chlorofluorocarbons affects all countries through long-term depletion of the ozone layer. With collective goods, market mechanisms break down. Alternative forms of management are needed.

IN FOCUS

COLLECTIVE GOODS

▶ Collective goods are available to all members of the group regardless of individual contributions.

▶ Some activities of states involve the provision of collective goods.

▶ Groups need to devise strategies to overcome problems of collective goods caused by the negative consequences of the actions of others—the "tragedy of the commons."

▶ Strategies include use of coercion, positive incentives to refrain from engaging in an activity, and altering the size of the group to ensure compliance.

Hardin proposed several possible solutions to the tragedy of the commons. First, use coercion. Force nations or peoples to control the collective goods by establishing organizations (such as world government) with effective police powers that coerce states to act in a mutually beneficial manner. Such organizations could, for example, force people to limit the number of children they have in order to prevent a population explosion that harms the environment by drawing heavily on scarce natural resources. Second, restructure the preferences of states through rewards and punishments. Offer positive incentives for states to refrain from engaging in the destruction of the commons; tax or threaten to tax those who fail to cooperate, say, by making it cheaper for a polluter to treat pollutants than to discharge them untreated. Third, alter the size of the group. Smaller groups can more effectively exert pressure, since violations of the commons will be more easily noticed. Small groups can also mobilize collective pressure more effectively. China's population policy of one child per couple is administered at the local level, by individuals residing on the same street or in the same apartment building. Close monitoring by these individuals, coupled with strong social pressure, is more apt to lead to compliance with the one-child policy. These alternatives can be achieved through organizations. At the international level, the first, use of coercion, would feel comfortable to the federalists; the second, restructuring preferences, to the functionalists; and the last, altering the size of the group, to proponents of a collective goods approach.

Each of these approaches has its own theoretical and practical shortcomings. States may be unwilling to weaken their sovereignty by turning control over to a federal body, as federalists advocate. The question of the composition of the governing body also arises: who would exert control? And what instruments would the governing body have at its disposal? It is unclear precisely how such bodies would prevent war. Federalists struggle with these issues.

Economic disparity, the focus of functionalists, is unlikely to be the main cause of war. Furthermore, habits of cooperation do not inevitably spill over into other issue areas. Individuals are often unwilling to shift loyalties beyond or outside of the nation-state. Despite the successes of the EU, the functionalists still are faced with these realities.

Collective goods theorists likewise confront practical difficulties. Institutions may not be able to alter their size and techniques to fit the characteristics of the collectivity.

The Role of International Organizations   **Intergovernmental organizations (IGOs)** such as the United Nations, the World Bank, and the International Civil Aviation Organization can play key roles at each of level of analysis, as highlighted in Table 9.1.[6] In the international system, IGOs contribute to habits of cooperation; through IGOs, states become socialized to regular interactions, a development that functionalists advocate. Such regular interactions occur between states in the United Nations. Some programs of IGOs such as the International Atomic Energy Agency's nuclear monitoring program establish regularized processes of information gathering, analysis, and surveillance which are particularly relevant to collective goods theory. Some IGOs such as the World Trade Organization develop procedures to make rules and settle disputes. Other IGOs like the World Health Organization conduct operational activities that help to resolve major substantive international problems, such as the transmission of communicable diseases, decolonization, economic disparity, and weapons proliferation. Some IGOs also play key roles in international bargaining, serving as arenas for negotiating and developing coalitions. They facilitate the formation of transgovernmental and transnational networks composed of both subnational and nongovernmental actors. And IGOs may be the place where major changes in the international distribution of power are negotiated.

The IGOs often spearhead the creation and maintenance of international rules and principles, which have come to be known generally as international **regimes.** Charters of IGOs incorporate the norms, rules,

	Roles of International Governmental Organizations	
Level	**Role**	**Example**
In the international system	Contribute to habits of cooperation—organizations and states become used to working together.	Work within U.N. system.
	Engage in information-gathering, surveillance.	World Bank gathers economic statistics; International Atomic Energy Agency monitors movement of nuclear materials across state boundaries.
	Aid in dispute settlement.	Dispute settlement procedures with the World Trade Organization or the International Court of Justice.
	Conduct operational activities.	Immunization campaigns for childhood diseases of the World Health Organization; refugee camps run by U.N. High Commission for Refugees.
	Serve as arena for bargaining.	European Council of Ministers, forums for different ministers to meet and negotiate.
	Lead to creation of international regimes.	International trade regime and international food regime.
With respect to states	Used by states as instrument of foreign policy.	Nordic states use U.N. to distribute international development assistance.
	Used by states to legitimate foreign policy.	U.S. legitimatizes military action in Korea and in Gulf War through U.N.
	Enhance information available to states.	Small states use in absence of extensive bilateral diplomatic network.
	Constrain state behavior—prevent states from taking certain action, punish states for acting in certain ways.	Embargoes against South Africa, Rhodesia, Iraq, and Serbia.
With respect to individuals	Place where individuals can be socialized to international norms.	U.N. delegates learn diplomatic norms.
	Place where individuals become educated about national similarities and differences.	Participants are educated at international meetings.

and decisionmaking processes of regimes. By bringing members of the regime together, IGOs help to reduce the incentive to cheat and enhance the value of reputation. The principles of the international human rights regime, for example, are articulated in a number of international treaties, including the Universal Declaration of Human Rights. Some IGOs, like the United Nations (through its High Commission for Human Rights), the European Union, and nongovernmental organizations like Amnesty International institutionalize those principles into specific norms and rules. They establish processes designed to monitor states' human rights behavior and compliance with human rights principles. These same organizations provide opportunities for different members of the regime— states, other IGOs, NGOs, and individuals—to meet and evaluate their efforts.

For states, IGOs enlarge the possibilities and add to the constraints under which states operate and implement foreign policy. States join IGOs to use them as instruments of foreign policy. The IGOs may serve to legitimate a state's viewpoints and policies; thus, the United States sought the support of the Organization of American States during the Cuban missile crisis. The IGOs increase the information available about other states, thereby enhancing predictability in the policymaking process. Small states, in particular, use the U.N. system to gather information about the actions of others. Some IGOs like the World Trade Organization may be used to settle disputes; the U.N. High Commission for Refugees may be used to conduct specific activities. These functions are compatible with or augment state policy.

But IGOs also constrain states. They constrain or affect member states by setting international and hence national agendas and forcing governments to make decisions; by encouraging states to develop specialized decisionmaking and implementing processes to facilitate and coordinate IGO participation; and by creating principles, norms, and rules of behavior with which states must align their policies if they wish to benefit from their membership. Both large and small states are subject to such constraints. Members of the U.N. General Assembly have at times set the international agenda to the displeasure of the United States, forcing the United States to take a stand it would not have taken otherwise. Small states, likewise, have to organize their foreign-policy apparatus to address issues discussed in IGOs.

The IGOs also affect individuals by providing opportunities for leadership. As individuals work with or in IGOs, they, like states, may become socialized to cooperating internationally.

Not all IGOs perform all of these functions, and the manner and extent to which each carries out particular functions varies. Clearly the United Nations has been given an extensive mandate to carry out many of the functions first discussed. Yet the United Nations itself is a product of a historical process, an evolution that permits it to play its designated roles.

A Historical Perspective   Events of the nineteenth century led to the development of international organizations generally and the United Nations in particular. In *Swords into Plowshares* political scientist Inis Claude described how three major strands of thinking and practice emerged in the nineteenth century.[7] The first strand involved the recognition of the utility of multilateral diplomacy. Beginning in 1815 the major European powers, including France, Russia, and Great Britain, participated in the Concert of Europe, a series of some thirty meetings intended to settle problems and coordinate actions. These meetings of like-minded dictators solidified the practices of multilateral consultation, collective diplomacy, and special status for great powers.

The second strand revolved around the Hague system, initiated in two conferences in 1899 and 1907. At the urging of Czar Nicholas II of Russia, the conferees thought proactively about techniques that states could utilize to prevent war, outlining the prerequisites for successful arbitration, negotiation, and legal recourse. Both small states and non-European ones participated in the discussions, which became increasingly formalized with the creation of committees, elected chairs, and roll-call votes.

The third strand involved the formation of public international unions. These agencies were initially established among European states to deal with problems stemming from expanding commerce, communications, and technological innovation, such as health standards for travelers, shipping rules on the Rhine River, increased mail volume, and the invention of the telegraph. In 1865, the International Telegraphic Union was formed, and in 1874, the Universal Postal Union. States began to cooperate to accomplish nonpolitical tasks. For the first time permanent secretariats were hired from a variety of countries to perform specific tasks.

Although World War I was not averted by the presence of these new multilateral forums, these nineteenth-century developments did serve as a vital precursor to twentieth-century intergovernmental organizations. In fact, World War I had hardly begun when private groups in both Europe and the United States began to lay the foundation for the postwar era. President Woodrow Wilson's proposal to incorporate a permanent international organization, the League of Nations, within the Versailles peace treaty was based on these plans.

The League Covenant, the founding document of the League of Nations, established an assembly and a council. The latter recognized the special prerogative of great powers (a lasting remnant of the European council system), and the former gave pride of place to universality of membership, about sixty states at the time. The League Council, composed of four permanent members and four elected members, was responsible for settling disputes, enforcing sanctions, and implementing peaceful settlements. However, the requirement of unanimity made action very difficult.

Liberals can rightly point to some successes of the League of Nations, many of them on territorial issues. It conducted plebiscites or referendums in disputed areas of Europe, notably Silesia and the Saar, and then, using the plebiscite results, demarcated the German-Polish border. It settled territorial disputes between Lithuania and Poland, Finland and Russia, and Bulgaria and Greece and guaranteed Albanian territorial integrity against encroachments by Italy, Greece, and Yugoslavia.

The United Nations *Basic Principles and Changing Interpretations* The United Nations was founded on three fundamental principles (see Table 9.2). Yet over the life of the organization, each of these principles has been significantly challenged by changing realities.

First, the United Nations is based on the notion of the sovereign equality of member states, consistent with the Westphalian tradition.

TABLE 9.2

U.N. Principles and Contemporary Realities

Principles	Changing realities
Sovereign equality of states.	Increasing number of members, including micro- and ministates that contribute little but still have equal votes in the General Assembly.
Only international problems are within U.N. jurisdiction.	Expansion of what is considered international because of changes in transportation, technology, and communication. For example, refugees can easily cross borders, this leads states to initiate humanitarian intervention without the consent of other states involved.
Primarily concerned with international peace and security.	Broadened view of security, to include economic and environmental security; international intervention to manage economic instability and to protect from environmental pollution.

Each state—the United States, Lithuania, India, or Suriname, irrespective of size or population—is legally the equivalent of every other state. This legal equality is the basis for each state having one vote in the General Assembly. However, the actual inequality of states is recognized in the veto power given to the five permanent members of the Security Council (China, France, Russia, the United Kingdom, and the United States), the special role reserved for the wealthy states in budget negotiations, and the weighted voting system used by the World Bank and the International Monetary Fund.[8]

No founders could have envisaged that there would be 189 members of the United Nations, as there are today. For many of the newer states, the United Nations serves as a badge of international legitimacy—a voice for small states. It is a place where they bargain with major powers, giving support on certain issues in return for economic concessions. The smaller, weaker states are the direct beneficiaries of most programs, averaging about 80 percent of the U. N. budget, yet they pay very little, each assuming only 0.01 percent of the United Nations' annual budget. Exercising effective leadership in the international arena is difficult when the demands for programs in the weaker states are many and only a few stronger states can actually pay.

Second is the principle that only international problems are within the jurisdiction of the United Nations. Indicative of the Westphalian influence, the U.N. Charter does not "authorize the United Nations to intervene in matters which are essentially within the domestic jurisdiction of any state" (Article 2, Section 7). Over the life of the United Nations, the once-rigid distinction between domestic and international issues has weakened and led to an erosion of sovereignty. Global telecommunications and economic interdependencies, international human rights, election monitoring, and environmental regulation are among the developments infringing on traditional areas of domestic jurisdiction and hence on states' sovereignty. War is increasingly civil war, which is not legally under the purview of the United Nations. Yet because international human rights are being abrogated, because refugees cross national borders, and because weapons of war are supplied through transnational networks, such conflicts are increasingly viewed as international, and the United Nations is viewed by some as the appropriate venue for action.

Based on the international ramifications of domestic and regional conflict, a growing body of precedent has developed for humanitarian intervention without the consent of the host country. During and after the Gulf War, efforts by western allies to protect the Kurdish people in northern Iraq clearly constituted intervention without Iraq's consent. This was true in Somalia as well, where there was no central government to give consent to the U.N. humanitarian relief operations in 1992, and in Kosovo, where the international community opposed Yugoslavia in its civil strife with the province of Kosovo. These cases testify to a clear modification of the principle of noninterference in domestic affairs.

The third principle is that the United Nations is designed primarily to maintain international peace and security, consistent with the Grotian tradition. This has meant that states should refrain from the threat or the use of force, settle disputes by peaceful means, and support enforcement measures.

While the foundations of both the League of Nations and the United Nations focused on security in the realist, classical sense—protection of national territory—the United Nations is increasingly confronted with demands for action to support a broadened view of security, as discussed in Chapter 7. Operations to feed the starving populations of Somalia and Rwanda or to provide relief in the form of food, clothing, and shelter for Kurds fleeing to the mountains of northern Iraq or to Kosovars forced out of their homes are examples of this broadened notion of security—human security. Expansion into these newer areas of security collides head-on with the domestic authority of states, undermining the principle of state sovereignty. The United Nations' founders recognized the tension between the commitment to act collectively against a member state and the affirmation of state sovereignty. But they could not foresee the dilemmas that changing definitions of security would pose.

Structure The structure of the United Nations was developed to serve the multiple roles assigned by its charter, but incremental changes in the structure have accommodated changes in the international system, particularly the increase in the number of states. The United Nations comprises six major bodies, as shown in Figure 9.2.

The power and prestige of these various organs has changed over time. The **Security Council,** responsible for ensuring peace and security and deciding enforcement measures, was very active during the 1940s. As the Cold War hardened between East and West, use of the Security Council diminished because of the Soviet Union's frequent use of the veto to block action. With the demise of the Cold War, the Security Council has again grown in power. Between 1987 and 1993, the number of annual official Security Council meetings rose from 49 to more than 171, and the number of annual resolutions passed increased from 13 to 93. This heightened activity reflects the absence of Cold War hostility and the permanent

FIGURE 9.2

STRUCTURE OF THE UNITED NATIONS

Principal Organs	Membership and Voting	Responsibilities
Security Council	15 members; 5 permanent with veto; 10 rotating on substantive issues	Peace and security: identifies aggressor; decides on enforcement measures
General Assembly	189 members; each state has one vote; work in 6 functional committees	Debates any topic within charter; admits states; elects members to special bodies
Secretariat, headed by secretary-general	Secretariat of 8,000+; secretary-general elected for 5-year renewable term by General Assembly and Security Council	Secretariat: gathers information, coordinates, and conducts activities Secretary-general: chief administrative officer, spokesperson
Economic and Social Council (ECOSOC)	54 members elected for 3-year terms	Coordinates economic and social welfare programs; coordinates action of specialized agencies (FAO, WHO, UNESCO)
Trusteeship Council	Originally composed of administering and non-administering countries; now made up of 5 great powers	Administers and supervises self-governing territories; only the trust territory of the Pacific Islands remains
International Court of Justice	15 judges	Noncompulsory jurisdiction on cases brought exclusively by states

members' newfound solidarity, as exemplified by increased use of secret meetings among the major powers. This practice has led to demands for restructuring the Security Council.

The **General Assembly,** permitted to debate any topic under the charter, has changed its method of operation in response to its increased membership. The bulk of the work of the General Assembly is done in six functional committees: Disarmament and Security; Economic and Financial; Social, Humanitarian, and Cultural; Political and Decolonization; Administrative and Budgetary; and Legal. These committees annually bring about 325 resolutions to the floor of the whole body. Debate on resolutions is typically organized around regionally based voting blocs, as member states coordinate positions and build support for them. These blocs facilitate the assembly's work, which became increasingly complicated as its membership grew from 51 to 189. In the early years, the Soviet Union and Eastern Europe formed the most cohesive bloc, voting together against three-quarters of the resolutions that passed. From the 1960s onward, the newly independent states of Africa and Asia joined with Latin American states to form a cohesive voting bloc in the assembly and other U.N. bodies. This group, the so-called Group of 77, dominated the General Assembly agendas and voting from the mid-1960s until the early 1990s. During this latter period, a bloc comprising the United States, some Western European countries, and Israel constituted the minority on many issues.

Since the end of the Cold War, the General Assembly's work has been increasingly marginalized, as the epicenter of U.N. power has shifted back to the Security Council and a more active Secretariat, much to the dismay of the states in the Group of 77. Over the years, the Secretariat has expanded to employ almost 8,000 individuals, although there has been a concerted effort by Secretary-General Kofi Annan to reduce its size.

In addition to the increase in the Secretariat, the role that the secretary-general plays has expanded significantly. Having few formal powers, the authority of the secretary-general depends on persuasive capability and an aura of neutrality. With this power, the secretary-general, especially in the post–Cold War era, can potentially forge an activist agenda, as former secretary-general Boutros Boutros-Ghali did: "He saw an opening for the UN in the post–Cold War disarray and plunged: prodding the United States to send thousands of American soldiers to rescue Somalis from famine; urging the United Nations into new terrain in Cambodia, Bosnia and Haiti; and . . . making a rare journey to North Korea to help solve an impasse over the nuclear program of the isolated Communist nation."[9] In 1998

Secretary-General Kofi Annan also seized the initiative. At the request of members of the Security Council, he traveled to Baghdad to negotiate a compromise between Iraq and the United States over the authority, composition, and timing of U.N. inspection teams searching for nuclear, biological, and chemical weapons in Iraq. The secretary-general's negotiated compromise averted a showdown between the two powers.

But the increased power and authority of the secretary-general has come at a cost. If the neutrality of the office is jeopardized and the autonomy of the office is threatened, the secretary-general loses legitimacy. This occurred during the Congo peacekeeping operation in the 1960s, when the secretary-general was viewed as supporting the West.

Throughout the United Nations, when one organ has expanded in importance, others have diminished, most notably the Economic and Social Council (ECOSOC) and the Trusteeship Council, albeit for very different reasons. The ECOSOC was originally established to coordinate the various economic and social activities within the U.N. system, including a number of specialized agencies. But the expansion of those activities and the increase in the number of programs has made ECOSOC's task of coordination a problematic one. A myriad of the system's most important activities formally lie outside the effective jurisdiction of ECOSOC, falling instead under the purview of autonomous agencies such as the World Bank, the World Health Organization (WHO), or the United Nations Educational, Scientific, and Cultural Organization (UNESCO). In contrast, the Trusteeship Council has worked its way out of a job. Its task was to supervise decolonialization and to phase out trust territories placed under U.N. guardianship during the transition from colonies to independent states. The number of trusts administered has dwindled from eleven to one. Thus, the very success of the Trusteeship Council has meant its demise. To avoid the necessity of altering the U.N. Charter, the council continues to exist but no longer holds annual sessions.

Possibilities for Reform Faced with escalating demands that challenge the very principles on which the organization is founded, and saddled with structures that no longer reflect the power realities of the international system, it is not surprising that the call for U.N. reform has been a loud and persistent one. Reforming the United Nations to participate more effectively in peace and security issues requires reorganization of both the Security Council and the office of the secretary-general. The "Report of the Panel on U.N. Peace Operations" (popularly known as the Brahimi Report, 2000) is the latest high-level attempt to evaluate peace and security operations. Among the proposals are calls for member states to form brigade-sized forces (about 5,000 troops) that could be deployed in the space of thirty to ninety days, a call for modernizing and equipping with intelligence capabilities the U.N. peacekeeping department in New York to be staffed by military and civilian personnel, and a proposal to permit the United Nations to identify aggressors and take appropriate action, rather than maintaining strict neutrality. The report did not, however, address the larger question of Security Council reform.[10]

The fact that membership and voting in the Security Council reflects Cold War politics undermines that organ's legitimacy. But what changes should be made? Should Japan and Germany be given status and responsibility commensurate with their power? Should middle states who have provided the peacekeepers and peacemakers in global conflicts continue to be excluded from decisionmaking? Should membership in the council be expanded and diversified to be more in accord with democratic principles? What about geographic representativeness? Efficiency? Should voting be modified to alter the antidemocratic bias of the permanent members' veto?

The office of the secretary-general has responded to the demands for reform. The report *An Agenda for Peace* is a comprehensive plan to buttress traditional U.N. peacekeeping and to initiate new activities in the area of peacemaking.[11] But should the secretary-general be given the power to respond more quickly and flexibly to situations? Should he or she have use of a force for preventive diplomacy? Should regional organizations be given new powers? Any changes that grant the secretary-general more authority will depend on strong intergovernmental support.

The United Nations also faces reform dilemmas in the promotion of sustainable development. Coordination of U.N. system organizations and activities is a critical problem. Boutros-Ghali told ECOSOC in June 1993, " . . . we have to recast our institutions in the light of our new thinking." That process, he said, "must start . . . in ECOSOC."[12]

All U.N. reforms begin and end with the willingness of states to commit financial resources to the organization. Getting enough money in the regular budget and making states pay for special operations has been a persistent problem. For example, during the Congo crisis of the early 1960s, the refusal by the Soviet Union and France to pay their financial obligations to the United Nations almost led to the end of the organization. In the 1980s and 1990s, financial problems have been exacerbated by the U.S. Congress's refusal to pay assessments until substantial reforms are implemented. In 1994, the crisis came to a head. The United States stopped paying its peacekeeping assessments and its contributions to the regular budget, which dipped to below 25 percent of total. Its arrears grew to between $1 billion and $1.7 billion. As a result, the United States lost its seat on the budget committee and almost lost its vote in the General Assembly. In November 1999, the Helms-Biden legislation was passed, permitting U.S. arrears to be paid in three installments, when specific conditions were met. This example of U.S. micro-management has isolated the United States from both allies and the majority of U. N. member states.

To address the financial problems, the members must pay, on time, and with penalties for late fees. New sources of revenue must be developed. But even more important, states must renew their commitment to provide leadership. The role of the United States will be determining, as one observer pointed out:

> The problem is not the system of collective security, or even its lack of resources. Rather it is the reluctance of the most influential member states—the United States first among them—to use it. Our thinking has still not adjusted to the realities of the post–Cold War world. If the member states see a U.N. that looks timid, weak, even anemic, it is in large part because they are looking at a reflection of their own policies. It is also because they are looking through myopic perspectives shaped by the history—not the potential—of internationalism.[13]

Reforms need to occur. "Fictitious forms cannot preserve an order now past, and international organizations that refuse to adapt to the new reality may do so at their institutional peril."[14]

Even with reform, the United Nations will probably be a less central player than it has been in the past because states can turn to alternative IGOs, and new entities, namely NGOs, are becoming increasingly salient.

REALIST VIEWS OF INTERNATIONAL LAW AND ORGANIZATION

Realists are skeptical about both international law and international organizations, though they do not completely discount their role. Recall that realists see anarchy in the international system, wherein each state is forced to act in its own self-interest and obliged to rely on self-help mechanisms. International law purportedly creates some order, as many realists acknowledge. But why do states choose to comply with these norms? The realist answer to this question is different from the response of the liberals. Realists contend that compliance occurs not because the norms are good and just in themselves but because it is in the state's self-interest to comply. States benefit from living in an ordered world, where there are some expectations about other states' behavior. A constant fear of infringement of territory and insecurity for their population is costly for states, in terms of both the economic cost of having to prepare for every possible contingency and the psychological cost of anxiety and fear. It is in the self-interest of most states to have their territory and airspace respected, to have their vessels free to navigate international waters, and to enjoy the secure procedures of diplomatic relations and international trade. Such is the rationale of international law, which realists admit is useful.

Realists are also skeptical about international organizations. The typical realist response is to emphasize the weaknesses of such organizations. For example, realists point to the failure of the League Council to act when Japan invaded Manchuria in 1931 and its slow response to the Italian invasion of Ethiopia in 1935. These failures confirm the fundamental weaknesses of the League and its collective approach to punishing aggressors. The Ethiopians appealed to the League Council to stop Italian aggression but were met by stalling actions. Eventually, the League Council did approve voluntary sanctions, but these had little effect, being too little and too late. Without the great powers to support the League's principles, especially its commitment to prevent war, the institution's power and legitimacy deteriorated.

Realists likewise do not put much faith in the United Nations. They can legitimately point to the Cold War era, when the Security Council proved impotent in addressing the conflict between the United States and the Soviet Union. The balance of power and deterrence, both realist approaches to insecurity, proved more effective in maintaining peace than the collectivist approaches of the United Nations.

Realists recognize that international law and international organizations potentially can prevent states from utilizing self-help alternatives. It may be in their self-interest to utilize these institutions. Yet they do not. States are uncertain whether such institutions will function as planned. There is an element of mistrust. They are skeptical about whether long-term gains can be achieved. Realists doubt that collective action is possible and refuse to rely on the collectivity for the protection of individual national interests.

THE RADICAL VIEW OF INTERNATIONAL LAW AND ORGANIZATION

Radicals in the Marxist tradition are also very skeptical about both international law and international organizations, albeit for very different reasons from those of the realists. Radicals see contemporary international law and organization as the product of a specific time and historical process, emerging out of eighteenth-century economic liberalism and nineteenth-century political liberalism. Thus, international law primarily comes out of Western capitalist states and is designed to serve the interests of that constituency. International law is biased against the interests of socialist states, the weak, and the unrepresented.

Similarly, international organizations, most notably the League of Nations, the United Nations, and the United Nations' specialized agencies, were designed to support the interests of the powerful. According to radicals, those institutions have succeeded in sustaining the powerful elite against the powerless mass of weaker states. For example, international legal principles, like the sanctity of national geographic boundaries, were developed during the colonial period to reinforce the claims of the powerful. Attempts to alter such boundaries are, according to international law, wrong, even though the boundaries themselves may be unfair or unjust. Marxists are quick to point out these injustices and support policies that overturn the traditional order. Thus, from the viewpoint of radicals, the actions by the United Nations following the Iraqi invasion of Kuwait in 1990, including a series of resolutions condemning Iraq and imposing sanctions on that country, were designed to support the position of the West, most notably the interests of the hegemonic United States and its capitalist friends in the international petroleum industry. To radicals, the U.N.-imposed sanctions provide an excellent example of hegemonic interests injuring the marginalized—Iraqi men, women, and children striving to eke out meager livings. Radicals also view the NATO actions in Kosovo as another example of hegemonic power, harming the poor and disenfranchised.

Radicals desire major political and economic change to overturn the contemporary international order in favor of one that distributes economic resources and political power more equitably. Since contemporary international law and organizations operate in favor of the status quo, radicals support more broad based change. Some changes may be accommodated under the rubric of *global governance,* a term currently prominent in liberal thinking.

TOWARD A BROADER VIEW OF GLOBAL GOVERNANCE

The general problems and weaknesses in international law and organizations that all three theoretical perspectives recognize and the stalemate in the U.N. reform process have renewed discussions about developing new forms of collective action, under the rubric of **global governance.**

Supporters of global governance, while they do not agree on a strict definition, do agree that *governance* is not synonymous with *government*, or with *more government*. For one prominent scholar, James Rosenau, governance is "a more encompassing phenomenon than government. It embraces governmental institutions, but it also subsumes informal, nongovernmental mechanisms whereby those persons and organizations within its purview move ahead, satisfy their needs, and fulfill their wants."[15] Global governance encompasses activities at all levels of human interaction that have international repercussions. It implies examination of various governance activities, from formal to informal, from law to rules to understandings, at a variety of locales. It is not the hierarchical approach of world government.

New forms of global governance are emerging as prominent pieces of international relations. Such forms include nongovernmental organizations, transgovernmental coalitions, members of various expert communities, and participants in international regimes.

Nongovernmental Organizations

Nongovernmental organizations (NGOs) are increasingly recognized as influential actors in global governance activities. Indeed, their very numbers have grown dramatically. The Union of International Associations recognizes about 14,500 nonprofit NGOs. If multinational corporations are included, the number approaches 25,000. The roots of many NGOs are at the local level.

The NGOs perform a variety of functions and roles. In Chapter 8, we looked at the role of NGOs in international economic issues, particularly in promoting sustainable development, but they play other roles as well. They act as advocates for specific policies and alternative channels of political participation, as Amnesty International has done through its letter-writing campaigns on behalf of victims of human rights violations. They mobilize mass publics, as Greenpeace did in saving the whales (through international laws limiting whaling) or labeling "green" (non–environmentally damaging) products in Europe and Canada. They distribute critical assistance in disaster relief and to refugees, as Médecins sans Frontières, World Catholic Relief, and Oxfam have done in Somalia, Yugoslavia, and Rwanda. They are the principal monitors of human rights norms and environmental regulations and provide warnings of violations, as Human Rights Watch has done in China, Latin America, and elsewhere. Increasingly they develop regional and global networks through linkages with other NGOs, like that which the Women's Environment and Development Organization has forged among its 283 worldwide member organizations. The NGOs are the primary actors at the grassroots level in mobilizing individuals to act. For example, during the 1990 meeting to revise the 1987 Montreal Protocol on Substances that Deplete the Ozone Layer, NGOs criticized U.N. Environmental Program secretary-general Mostafa Tolba for not advocating more stringent regulations on ozone-destroying chemicals. Friends of the Earth International, Greenpeace International, and the Natural Resources Defense Council held press conferences and circulated brochures to the public, media, and officials complaining of the weak regulations. The precise strategy of each group varied. Friends of the Earth approached the matter analytically, while Greenpeace staged a drama to show the effects of environmental degradation. But the intent of each was the same—to focus citizen action on strengthening the Montreal Protocol. By publicizing inadequacies, NGOs force discussion both within states and between states in international forums.

Nowhere has the impact of NGOs been felt more strongly than at the 1992 U.N. Conference on the Environment and Development (UNCED) in Rio de Janeiro. The NGOs played key roles in both the preparatory conferences and the Rio conference, adding representation and openness (or "transparency") to the process. For the first time, they made statements from the floor during official working group and plenary meetings. They drafted informational materials, which were circulated on tables inside meeting rooms for easy access by government delegations. They scrutinized working drafts of U.N. documents, reviewing and passing on comments to influential officials and delegates. They spoke up to support and refute specific phrasing. The UNCED provided extensive opportunities for NGO networking. More than four hundred environmental organizations were accredited at the conference, including not only traditional, large, well-financed NGOs such as the World Wildlife Fund but also those working on specific issues and those with grassroots origins in developing countries, many of which were poorly financed and had few previous transnational linkages.

The persistence of the NGOs paid off. Agenda 21, the official document produced by the conference, recognized the unique capabilities of NGOs and recommended their participation at all levels from policy formulation and decisionmaking to implementation. What began as a parallel informal process of participation within the U.N. system evolved into a more formal role, a role replicated at the 1994 International Conference on Population and Development in Cairo and at the 1995 Fourth World Conference on Women in Beijing.

The NGOs are privileged over other types of actors in conducting global governance. They are usually politically independent from any sovereign state, so they can make and execute international policy more rapidly and directly, and with less risk to national sensitivities, than IGOs can. They can participate at all levels, from policy formation and decisionmaking to implementation. Yet they can also influence state behavior by initiating formal, legally binding action, pressuring authorities to impose sanctions, carrying out independent investigations, and linking issues together in ways that force some measure of compliance. Thus, NGOs are versatile and increasingly powerful actors.

Transgovernmental Coalitions

When political agendas broaden into many different issues and the state no longer acts as a unified entity (unitary actor), then transgovernmental coalitions can play special roles in organizing substate actors in global governance activities. Bureaucracies in different states, such as the ministries of transportation, trade, or agriculture, find in some cases that they need to deal with each other directly, rather than indirectly through their foreign ministries, particularly when there is no central policy or where strikingly different interests are at stake.

The coordination evidenced by the major economic powers in bargaining over issues of the New International Economic Order (NIEO) with the Third World countries is an excellent example of the effective use of transgovernmental coalitions. On the issue of debt relief and the establishment of the Common Fund, "hardliners" (opponents of change) were typically located in the finance and economic ministries of the United States, Japan, Great Britain, and France, while the "softliners" (supporters of change) were those in the foreign affairs and foreign-aid bureaus. Members of these ministries found it useful to forge transgovernmental coalitions with their counterparts in ministries sharing similar views. Four separate transgovernmental coalitions formed. One, composed of finance ministry officials, blocked concessions on the issue of debt relief in both Third World countries and from their own foreign ministries or foreign-aid agencies. The foreign ministry and foreign-aid coalitions won concessions on behalf of the developed countries to establish the Common Fund. As political scientist Barbara Crane concludes, "The coalitions may therefore have prepared the way for some incremental change in the international economic order. Their actions also helped to diminish overt tensions in North-South relations."[16]

Transgovernmental groups played a similar role with respect to oceans policy. The navies, fisheries ministries, and the ministries of oceanographic scientific research of different countries have worked together to forge policies reflecting common interests and to oppose others that are contrary to the coalition's interests. Through transgovernmental coalitions, small and poor states have been able to gain access to larger and stronger states, thus enabling weak states to play a role in global governance. In both the NIEO and oceans cases, transgovernmental coalitions formed in and around international organizations and ad hoc global conferences. In each case they successfully forged compromises that states acting as unified actors could never achieve.

Transnational Communities of Experts

In some issue areas, a broader group of elites is engaged in global governance. Expert communities have formed just as the functionalists predicted. Such communities are composed of individual experts and technical specialists from IGOs, NGOS, and state and substate agencies. These communities share expertise as well as a set of beliefs. They share notions of validity and a set of practices organized around solving a particular problem.[17] Members of transnational knowledge communities can influence both state and international secretariat behavior.

One example of a transnational expert community can be found in the Mediterranean Action Plan of the U.N. Environmental Program (UNEP). After 1972, individual experts were invited to meetings in a professional, nonofficial capacity to discuss ways to improve the water quality of the Mediterranean Sea. Meetings bound the experts in the process, and UNEP administrators relied on this expert community for the data to establish the water-monitoring program and for modifications in the program in accord with the data received. These same individuals also became active in the domestic bargaining process, fostering learning among governmental elites. Thus individuals outside the government also can be instrumental in global governance.

International Regimes

One of the earliest references to international regimes recognizes them as one of the key parameters of international governance. Although regimes can be the embodiment of governance, today the more accurate assessment is that global governance occurs, in part, through international regimes.

The term *regime* has been used by scholars to refer to high levels of cooperation—beyond the willingness to negotiate internationally and to coordinate policy outcomes on a periodic basis. The notion of a regime suggests that states develop principles about how certain problems *should* be addressed. Over time, these principles solidify. Such rules and principles may be explicit—as indeed some international law is when it is codified—or they may be implicit. Regimes are "principles, norms, rules, and decision-making procedures around which actors' expectations converge in a given issue area."[18]

Whether or not the principles are formalized in an organization or an international treaty, regimes guide state actions. Realists accept the notion of international regimes because states agree to participate in regimes out of their own self-interest. States benefit from the increased information and from the stable expectations created by regimes. Not surprisingly, given the vague definition of the term, scholars do not always agree on whether the expectations in a certain issue area have sufficiently converged to be considered an international regime.

An example of an international regime is found in the area of international food policy.[19] Formal organizations are an important part of the international food regime, including six U.N.-based organizations—the Food and Agriculture Organization (FAO), the World Food Program (WFP), the International Fund for Agricultural Development (IFAD), the Consultative Group of International Agricultural Research (CGIAR), the World Food Council, and the less well known International Wheat Council. Other organizations have specific interests and responsibilities: these groups include the Organization for Economic Cooperation and Development (OECD) and its committees on Agriculture and Development Assistance, the World Trade Organization (WTO), and the World Health Organization (WHO).

The NGOs are integral to the food regime. Prominent in this sector are the International Committee of the Red Cross, CARE, and Médecins sans Frontières, each of which organizes emergency food programs; health clinics for children, pregnant women, and mothers; and supplementary food programs.

Yet the international food policy regime is more than the sum of IGOs and NGOs, or even of transgovernmental or transnational coalitions. It rests on principles. Between 1944 and 1960, the thrust of the regime was toward harmonizing agricultural policies with free trade principles. Between 1960 and 1973, the emphasis moved toward economic development in the South through the transfer of financial resources and technical expertise. During the 1970s, the North-South struggle dominated the food regime, as the developing countries sought greater influence in reshaping the principles of the regime.

These principles have not been achieved uniformly. The principle of multilateral food aid has become firmly embedded in the food regime, largely as a response to a series of international crises in Africa in the 1970s. Yet the principle of freer trade in agriculture has not been achieved; agricultural crops continue to enjoy protected status in most states.

A regime is nevertheless a useful concept for evaluating cooperation. Most regimes comprise a web of organizations—global and regional, general purpose and specialized—that are engaged in activities. Most important, these various actors operate within sets of explicit principles, norms, and procedures. Regimes do evolve; their principles change to meet new international demands and responsibilities.

PUTTING THE PIECES OF GLOBAL GOVERNANCE TOGETHER

Various participants in global governance are in place (see Figure 9.3). Their processes of interaction are more frequent and intense than they have been in the past, ranging from conventional ad hoc cooperation and formal interorganizational collaboration to social networks and even computer-based communities on the World Wide Web. "The processes can be direct or circuitous, spontaneous or mobilized, brief or prolonged, intended or unintended, subsystemic or global."[20]

Yet for global governance to come together, for the international relations puzzle to be whole and complete, there must be a global civil society.

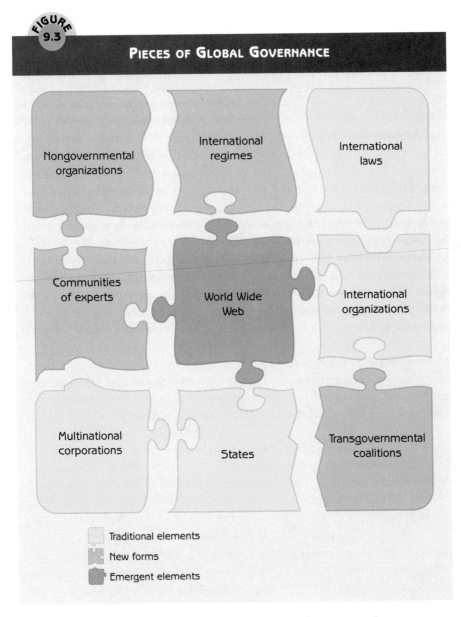

FIGURE 9.3

PIECES OF GLOBAL GOVERNANCE

Nongovernmental organizations

International regimes

International laws

Communities of experts

World Wide Web

International organizations

Multinational corporations

States

Transgovernmental coalitions

Traditional elements

New forms

Emergent elements

Political scientist Ronnie Lipschutz describes the essential component: "While global civil society must interact with states, the code of global civil society denies the primacy of states or their sovereign rights. This civil society is 'global' not only because of those connections that cross national boundaries and operate within the 'global, nonterritorial region,' but also as a result of a growing element of global consciousness in the way the members of global civil society act."[21] Some liberals would find this a desirable direction in which to be moving—a goal to be attained.

Skeptics of global governance do not believe that anything approaching governance, however defined, is possible or desirable. For realists, there can never be governance in anarchy; outcomes are determined by relative power positions rather than law or other regulatory devices, however decentralized and diffuse those devices might be. For Kenneth Waltz, the quintessential neorealist, the anarchical structure of the international system is the core dynamic. For other realists, like Hans Morgenthau, there is space for both international law and international organization; his textbook includes chapters on both, but each is relatively insignificant in the face of power politics and the national interest. Few realists would talk in governance terms. Radicals are also uncomfortable with global governance discourse. Rather than seeing global governance as a multiple-actor, multiple-process, decentralized framework, radicals fear domination by hegemons who would structure global governance processes to their own advantage. Some liberals are also skeptical because of their fear that global governance might undermine democratic values. As the locus of governance moves further from the population, democracy becomes more problematic.

In Sum: Toward Global Governance

In the next century, much of international relations discourse will revolve around these issues of global governance. In this chapter we have explored the historical roots of global governance in traditional liberal notions of international law and organization. We have analyzed how international law and organization have functioned in international relations, with particular emphasis on the United Nations. Then we turned to a discussion of the broader view of global governance, which includes at least four other forms: nongovernmental organizations, transgovernmental coalitions, members of various expert communities, and participants in international regimes. Finally, we have put the pieces of the global governance puzzle together by suggesting the need for a global civil society.

Skepticism about the *possibility* of global governance does not diminish the fact that there is a *need* for such actions. In the next chapter, we turn to a survey of selected globalizing issues which have stimulated the demand for global governance and discuss the effects of the globalizing issues on state practices, core international relations concepts, and international relations theory.

NOTES

1. Louis Henkin, *How Nations Behave: Law and Foreign Policy* (2d ed.; New York: Columbia University Press, 1979), 2.
2. Jean-Jacques Rousseau, "Extrait du projet de paix perpétuelle," from *Ouevres complètes bibliothèque de la pleiade* III (Paris, 1760), 564, as translated and quoted in Torbjörn L. Knutsen, *A History of International Relations Theory* (Manchester, Eng.: Manchester University Press, 1997), 120.
3. David Mitrany, *A Working Peace System* (London: Royal Institute of International Affairs, 1946), 7.
4. Ibid., 40.
5. Garrett Hardin, "The Tragedy of the Commons," *Science* 162 (December 13, 1968), 1243–48. See also Mancur Olson, Jr., *The Logic of Collective Action: Public Goods and the Theory of Groups* (New York: Schocken, 1968).
6. Margaret P. Karns and Karen A. Mingst, "The United States and Multilateral Institutions: A Framework," in *The United States and Multilateral Institutions: Patterns of Changing Instrumentality and Influence*, eds. Margaret P. Karns and Karen A. Mingst (Boston: Unwin Hyman, 1990), 1–24.
7. Inis Claude, *Swords into Plowshares: The Problems and Progress of International Organization* (4th ed.; New York: Random House, 1971).
8. Karen A. Mingst and Margaret P. Karns, *The United Nations in the Post–Cold War Era* (2d ed.; Boulder, Colo.: Westview, 2000).
9. Julia Preston, "Boutros-Ghali Rushes in . . . in a Violent World: The U.N. Secretary General Has an Activist's Agenda," *Washington Post National Weekly Edition*, January 10–16, 1994, 10–11.
10. United Nations, "Report on the Panel on U.N. Peace Operations" (August 2000). www.unorg/peace/reports/peace_operations/doc.part1.htm.
11. Boutros Boutros-Ghali, *An Agenda for Peace*, (2d ed.; New York: United Nations, 1995).
12. As quoted in Nancy Seufert-Barr, "Towards a New Clarity for UN Work," *UN Chronicle* 30:4 (December 1993), 39.
13. Edward C. Luck, "Making Peace," *Foreign Policy*, no. 89 (Winter 1992–93), 155.
14. Peter J. Spiro, "New Global Communities: Nongovernmental Organizations in International Decision-Making Institutions," *Washington Quarterly* 18:1 (1994), 54.
15. James N. Rosenau, "Governance, Order and Change in World Politics," in *Governance without Government: Order and Change in World Politics*, eds. James N. Rosenau and Ernst-Otto Czempiel (Cambridge, Eng.: Cambridge University Press, 1994), 4.
16. Barbara Crane, "Policy Coordination by Major Western Powers in Bargaining with the Third World: Debt Relief and the Common Fund," *International Organization* 38:3 (Summer 1984), 427.

17. Peter M. Haas, "Introduction: Epistemic Communities and International Policy Coordination," *International Organization* 46:1 (Winter 1992), 3.

18. Stephen D. Krasner, "Structural Causes and Regime Consequences: Regimes as Intervening Variables," *International Organization* 36:2 (Spring 1982), 186.

19. Raymond Hopkins, "International Food Organizations and the United States: Drifting Leadership and Diverging Interests," in *The United States and Multilateral Institutions: Patterns of Changing Instrumentality and Influence,* eds. Margaret P. Karns and Karen A. Mingst (Boston: Unwin Hyman, 1990), 177–204.

20. James N. Rosenau, *Turbulence in World Politics: A Theory of Change and Continuity* (Princeton, N.J.: Princeton University Press, 1990), 158.

21. Ronnie Lipschutz, "Reconstructing World Politics: The Emergence of Global Civil Society," *Millennium: Journal of International Studies* 21:3 (1992), 398–99.

GLOBALIZING ISSUES

10

- *What are the critical characteristics of globalizing issues?*
- *How do the concepts collective goods and sustainability help us think about environmental issues?*
- *What makes the population issue difficult to address?*
- *What environmental issues may lead to international conflict?*
- *What are the different generations of human rights?*
- *How can international human rights standards be enforced?*
- *How have women's rights issues been transformed into human rights issues?*
- *How have the contending theories of international relations been modified or changed to accommodate globalizing issues?*

The need for global governance structures has never been greater. States are interconnected and interdependent to a degree never previously experienced. These interconnections are clearly illustrated in the globalizing issues of the twenty-first century. In this chapter, we examine selected globalizing issues, specifically the environment and human rights among a plethora of issues including AIDS and drugs. For these issues we show interconnectedness, the interaction among various international actors, and the impacts of these changes on core concepts and on the study of international relations.

In the twenty-first century, more different kinds of actors than ever participate in international politics, including the state, ethnonational challengers, multinational corporations, international organizations, nongovernmental organizations, civil society actors and movements, and transnational networks. The movement of actors from the state to others portends a significant power shift. These actors address a great variety of issues which are substantively and geographically interlinked from the local to the global level. Chapters 6 and 7 introduced two of the core issues—security and the international political economy. These two issues have evolved in new ways. State security is now human security; interstate wars may be less prevalent than civil wars or terrorist operations. The international political economy is just part of the broader process of globalization, dominated by actors other than the state. Economic decisions made by multinational corporations affect national balances of payments and the ability of workers at the local level to hold a job and make a living wage. New issues such as the environment and human rights may be as salient to states and individuals as traditional "guns or butter" issues. Finally, the changes wrought by the global communications and technology revolution lessens the determinacy of geography and undermines the primacy of territorial states. Distance and time are compressed; important issues can be communicated virtually instantaneously around the globe to the most remote villages of the developing world. The ability of state leaders to manage this flow of information has diminished. One aspect of the sovereignty of the state, namely internal control over its citizens, has eroded.

As a result of these changes, globalizing issues demand further discussion. These issues are not new. Interest at the local and state level in the environment and human rights has been expressed for generations, because these issues touch the quality of people's lives directly. These issues are closely connected to war and strife and political economy. What is new is that there is now *international* interest and action. And these issues are likely to be at the forefront in the twenty-first century. How can we think conceptually about the globalizing issues of environment and human rights? How do these issues crosscut with the traditional issues of security and economics? Who are the various actors with interests? How would a realist, a liberal, a radical, or a constructivist approach these globalizing issues?

THE ENVIRONMENT

Among the plethora of new issue areas, the environment stands out as directly affecting the quality of our individual and collective lives, as well as the political and economic choices we make. A contemporary perspective on the environment confirms that multiple issues of population, natural resources, energy, and pollution are integrally related. Trends in one of these issues affect each of the others. Policy decisions taken to address one issue have impacts on each of the others.

Conceptual Perspectives

Two conceptual perspectives help us think about the suite of environmental issues. These perspectives are not contending approaches; rather they augment each other. First is the notion of collective goods. Collective goods help us conceptualize how to achieve shared benefits that depend on overcoming conflicting interests. How can individual herders in the commons be made not to pursue their own self-interest (increasing grazing on the commons) in the interests of preserving the commons for the collectivity? How can individual contributors to air pollution or ocean pollution be made to realize that their acts jeopardize the very collective good they are utilizing (the air and the ocean)? Collective goods theory provides the theoretical explanation for why there are environmental problems, as well as some ideas on how to address these problems.

The second conceptual perspective is sustainability. This newer concept provides the criterion to evaluate the soundness of environmental policies from scientific and economic perspectives. Can the policy be implemented without using up the precious capital of the Earth? How can development proceed and the Earth and its resources be maintained? Employing the criterion of sustainability forces individuals to think about policies to promote change that neither damage the environment nor use up finite resources.

Three key topics provide a foundation for understanding environmental issues. While each topic may be treated separately, and often are, they are integrally related.

Population Issues

Recognition of the potential population problem occurred centuries ago. In 1798 Thomas Malthus posited a key relationship. If population grows unchecked, it will increase at a geometric rate (1,2,4,8, . . .), while food resources will increase at an arithmetic rate (1,2,3,4, . . .). Very quickly, he postulated, population increases will outstrip food production. This phenomenon is referred to as the **Malthusian dilemma**.[1] Three centuries later, an independent report (*The Limits to Growth*) issued by the Club of

Rome in 1972 systematically investigated the trends in population, agri-cultural production, natural resource utilization, and industrial produc-tion and pollution and the intricate feedback loops that link these trends. Its conclusions were pessimistic: the Earth would reach natural limits to growth within a relatively short period of time.[2]

Neither Malthus nor the Club of Rome proved to be correct. Malthus did not foresee the technological changes that would lead to much higher rates of food production, nor did he predict the **demographic transition**—that population growth rates would not proceed unchecked. While improvements in economic development would lead at first to lower death rates and hence a greater population increase, over time, as the lives of individuals improved and women became more educated, birth rates would dramatically drop. Likewise, the Club of Rome's predictions proved too pessimistic, as technological change stretched resources beyond the limits predicted in the 1972 report.

Although Malthus and the Club of Rome missed some key trends, their prediction that population growth rates would increase dramatically has been proven true. Figure 10.1 shows the world population growth line projected over the next fifty years. Note the accelerating rate of population growth and the distribution by region.

Three key observations make these population growth rates all the more disturbing. First, the population increase is not uniformly distrib-uted. The developing world has much higher population growth rates than the developed world. Fertility rates in the developing world have averaged 3.4 children per woman, while in the developed world fertility has de-clined to 1.6 children per woman as a result of the demographic transi-tion. Thus, there is a significant demographic divide between the rich North with low population growth rates and the poor South with high population growth rates; 98 percent of the growth in world population is occurring in the developing countries. This divide has politically sensitive consequences, as those in the South, laboring under the burden of the population explosion, attempt to meet the economic consumption stan-dards of the North. Realists fear this could potentially lead to a shift in the balance of power, while radicals view the data as confirmation that the few (the rich) dominate the many (the poor).

Second, both rapid rates of overall population growth and high levels of economic development mean increased demands for natural resources. For certain countries like China, India, and Bangladesh with large popula-tions already, the problem is severe. In Bangladesh and Nepal, the grow-ing population is forced onto increasingly marginal land. In Nepal, human

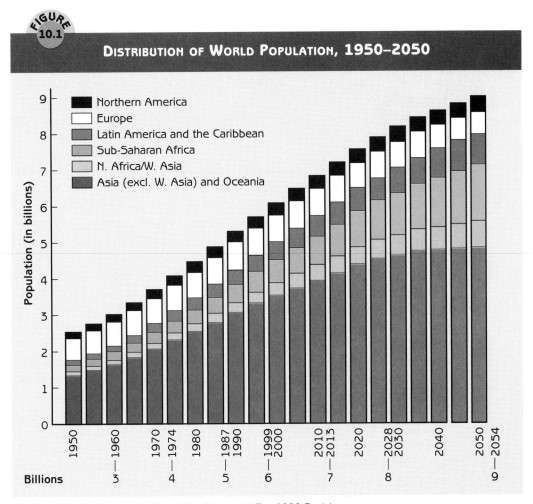

FIGURE 10.1

DISTRIBUTION OF WORLD POPULATION, 1950–2050

SOURCE: United Nations, *World Population Prospects: The 1998 Revision.*

settlements at higher elevations have resulted in deforestation, as individuals utilize trees for fuel, resulting in hillside erosion, and landslides and other "natural" disasters. In Bangladesh, population pressures have led to settlements on deltas, vulnerable to monsoonal flooding, which strips the top soil, decreases agricultural productivity, and periodically dislocates millions of individuals.

Accelerating demands for natural resources occur in the developed world as well. As the smaller (even slightly declining) population becomes more economically affluent, there is increasing demand for more energy and resources to support higher standards of living. People clamor for more living space, larger houses and more highways, creating more demand for energy and resources.

Third, high population growth rates lead to numerous ethical dilemmas for state and international policymakers. How can population growth rates be curbed without infringing on individual rights to procreate? How can the developed countries promote lower birth rates in the developing world without sounding like supporters of eugenics? Can policies be developed that both improve the standard of living for individuals already born and guarantee equally high standards and improvements for future generations?

Population becomes a classic collective goods problem. It is eminently rational for an individual or couple in the developing world to have more children: children provide valuable labor in the family and often earn money in the wage economy, contributing to family well-being. Children are the social safety net for the family in societies where no governmental programs exist. But what is economically rational for the couple is not economically sustainable for the collectivity. The amount of land in the commons shrinks on a per capita basis, and the overall quality of the resource declines. What is economically rational for a family is not environmentally sustainable. The finite resources of the commons over time have a decreasing capacity to support the population; policies are not sustainable over time.

What actions can be taken with respect to population to alleviate or mitigate the dilemmas just discussed? Biologist Garrett Hardin's solution, using coercion to prohibit procreation, is politically untenable and pragmatically difficult, as China discovered with its one-child policy. Relying on group pressure to force individual changes in behavior is also unlikely to work in the populous states.[3] What is clear about the population problem is that it is an international problem affecting the one globe. The photographs taken by the Apollo 2 astronauts in 1969 showed in a dramatic way Spaceship Earth. We no longer live on isolated islands; the decisions of each affect the whole.

The issue is a classically global one, affecting not just states with high rates of population growth but their neighbors, as people on overcrowded land contend for scarce resources and seek a better life in other countries through migration or turn to violence to get more desirable space.

States are not the only actors affected: this issue involves individuals, couples, and communities and their deepest-held religious and humanistic values. It also involves the nongovernmental community, those groups like Zero Population Growth or the Population Council in the business of trying to change public attitudes about population and procreation, as well as the Catholic Church and fundamentalist Islamic sects that oppose artificial restrictions on the size of families. It involves international organizations like the World Bank, charged with promoting sustainable development and yet hamstrung by the wishes of some member states to refrain from directly addressing the population issue. Perhaps, most importantly, the population issue intersects with other environmental issues in an inextricable way. Populations put demands on land use for enhanced agricultural productivity; they need natural resources and energy resources. Thus, ironically, population may well be the pivotal global environmental issue, but it may be the one that states and other international actors can do the least about.

Natural Resource Issues

The belief in the infinite supply of natural resources was a logical one throughout much of human history, as peoples migrated to uninhabited lands. Trading for natural resources became a necessary activity as it was recognized that those resources were never uniformly distributed.

The belief in the infinite supply of key economic resources was dramatically challenged by radical Marxist thinkers. One of the reasons for imperialism, according to Lenin, was the inevitable quest for sources of raw materials. Capitalist states depended on overseas markets and resources, precisely because resources are unevenly distributed. Petroleum is one of those key resources. Demand in the industrialized world has increased dramatically, and those countries which are major consumers are increasingly relying on foreign supplies, leading to unprecedented economic vulnerability.

The 1973 oil shortage, exacerbated by the imposition of an oil embargo by Arab members of OPEC against countries supportive of Israel in the 1973 Yom Kippur War against Egypt, brought home to U.S. policymakers and public the issue of natural resource interdependency and potential scarcity. Americans were forced to cut back on driving to conserve fuel. They were relegated to long and inconvenient lines to get their share of gasoline. They literally fought with fellow citizens for oil, all because of actions taken by Middle East oil suppliers who were punishing the United States for its pro-Israeli stance. For the first time since World War II, it was the U.S. public that was dramatically affected by natural resource shortages. Since then, the point has been repeated. Another oil shock occurred at the end of the 1970s when panic hit following the seizure of power by Islamic fundamentalists in oil-rich Iran. Oil prices have dramatically escalated in the face of the shortage of supply and the use of oil as a political weapon. In the energy profligate economies of the twenty-first century, the direct correlation between population pressures and natural resource utilization and dependency has been made clear.

Population pressures and increased per capita consumption of resources has also made water a natural resource issue of the twenty-first century. Freshwater is a key natural resource necessary for all forms of life—human, animal, and plant. Only 3 percent of the Earth's water is fresh, and that supply is one-third lower than in 1970, at the same time that demand is increasing. Agriculture accounts for about two-thirds of the use of water, industry about one-quarter, and human consumption slightly less than one-tenth. It is estimated that by 2025, two-thirds of the world's people will live in countries facing moderate or severe water problems. While most freshwater issues are national problems, increasingly such problems have an international dimension.

Two examples illustrate the international controversies. The U.S. use of the Colorado River for irrigation has not only reduced the flow of that river but also diminished the quality of the water that ends up in Mexico, the downstream user. By the time the river crosses the border, the flow is a trickle and is highly saline, driving Mexican agricultural users out of business. Similarly, Israel's control of scarce water on the West Bank has resulted in rationing in neighboring regions. Hence, the World Bank predicts that in the twenty-first century, water could be the major political issue not only between Israel and Jordan, but between Turkey and Syria and between India and Bangladesh.

Pollution

As pressures on the commons mount, the quality of geographic space and landscapes diminish. In the 1950s and 1960s, several events dramatically publicized the deteriorating quality of the commons. Oceanographer Jacques Cousteau warned of the degradation of the ocean, a warning confirmed by the Torrey Canyon oil spill off the coast of England. Rachel Carson's *Silent Spring* warned of the impact of chemicals on the environment.[4] The natural world was being degraded by human activity associated with agricultural and industrial practices. Economic development both in agriculture and industry has **negative externalities,** costly unintended consequences, for everyone, as well as positive effects.

While many of these negative externalities may be local, others have national or international implications. Nowhere is this more true than for two issues on the agenda of the twenty-first century: ozone depletion and global warming. Both pollution issues share characteristics in common. They concern pollution in spaces which belong to no one state. They both result from unintended negative externalities associated with rising levels of economic development. They both pit groups of states against others, and they both have been the subject of highly contested international negotiations.

Ozone depletion was thrust onto the international agenda in 1975, following a report submitted by two U.S. scientists attributing the depletion of the ozone layer to the use of chlorofluorocarbons (CFCs), a widely used chemical in refrigeration systems. The correlation between the use of CFCs and ozone depletion was a contested one for several years. But in a little less than a decade, following the publication of new data confirming a widening ozone hole over Antarctica, most states and scientific experts acknowledged the problem. The United States and European states were both the major producers of CFCs and the major consumers, although usage in the large rapidly developing countries like India, China, Brazil, and Mexico was rising at about 10 percent annually, as industrialization accelerated.

Beginning in 1985, states promised to cooperate on research and data acquisition. Under both the 1987 Montreal Protocol on Substances That Deplete the Ozone Layer and the 1990 London Agreement, states agreed to a phasing out of ozone-depleting chemicals.[5] During the early 1990s, as evidence of further ozone depletion mounted, the bans on CFCs were accelerated and the timetables for the phaseout of other similar chemicals shortened. In an unprecedented move during the international negotiations, the developed countries promised technological assistance to developing economies to finance substitute technologies. The case of ozone depletion illustrates the rather unusual circumstance where states recognize a problem before it takes on crisis proportions and react with increasingly strong measures involving both developed and developing countries.

While the final verdict on whether ozone depletion has been curbed is not clear, the evidence is promising. Global production of CFCs has declined, although production in the developing world has grown slightly. There is a continued demand for products using CFC-like compounds, but research for substitutes has been promising.

The issue of global climate change or greenhouse warming has proved more complicated. On the one hand, there are scientific facts that are indisputable. The preponderance of greenhouse gas emissions comes from the burning of fossil fuels in the industrialized northern countries. But sources are also found in the developing countries, most notably from deforestation of the tropics caused by agriculture and the timber industry. Figure 10.2 shows per capita carbon dioxide emissions by region in the absence of any international agreement.

On the other hand, the models of climate change are rudimentary. There is dispute about whether global temperatures have actually risen and, if so, by how much. While most agree that the globe's temperature

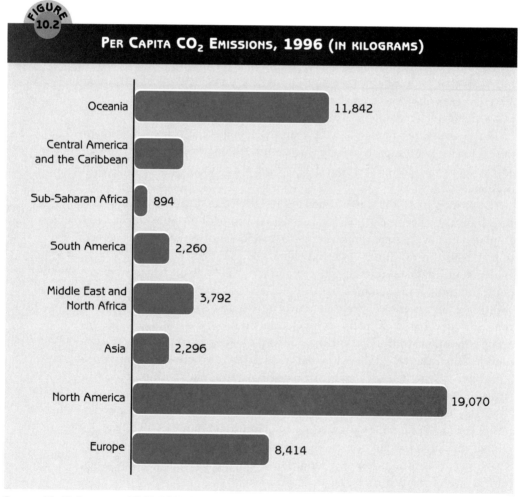

FIGURE 10.2

PER CAPITA CO$_2$ EMISSIONS, 1996 (IN KILOGRAMS)

Oceania — 11,842
Central America and the Caribbean
Sub-Saharan Africa — 894
South America — 2,260
Middle East and North Africa — 3,792
Asia — 2,296
North America — 19,070
Europe — 8,414

SOURCE: *World Resources 2000–2001* (Washington D.C.: World Resource Institute, 2000). Reprinted with Permission.

appears to be between 0.3 and 0.6 degrees Centigrade higher than in 1990, scientists disagree about projected increases in the future. Some predict as much as a 3.6-degree-Centigrade increase in the next hundred years; others are more skeptical about the rate of increase. And there is controversy over what impacts the temperature increases will have. Will sea levels rise? Will winter in some locales be warmer? Will rainfall be affected? Will some ecosystems be more affected than others? Global warming may positively affect some, while negatively impacting others.

There is also disagreement about the appropriate scientific strategies to be taken. Are voluntary restraints sufficient or are authoritative regulations needed? Finally, to complicate the picture further, the burning of fossil fuels for energy, one of the acknowledged causes of global warming, is viewed as a necessity, both for the industrialized countries to continue high rates of economic growth and for the developing countries to become industrialized. Under these exigencies, negotiating an international agreement on greenhouse gas emissions has proved to be a highly contested political process.[6]

With scientific uncertainty and differing political interests, the negotiations have resulted in a series of confrontations over timetables and targets. A relatively weak U.N. Framework Convention on Climate Change was signed in 1992 in Rio de Janeiro and became effective in 1994. That document, however, did not include legally binding obligations to reduce carbon dioxide emissions to an agreed level.

The Kyoto Protocol of 1997 amended the 1992 U.N. document. It provided for stabilizing the concentration of greenhouse gases and delineated international goals for reducing emissions by 2010. Under the protocol, developed countries (including the United States, Europe, and Japan) were required to reduce their overall greenhouse gas emissions by at least 5 percent below 1990 levels over the next decade; Japan committed to 6 percent, the United States to 7 percent, and the European Union to 8 percent. In neither the Kyoto Protocol nor the earlier agreement were developing countries included in the emission limitation requirement.

The protocol does provide for flexibility mechanisms designed to make the emission targets more cost efficient. Trading of international emission shares is permitted. This allows countries that achieve deeper reductions than their targets to trade their surplus shares to other countries. Credits can be earned from *carbon sinks*. Since forests absorb the carbon dioxide from the air as they grow and help slow the buildup of the gas in the atmosphere, states could offset emissions through credits for carbon sinks. The debate focuses on whether sinks can be used to meet all or only part of the emission reduction. Joint implementation permits countries to participate in projects for emission reductions and allows each to receive part of the credit. Each mechanism represents a highly complex scientific technique designed to reduce emissions, yet each comes with economic costs that are often difficult, if not impossible, to estimate.

While the United States signed the Kyoto Protocol, it has not been ratified by the U.S. Congress, nor has it been ratified by the 55 other states needed for implementation, nor by those states accounting for 55 percent of the carbon dioxide emissions. As stipulated, failure of the United States, the Russian Federation, or any of the other major developed countries to ratify prevents the protocol from becoming operational.

The United States objects to the protocol for several reasons. Some members in Congress argue that the required cutbacks for the developed countries are too high and that the developing countries would gain an unfair economic advantage since they would not be restricted in the emission of greenhouse gases. That view was not shared by the Europeans and Japanese, all of whom signed the protocol and have already made significant efforts to reduce emissions, stabilizing 2000 emissions at the 1990 level. The United States wants to be able to use its vast carbon sinks to offset the preponderance of its required emission reductions, and again the Europeans disagree. Meanwhile, as the U.S. objections are registered, its emissions have continued to increase. In 2000, U.S. emissions were 13 percent higher than in 1990. And, if no action is taken, it is projected that U.S. emissions will increase by a total of 26 percent by 2010. The longer the negotiations continue without agreement on emission reduction, the more problematic successful negotiations will be in the future.

Global warming thus remains on the international agenda, despite subsequent international conferences charged to iron out the differences. As with ozone depletion, states, multinational corporations, and nongovernmental organizations have taken strong stands, although these positions are clearly at odds.

A Theoretical Take

What has made many environmental issues so politically controversial at the international level is that states have tended to divide along the developed-developing—North-South—economic axis, although some developed states have been more accommodating than others. To the developed world, many environmental issues stem from the population explosion, a developing world problem. Population growth rates must decline; then pressure on scarce natural resources will decrease and the negative externality of pollution will diminish. Those in the developed world who have enjoyed the benefits of economic growth and industrialization may now be willing to pay the costs in order to achieve human security—ensuring that the population enjoys a safe and healthy environment.

States of the developing South perceive the environmental issue differently. These states correctly point to the fact that many of the environmental problems—including the overutilization of natural resources and the pollution issues of ozone depletion and greenhouse emissions—are the result of excesses of the industrialized world. By exploiting the environment, by misusing the commons, the developed countries were able to achieve high levels of economic development. Putting restrictions on developing countries, not allowing them to exploit their natural resources or restricting their utilization of vital fossil fuels, may impede their development. Thus, since the developed states have been responsible for most of the environmental excesses, it is they who should pay for the cleanup.

The challenge in addressing globalizing issues is to negotiate a middle ground that reflects the fact that both sides are, in fact, correct. High population growth rates is a problem of the South—one which will not be alleviated until higher levels of economic development are achieved. Overutilization of natural resources is primarily a problem of the North. Powerful economic interests in the North are constantly reminding us that changes in resource utilization may lead to a lower standard of living. Pollution is a by-product of both, which in the South, tends to be in the form of land and water resource utilization because of excessive population, whereas in the North, it stems from the by-products and negative externalities of industrialization. Thus, the environmental issue, more than the other globalizing issues, involves trade-offs with economic interests. Economic security is more likely to lead to environmental security.

Realists, liberals, and radicals do not have the same degree of concern for environmental issues, although each of the perspectives has been modified in response to external changes. Realists' principal emphasis has been on state security, although in some quarters that has recently expanded to include human security. Either version of security requires a strong population base, a nearly self-sufficient source of food, and a dependable supply of natural resources. Making the costs of natural resources or the costs of pollution abatement too high diminishes the ability of a state to make independent decisions. Thus realists fit environmental issues into the theoretical concepts of the state, power, sovereignty, and the balance of power.

Radicals, likewise, are concerned with the economic costs of the environmental problem. Radicals are apt to see the costs borne disproportionately by those in the South and by the poorer groups in the developed North. Neither of these burdens is acceptable.

Both realists and radicals clearly recognize that controversies over natural resources and resource scarcity can lead to violence and even war. Political scientist Thomas Homer-Dixon has proposed one model that directly links the environment to conflict.[7] Figure 10.3 shows these hypothesized relationships. While not all would agree with the lines of causation, they are intellectually provocative and a source of concern for policymakers.

In contrast, liberals have typically seen the environmental issue as appropriate to the international agenda for the twenty-first century. Their broadened view of security, coupled with the credence given to the notion of an international system described as interdependent, perhaps even one

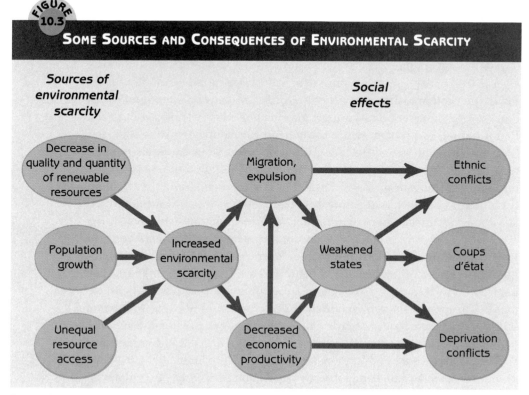

FIGURE 10.3

SOME SOURCES AND CONSEQUENCES OF ENVIRONMENTAL SCARCITY

Source: Thomas F. Homer-Dixon, "Environmental Scarcities and Violent Conflict: Evidence and Cases," *International Security* 19:.1 (Summer 1994), 31. Reprinted with Permission.

so interconnected as to be called an international society, makes environmental issues ripe for international action. Because liberals can theoretically accommodate a greater variety of different international actors, including nongovernmental actors from global civil society, environmental issues and human rights issues are legitimate, if not key, international issues of the twenty-first century. Unlike realists and radicals who fear dependency on other countries because it may diminish state power and therefore limit state action, liberals welcome the interdependency and have faith in the technological ingenuity of individuals to be able to solve many of the natural resource dilemmas.

Constructivists, too, are comfortable with environmental issues. Environmental issues bring out the salience of discourse. Constructivists are interested in how political and scientific elites define the problem and how that definition changes over time and new ideas become rooted. Constructivists also realize that environmental issues challenge the core concepts of sovereignty. One of the major intellectual tasks for constructivists has been to uncover the roots and practices of sovereignty.

HUMAN RIGHTS

The issue of human rights, the treatment of individuals and groups of individuals, has a longer historical genesis than environmental issues, but its global dimension is of more recent vintage. Prior to 1945, relations between a state and the individuals within the state was largely that state's concern. Over these individuals, the state had absolute sovereignty, supreme legal authority. Gradually five exceptions developed. In 1815 the major European powers began to negotiate a treaty, which was finally concluded in 1890, which recognized the obligation of states to abolish the slave trade. But it was not until 1926 that the practice of slavery was abolished by the international community. During the nineteenth century, individuals became entitled to medical treatment by belligerent states during war. In the twentieth century, legal aliens became entitled to minimum civil rights within a state. Laborers achieved some protection under the International Labor Organization, and specific minorities from the vanquished states of World War I were granted nominal international rights by the League of Nations. But the protection of individuals for all other purposes remained solely a state responsibility.[8]

Like the issue of population, the issue of human rights addresses core values in which there are fundamental disagreements about what rights should be protected and what the role of the state and international community should be in the protection of such rights. And realists, liberals, and radicals offer contrasting perspectives.

Conceptualizing Human Rights

Political theorists have long been in the business of conceptualizing human rights. Three different kinds of rights have been articulated. The first group of human rights to be formulated (**first generation human rights**) is rights possessed by an individual which the state cannot usurp. John Locke (1632–1704), among others, asserted that individuals are equal and autonomous beings whose natural rights predate both national and international law. Public authority is designed to secure these rights. Key historic documents detail these rights, beginning with the English Magna Charta in 1215, the French Declaration of the Rights of Man in 1789, and the U.S. Bill of Rights in the 1791 Constitution. These documents listed rights of the individual which the government could not take away. No individual should be "deprived of life, liberty, or property, without due process of law." Political and civil rights dominate first generation rights: the right to free speech, free assembly, free press, and freedom of religion. To some theorists and to many U.S. pundits, these are the only recognized human rights. First generation rights are squarely within the liberal tradition and are widely accepted by realists. Even Karl Marx regarded some civil rights as good, though not the emphasis on property rights.

Second generation human rights developed in large part under the disciples of Marx and other radical socialist thinkers. Marx's concern was for the welfare of industrialized labor. The duty of states is to advance the well-being of its citizens; the right of the citizens is to benefit from these socioeconomic advances. This view emphasizes minimum material rights that the state must provide to individuals. The state has the responsibility to provide for the social welfare of individuals, and thus, individuals have the right to education, health care, social security, and housing, although the amount guaranteed is unspecified. Without guarantees of those economic and social rights, political and civil rights are largely meaningless. The socialist states of the former Soviet Union, as well as many social welfare states of Europe, recognize economic and social rights either as important as political and civil rights or more important.

Third generation human rights, a product of late twentieth-century thinking, specify rights for groups. Groups that have rights include ethnic or indigenous minorities within a polity or designated special groups such as women or children. Some theorists have even added group rights to the list of human rights: the right to a safe environment, the right to peace and human security, the right to live in a democracy.

Is each of these different conceptions of human rights applicable universally? Is there a set of rights which should be **universal rights?** There is disagreement. Clearly, some states give priority to one generation of rights over others. Pundits from different regions of the world have argued **cultural relativism,** that is, that rights are culturally determined, and hence different rights are relevant in different cultural settings. A group of Asian writers, including some in China, Indonesia, Malaysia, Singapore, and Vietnam, have made this argument. Global human rights are a misnomer; human rights are culturally relative. In their view, when regional population and land pressures are so severe, to advocate the rights of the individual over the welfare of the community as a whole is unsound and potentially dangerous. The rights of the individual in first and second generation rights may conflict with the collective rights of groups. Asian culturalists give primacy to the latter over the former.[9] Others disagree. The final document of the Vienna World Conference on Human Rights in 1993 asserts, "All human rights are universal, indivisible and interdependent and related." Perhaps, Secretary-General Kofi Annan put it most persuasively: "It was never the people who complained of the universality of human rights, nor did the people consider human rights as a Western or Northern imposition. It was often their leaders who did so."[10]

Enforcing Human Rights

Not only is there controversy over which human rights should be protected, but there is also disagreement about the proper agency for enforcement. Are human rights primarily the responsibility of the local community, the state, or a culturally homogeneous subregion? Or is there an international collectivity, a formal IGO, or a nongovernmental group from civil society that is responsible for enforcement?

Most states contend that the protection of human rights are the primary prerogative of the state. States are to refrain from interfering with the political and civil liberties of their citizens, and states are to guarantee the social and economic, as well as group, rights. That is largely a state's sovereign prerogative, limited only by a state's own constitutional processes. The United States made this argument during the era of civil rights in the 1950s and 1960s. Discrimination against African Americans was a U.S. problem to be handled by federal authorities. The People's Republic of China has been one of the more vocal supporters of this point of view, disdainful of any interference in its domestic rights policy.

During the twentieth century with mass communication and the spread of information about how countries were treating their populations, a contending position emerged. That position was based on the realization that how a government treats its own citizens can affect the larger global community. Mistreatment of individuals and minorities can inflame ethnic tensions, causing unrest across national borders. Mistreatment of individuals debases humans everywhere, threatening to undermine the essence of humanity worldwide. The Holocaust, the German Nazi genocide against Jews, gypsies, and countless minorities, brought the issue to the attention of the international community in a way that had not been done previously. Nongovernmental groups participating in the U.N. founding conference in San Francisco pushed for the inclusion of human rights in the new organization's agenda. The international community, namely but not exclusively, should assume responsibility for the promotion and encouragement of global human rights standards.

While most realist, liberals, and radicals would now agree at least theoretically that genocide should lead to a concerted international response, in specific cases the actual decision may be different. Realist would generally couch their response in the national interest. If genocide by others jeopardizes a state's national interest, including intruding on its core values, then it may act. As former U.S. national security adviser Henry Kissinger has warned, a wise realist policymaker would not be moved by sentiment alone or by personal welfare, but by the calculation of the national interest.[11] But the definition of that national interest may be broad, based on historical tradition or domestic values.

Liberals have less inhibition about responding not only to genocide but also to less dramatic abuses. Their emphasis on individual welfare and on the malleability of the state makes such intrusions into the actions of other states less offensive to them. Like the realists, they may prefer that nongovernmental actors take the initiatives, but they generally see it to be a state's duty to intercede in blatant cases of human rights abuse.

Radicals, too, have no restraints against taking actions against other states. However, for them, the real culprit is the nemesis of an unfair economic system, namely, the international capitalist system, so the target is much more diffuse.

What can the international community actually do? What can the United Nations do when the United Nations itself is composed of the very sovereign states that threaten individual rights? The United Nation's activities have been confined to several areas.[12] First, it has been involved in the setting of international human rights standards, beginning with the Universal Declaration of Human Rights in 1949 and followed by numerous other legal conventions, including the International Covenant on Economic, Social, and Cultural Rights; the International Covenant on Civil and Political Rights (passed in 1966, operative in 1976); and specific conventions for human rights of women, children, refugees, and indigenous peoples.

Second, the United Nations has worked to monitor state behavior, establishing procedures for complaints about state practices, compiling reports from interested and neutral observers about state behavior, and investigating alleged violations. Monitoring has generally focused on political rights associated with democracy or on civil rights, rather than on second generation rights.

Third, the United Nations has taken measures to promote human rights by assuring fair elections with neutral monitors and providing a focal point for global human rights activity in the person of the high commissioner for human rights.

Fourth, the United Nations and its member states have occasionally been involved in direct enforcement. In the case of apartheid—legalized racial discrimination against the majority black population in South Africa and a comparable policy in Southern Rhodesia (now Zimbabwe)— the international community under U.N. authority instituted economic embargoes, seeking to punish those responsible for violating human rights standards and hoping to cause a change in the states' aberrant behavior. In other cases such as the Iraqi treatment of the Kurds and "ethnic cleansing" in Bosnia and Kosovo, the United Nations and NATO authorized military action on behalf of beleaguered peoples.

All of these approaches to human rights enforcement are fraught with difficulties. A state's signature on a treaty is no guarantee of its willingness or ability to follow the treaty's provisions. Monitoring state compliance using self-reporting systems presumes a willingness to comply and to be transparent. Taking direct action by imposing economic embargoes may not achieve the announced objective—change in human rights policy—but may actually be harmful to those very individuals whom the embargoes are trying to help. It has been reported that the international community's economic sanctions against Iraq since the Gulf War have resulted in a lower standard of living for the population and an imposition of real economic hardship on the masses, while the targeted elites remain unaffected. The sanctions have not had the intended affect of securing the elimination of weapons of mass destruction.[13]

Even NATO's bombing of Kosovo and Serbia in 1999, designed to stop Serbian atrocities against the Albanian Kosovars and punish the Milosevic regime, resulted in unintended Kosovar casualties and increased hardship for all peoples, while the regime went unpunished, at least in the short run. International and national actions on behalf of human rights objectives remains a very tricky business. Use of power, whether hard or soft power, does not always result in its intended consequences.

While the enforcement of human rights standards by the international community is clearly the exception rather than the norm, important precedents were established in the late twentieth century. Some kind of international action is acceptable, though such actions are not always taken. The international community may be closer to saying it has a responsibility, even an obligation, to intervene, though the same community has not chosen to intervene the same way in similar situations. Constructivists are mindful of the possibilities. The more international norms fit in with collective understandings embedded in domestic institutions and political culture, the more likely international norms will be implemented.[14]

States acting alone are unlikely to intervene. To realist decisionmakers, national interests are not directly engaged. Radicals are generally pessimistic that any state action alters underlying structural relationships. Yet, for liberals in a few cases, the argument has been made that the norms of international society are jeopardized by the actions of an aberrant few. The situation must be remedied by direct action. But such humanitarian intervention is highly contested and often influenced by other considerations, including power, politics, economic prowess, and even race.

Other Human Rights Actors

Similar to the global environmental issue, human rights issues involve a multiplicity of actors, not only state actors and international organizations. The NGOs have been particularly vocal and sometimes very effective in the area of human rights. Of the over 250 human rights organizations having interests that cross national borders, there is a core group that has been the most vocal and attracted the most attention. It includes Amnesty International, the International Committee of the Red Cross, Human Rights Watch, and the International Commission of Jurists. These organizations have played a key role in publicizing the issues, including the abuses; of putting pressure on states (both offenders and enforcers); and of lobbying international organizations capable of taking concerted action. The groups have often formed coalitions, leading to advocacy networks and social movements.[15]

The work of human rights NGOs, like environmental NGOs, has become more effective with the use of the Internet and the World Wide Web. Individuals and groups are able to voice their grievances swiftly and to a worldwide audience. Individuals in Chiapas, southern Mexico, for example, were able to mobilize an international audience against the abuses of the Mexican government and against NAFTA. The NGOs are able to communicate with their far-flung constituencies through the World Wide Web and solicit sympathizers to take direct actions, e-mailing individuals and groups who can change the situation. They can disseminate information quickly and to maximum effect. In constructivist discourse, they can aid in the spread of ideas.

Environmentalists and human rights advocates have not been the only groups able to utilize the new technologies effectively. But they, like their counterparts concerned with other issue areas such as gender, labor, and social welfare, have utilized the new communications and, by doing so, have engaged directly and indirectly a larger and more-committed audience.

Women's Rights as Human Rights

A cursory examination of women's rights moving from the national to the international agenda illustrates many of the principles and problems we have just delineated. Women's rights, like other human rights issues, touch directly on cultural values and norms, yet like other human rights issues, they have gradually become a globalizing issue.[16] As a U.N. poster prepared for the Vienna Conference in 1993 headlined: Women's Rights Are Human Rights. This has not always been the case.

Women first took up the call for political participation within national jurisdictions, demanding their political and civil rights in the form of women's suffrage. Although British and U.S. women won that right in 1918 and 1920, respectively, women in many parts of the world waited until World War II (France 1944) and after (Greece 1952, Switzerland 1971, Jordan 1974, and El Salvador 1991). In many Middle Eastern countries (Brunei, Kuwait, Oman, Qatar, and Saudi Arabia), women still do not have that right. Thus, although the efforts of Eleanor Roosevelt and her Latin American colleagues led to gender's being included in the

Universal Declaration of Human Rights (1945), at the time, gender was not seen as a human rights issue. In the immediate aftermath, the priority of the United Nations and its Commission on the Status of Women was on getting states to grant women the right to vote, hold office, and enjoy legal rights, part of the first generation human rights.

During the 1960s and 1970s, more attention was paid by the United Nations to the economic and social rights of women, the second generation human rights. Issues such as equal remuneration for men and women workers, minimum standards of social security, maternity protection, and nondiscrimination in the workplace were squarely on the agenda. Some of these issues resulted in international conventions, and international agencies like the U.N. Development Programme and the International Labor Organization worked to create economic equality for participants in their funded programs. Most implementation remained in the hands of the states. A weak system for states to report their progress and their impediments was put into place, giving a degree of transparency to highly controversial endeavors.

By the 1990s, the discussion of women's rights became viewed as one of human rights. This shift was solidified in the 1993 Vienna Conference on Human Rights. As the Vienna Declaration asserted, "The human rights of women and of the girl-child are an inalienable, integral and indivisible part of universal human rights. . . . The human rights of women should form an integral part of the United Nations human rights activities, including the promotion of all human rights instruments relating to women."[17] Included was not only human rights protection in the public sphere (first and second generation human rights) but protection against human rights abuses in the private sphere, notably gender-based violence against women. The latter includes violence against women in the family and domestic life; gendered division of labor in the workplace, including work in the informal sector and sexual work; and violence against women in war, particularly rape and torture. The rape of 60,000 Bosnian women in 1993 by Serb forces, as well as the rape of 250,000 women in Burundi's and Rwanda's ethnic conflicts in 1993–94 brought home the extent of the unique violence against women. In 1995 rape was recognized as a distinct and prosecutable crime of war.

But the 1993 Vienna conference did not end the debate. Women's rights as human rights have continued to be discussed most vigorously with respect to reproductive rights. If human rights are culturally based and not universal, then women's reproductive rights would be limited to those countries approving the measures. If human rights are universal, then women's reproductive rights and the rights of girls would be universally applicable. Women would have the right to decide issues related to their sexuality; violence against women in the home, workplace, and society would be prohibited; and political and economic discriminatory practices against women would be illegal. The debate still rages.

Different feminist groups have placed different priorities on the various types of human rights protection. Liberal feminists have found solace in granting women political and civil human rights, providing them the opportunity to secure privileges which were once exclusively male prerogatives. Socialist feminists point to the economic forces that have disadvantaged women and sought economic changes. In their view, as women become economically empowered, they will be able to alter patriarchal gender relations. More-radical feminists highlight the distinctiveness of women and seek protection from all forms of gendered violence in both the public and private spheres.

Like other human rights issues, women's rights have spawned a plethora of NGOs from different parts of the world, with differing agendas. The number of women's international NGOs grew from 16 in 1973 to 61 in 1993 alone. These groups coalesced in 1993 into two networks, the International Feminist Network and the Asian Women's Research and Action Network. Each have become key actors in the U.N. system, participating in international meetings, developing strategies to push selected issues, gathering information, and monitoring governmental and IGO positions. All groups within these coalitions clearly do not share cultural similarities, nor do they have the same issue priorities. However, women's rights as human rights have gained a critical following.

While the legal stage has been set by protection in various human rights treaties under the auspices of international organizations, the mainstay of enforcement will continue to be at the state level. It is states prodded by the normative requirements of international treaties and lobbied by prominent individuals and human rights networks that undertake domestic reform. It is states that unilaterally or multilaterally undertake punitive action against offending states.

IMPACT OF GLOBALIZING ISSUES

Globalizing issues have affects on four major areas of international relations theory and practice.

First, the interconnectedness of the plethora of subissues within both environmental and human rights issues affect international bargaining.

When states choose to go to the bargaining table, a multiplicity of issues is often at stake. Many issues are fungible; states are willing to make trade-offs between issues to achieve the desired result. For example, in the aftermath of the 1973 oil embargo and in the face of supply short-ages, the United States was willing to negotiate with Mexico on cleaning up the Colorado River water. The United States built a desalinization plant at the U.S.-Mexican border and helped Mexican residents reclaim land in the Mexicali Valley for agriculture. To win an ally in the supply of petroleum resources, the United States made the major concession and accepted responsibility for past legal violations.

Other issues, however, are less fungible, particularly if key concerns of national security are at stake. The United States was unwilling to compro-mise by signing the Anti-Personnel Land Mine Treaty (Land Mines Treaty)—a treaty designed to prohibit and eliminate the use of land mines—because of the security imperative to preserve the heavily mined border between North and South Korea. Supporters of the treaty framed the argument in human rights terms: innocent individuals, including vul-nerable women and children, are being maimed by the use of such weapons; these weapons need to be eliminated. Yet in this case, the United States decided not to sign the treaty because of Korean security. While some states, eager for U.S. participation, were willing to make con-cessions, others, afraid that the treaty would be weakened by too many ex-ceptions, were not. Bargaining is a much more complicated process in the age of globalizing issues.

Second, these globalizing issues themselves may be the source of con-flict, just as the Marxists predicted in the nineteenth century. The need to protect the petroleum supply was the primary motivation for the West's involvement in the Gulf War. Population pressures in Rwanda and Bu-rundi have escalated the level of violence between the Tutsis and Hutus. The relationship between environmental and resource issues and conflict is a complex one.

Issues of resource depletion and degradation, usually attenuated by population increase and pressure on resources, are apt to result in conflicts when some groups try to capture use of the scarce resource. For example, on the West Bank of the Jordan River where Israeli authorities control ac-cess to scarce water, conflict between the Israelis and the Palestinians is exacerbated. Israel permits its own settlers greater access to the resource and restricts access to the Palestinians. In cases where conflict does not erupt, the groups experiencing resource depletion are marginalized.

Nonrenewable resources like oil lead to particularly violent conflicts, because these resources are vital; there are few viable substitutes. Changes in the distribution of these resources may lead to a shift in the balance of power, creating an instability that leads to war, just as realists fear. In contrast, issues such as ozone depletion or global warming are not particularly conducive to violent interstate conflict. In both cases, the commons and responsibility for its management is diffuse. The detrimental impact may be displaced to future generations.

Third, these globalizing issues pose direct challenges to state sovereignty. Thus, these new issues have set off a major debate about the nature of sovereignty. In Chapter 2, we traced the roots of sovereignty in the Westphalian revolution. The notion developed that states enjoy an internal autonomy and cannot be subjected to external authority. That norm—noninterference in the domestic affairs of other states—was embedded in the U.N. Charter. Yet the rise of nonstate actors, including multinational corporations, nongovernmental organizations, and supranational organizations like the European Union, and the forces of globalization, whether economic, cultural, or political, undermine the Westphalian notions of state sovereignty.

Likewise, the globalizing issues pose direct challenges to state sovereignty. The issues of the environment and of human rights were traditionally sovereign state concerns, where interference by outside actors was unacceptable. After World War II, those norms began to change and are still in the process of changing. This is one of the main reasons that discussion has turned to a power shift, an erosion of state authority, to a potential demise of state power. Issues that once were the hallmark of state sovereignty are increasingly susceptible to scrutinizing by global actors.

How then should sovereignty be reconceptualized? How has sovereignty been transformed? Mainstream theories in the realist and liberal traditions tend to talk of an erosion of sovereignty. Constructivists go further, probing how sovereignty is and has always been a contested concept. There have always been some issues where state control and authority are secure and others where authority is shared or even undermined. After all, sovereignty is a socially constructed institution that varies across time and place. Globalizing issue like the environment and human rights permit us to examine long standing but varying practices based on sovereignty in depth. They give rise to new forms of authority and new forms of governance. They stimulate us to reorient our views of sovereignty.[18]

Fourth, globalizing issues pose critical problems for international relations scholars and for the theoretical frameworks introduced at the beginning of the text. Each of the frameworks has been forced to rethink key assumptions and values, as well as discourse, to accommodate globalizing issues.

IN FOCUS

EFFECTS OF GLOBALIZING ISSUES

▶ On international bargaining
  More policy trade-offs
  Greater complexity
▶ On international conflict
  May increase at international and
  substate level
▶ On state sovereignty
  Traditional notion challenged
  Need for reconceptualization
▶ On study of international relations
  Core assumptions of theories jeopardized
  Theories modified and broadened

For realists, the very core propositions of their theory—including the primacy of the state, the clear separation between domestic and international politics, and the emphasis on state security—are made problematic by the globalizing issues. The globalizing issues of environment, human rights, epidemics, drugs, and crime are problems that no one state can effectively address alone. These are issues in which the divide between the international and the domestic has broken down. These are issues which may threaten state security yet for which there may be no traditional military solution.

Responding to the issues, realists have generally adopted a more-nuanced argument consonant with realist precepts. While most realists admit that there may be other actors that have gained power relative to the state, they contend that state primacy is not in jeopardy. Competitive centers of power either at the local, transnational, or international level do not necessarily or automatically lead to the erosion or demise of state power. Most importantly, the fundamentals of state security are no less important in an age of globalization than they were in the past. What has changed is that security discourse has been broadened to encompass human security. For humans to be secure, not only must state security be assured but economic security, environmental security, and human rights security as well. One form of security does not replace the other; the latter augments the former. Thus, while adding qualifications to realism, the theory is preserved and its theoretical usefulness enhanced.

For liberals, the globalizing issues can be more easily integrated into their theoretical picture. After all, liberals at the outset asserted the importance of individuals and the possibility of both cooperative and conflictual interests. They introduced the notion of multiple issues which may be as important as security. They see power as a multidimensional concept. Later versions of liberal thinking like neoliberal institutionalism recognized the need for international institutions to facilitate state interactions to ensure transparency and to add the new issues to the international agenda. While not denying the importance of state security, they quickly embraced the notion of other forms of security, compatible with environmental and human rights issues.

Radicals have never been comfortable with the primacy of the state and the international system that the dominant coalition of states created. A shift in power away from the state and that international system is a desired transition. With their pronounced emphasis on economics over security, radicals may be able to accommodate globalizing issues like the environment and human rights. A prominent interpretation of the environmental dilemma, according to radical thought, is that economic deprivation and perceived relative economic deprivation is the root cause of environmental degradation. Human rights violations are caused by elites and privileged groups trying to maintain their edge over the less fortunate.

Constructivists have presented a different approach for tapping into the globalizing issues. They have alerted us to the nuances of the changing discourse embedded in discussions of the environment and human rights. They have illustrated how both material factors and ideas shape the debates over the issues. They have called attention to the importance of norms in influencing and changing individual and state behavior. Better than other theorists, constructivists have begun to explore the variable impacts of these issues on the traditional concepts of the state, national identity, and sovereignty. Yet while sometimes pathbreaking and often suggestive, constructivism itself remains under construction.

As all globalizing issues assume greater salience in the twenty-first century, there are bound to be theoretical modifications to realism, liberalism, and radicalism. Among the three, realists and liberals are well on their way to theoretical reformulations that give space to the state, expand the notions of power and security, and accommodate globalizing concerns at all levels of analysis.

IN SUM: CHANGING YOU

In these ten chapters, we have explored the historical development of international relations from feudal times, to the development of the state system, and to notions of an international system and community and global governance. We have introduced different theories—namely liberalism, realism, and radicalism—that help us organize our perspectives about the role of the international system, the state, and the individual in international relations. And we have introduced constructivist thinking on several issues. Using these perspectives, we have examined two of the major issues of the day—security and war, and the international political economy. To more adequately prepare ourselves for discussions in this new century, we have explored the roots of cooperation in international law and organizations and in the broader notions of global governance. And we have confronted the emerging globalizing issues of the twenty-first century—the environment and human rights—and analyzed how these issues affect interstate bargaining, conflict, sovereignty, and even how we study international politics.

A citizenry able to articulate these arguments is a citizenry better able to explain the whys and hows of events that affect our lives. A citizen who can understand these events is better able to make informed policy choices. In the globalizing era of the twenty-first century, as economic political, social, and environmental forces both above the state and within the state assume greater saliency, the role of individuals becomes all the more demanding.

NOTES

1 Thomas Malthus, "An Essay on the Principle of Population: Text, Sources, and Background Criticism" (1789), ed. Philip Appleman, (New York: Norton, 1976).

2. Dennis Meadows et al., *The Limits to Growth* (New York: Signet, 1972).

3. Garrett Hardin, "The Tragedy of the Commons," *Science* 162 (December 13, 1968), 1243–48.

4. Rachel Carson, *Silent Spring* (Boston: Houghton Mifflin, 1962). See also Jacques Yves Cousteau with Frederick Dames *The Silent World* (New York: Harper and Row, 1953); and Jacques Yves Cousteau with James Dugan, *The Living Sea* (New York: Harper and Row, 1963).

5. For an excellent history of the negotiations, see Richard Elliott Benedick, *Ozone Diplomacy: New Directions in Safeguarding the Planet* (Cambridge, Mass.: Harvard University Press, 1997). For a constructivist view, see Karen T. Litfin, *Ozone Discourses: Science and Politics in Global Environmental Cooperation* (New York: Columbia University Press, 1994).

6. Gareth Porter, Janet Welsh Brown, and Pamela S. Chasek, *Global Environmental Politics* (3d ed.; Boulder, Colo.: Westview, 2000).

7. Thomas F. Homer-Dixon, "Environmental Scarcities and Violent Conflict: Evidence and Cases," *International Security* 19:1 (Summer 1994), 5–40.

8. For excellent overviews, see Jack Donnelly, *International Human Rights* (2d ed.; Boulder, Colo.: Westview, 1998); and David P. Forsythe, *Human Rights in International Relations* (Cambridge, Eng.: Cambridge University Press, 2000).

9. See Joanne R. Bauer and Daniel A. Bell, eds., *The East Asian Challenge for Human Rights* (Cambridge, Eng.: Cambridge University Press, 1999).

10. Quoted on the U.N. high commissioner for human rights website, available at http://www.unhchr.ch.

11. Henry Kissinger, *Diplomacy* (New York: Simon and Schuster, 1994).

12. Karen A. Mingst and Margaret P. Karns, *The United Nations in the Post–Cold War Era* (2d ed.; Boulder, Colo.: Westview, 2000). Chap. 6.

13. David Cortright and George A. Lopez, *The Sanctions Decade: Assessing UN Strategies in the 1990s* (Boulder, Colo.: Lynne Rienner, 2000).

14. See Thomas Risse, Stephen C. Ropp, and Kathryn Sikkink, *The Power of Human Rights: International Norms and Domestic Change* (Cambridge, Eng.: University of Cambridge Press, 1999).

15. See Margaret E. Keck and Kathryn Sikkink, *Activists Beyond Borders: Advocacy Networks in International Networks* (Ithaca, N.Y.: Cornell University Press, 1998).

16. V. Spike Peterson and Anne Sisson Runyan, *Global Gender Issues* (2d ed.; Boulder, Colo.: Westview, 1999).

17. U.N. Conference on Human Rights, *Declaration* (Vienna, 1993), Art. 18.

18. See Stephen D. Krasner, *Sovereignty: Organized Hypocrisy* (Princeton, N.J.: Princeton University Press, 1999); and the articles in *The Greening of Sovereignty in World Politics*, ed., Karen T. Litfin, (Cambridge, Mass.: MIT Press, 1998).

GLOSSARY

anarchy   the absence of governmental authority (7)

arms control   agreements among states to restrict the research, manufacture, or deployment of weapons systems and certain types of troops (156)

balance of payments   the flow of money into and out of a country from trade, tourism, foreign aid, sale of services, profits, etc., for a period of time (185)

balance of power   an international system in which states enjoy relatively equal power, states form alliances or make policies to counteract the acquisition of power by other states, and no one state is able to dominate the international system (32)

behavioralism   an approach to the study of social science and international relations that posits that individuals and units like states act in regularized ways; leads to a belief that behaviors can be described, explained, and predicted (10)

belief system   the organized and integrated perceptions of individuals in a society, including foreign-policy decisionmakers, often based on past history, that guide them to select certain policies over others (139)

bipolar   an international system with two major powers or two groups of states having relatively equal power (52)

bureaucratic politics   the model of foreign-policy decisionmaking that posits that national decisions are the outcomes of bargaining among bureaucratic groups having competing interests; decisions reflect the relative strength of the individual bureaucratic players (122)

capitalism the economic system where the ownership of the means of production is in private hands; the system operates according to market forces where capital and labor move freely. According to radicals, an exploitative relationship between the owners of production and the workers (42)

civil war armed conflict within a state between factions that wish to control a government or exercise jurisdiction over territory; may have international repercussions with the flow of armaments and refugees, often leading to intervention by other states (178)

cognitive consistency the tendency of individuals to accept information that is compatible with what has previously been accepted, often by ignoring inconsistent information; linked to the desire of individuals to be consistent in their attitudes (140)

Cold War the era in international relations between the end of World War II and 1990, distinguished by ideological, economic, and political differences between the Soviet Union and the United States (40)

collective goods public goods that are jointly provided for—the air, the oceans, or Antarctica—but that no one owns or is individually responsible for; with collective goods, decisions by one group or state have effects for other groups or states (225)

collective security concept that aggression against a state should be defeated collectively because aggression against one state is aggression against all; basis of League of Nations and United Nations (64)

comparative advantage the ability of a country to make and export a good relatively most efficiently; the basis for the liberal economic principle that countries benefit from free trade among nations (190)

compellence the policy of threatening or intimidating an adversary to take or refrain from taking a particular action (116)

constructivism an alternative international relations theory that hypothesizes how ideas, norms, and institutions shape state identity and interests (76)

containment a foreign policy designed to prevent the expansion of an adversary by blocking its opportunities to expand, by supporting weaker states through foreign aid programs, and by using coercive force against the adversary to harness its expansion; the major U.S. policy toward the Soviet Union during the Cold War era (41)

cultural relativism the belief that human rights, ethics, and morality are determined by cultures and history and therefore are not universally applicable (267)

democratic peace the classical theory now being empirically tested that democratic states are least likely to wage war against each other (13)

demographic transition   the situation where increasing levels of economic development lead to falling death rates, followed by falling birthrates (254)

dependency theory   derived from radicalism, an explanation of poverty and underdevelopment in developing countries based on their historical dependence and domination by rich countries (74)

deterrence   the policy of maintaining a large military force and arsenal to discourage any potential aggressor from taking actions; states commit themselves to punish an aggressor state (52)

diplomacy   the practice of states trying to influence the behavior of other states by bargaining, negotiating, taking specific noncoercive actions or refraining from such actions, or appealing to the public for support of a position (111)

disarmament   the policy of eliminating a state's offensive weaponry; may occur for all classes of weapons or for specified weapons only; the logic of the policy is that fewer weapons leads to greater security (156)

domino effect   a metaphor that posits that the loss of influence over one state to an adversary will lead to a subsequent loss of control over neighboring states, just as dominos fall one after another. Used by the United States as a justification to support South Vietnam, fearing that if that country became communist, neighboring countries would also fall under communist influence (48)

ethnonationalist movements   self-conscious communities sharing an ethnic affiliation that decide to participate in organized political activity; some movements seek autonomy within an organized state; others desire separation and the formation of a new state; still others want to join with a different state (127)

European Union (EU)   a union of fifteen European states, formerly the European Common Market. Designed originally during the 1950s for economic integration, but since expanded into a closer political and economic union (197)

evoked set   tendency to look for details in a contemporary situation that are similar to information previously obtained; leads to outcomes that are similar to those of the past (140)

externalities   in economics, unintended side effects which can have positive or negative consequences (258)

first generation human rights   political or civil rights of citizens that prevent governmental authority from interfering with private individuals or civil society (negative rights) (266)

first strike   a nuclear attack against an enemy that is designed to eliminate the possibility of its being able to make *second strike* (156)

first-generation peacekeeping   the use of multilateral forces to achieve several different objectives, including the enforcement of cease-fires and separation of forces; used during the Cold War to keep the great powers out of international conflicts (164)

game theory   a technique developed by mathematicians and economists and used by political scientists to evaluate the choices made in decision situations, where one state's or individual's choice affects that of other actors; based on the assumption that each player knows its and the others' unique sets of options and the payoffs for each associated with these options. Among the various types of games is the *prisoner's dilemma* (117)

general war   war designed to conquer and occupy enemy territory, using all available weapons of warfare and targeting both military establishments and civilian facilities (177)

General Assembly   one of the major organs of the United Nations which generally addresses issues other than those of peace and security; each member state has one vote; operates with six functional committees of the whole (235)

General Agreement on Tariffs and Trade (GATT)   founded by treaty in 1947 as the Bretton Woods institution responsible for negotiating a liberal international trade regime that included the principles of nondiscrimination in trade and most-favored-nation status. Re-formed itself as the World Trade Organization in 1995 (207)

global governance   the rules, norms, and organizations that are designed to address international problems that states alone cannot solve (241)

globalization   the process of increasing integration of the world in terms of economics, politics, communications, social relations, and culture (126)

Group of 77   a coalition of about 125 developing countries that press for reforms in economic relations between developing and developed countries; also referred to as the *South* (192)

groupthink   the tendency for small groups to form a consensus and resist criticism of a core position, often disregarding contradictory information in the process; group may ostracize members holding a different position (141)

hegemon   a dominant state that has a preponderance of power; often establishes and enforces the rules and norms in the international system (33)

hypothesis   a tentative assumption about causal relations put forward to explore and test its logical and usually empirical consequences (60)

imperialism   the policy and practice of extending the domination of one state over another through territorial conquest or economic domination. In radicalism, the final stage of expansion of the capitalist system (73)

intergovernmental organizations (IGOs)   international agencies or bodies established by states and controlled by member states that deal with areas of common interests (227)

International Monetary Fund (IMF)   the Bretton Woods institution originally charged with helping states deal with temporary balance-of-payments problems; now plays a broader role in assisting debtor developing states by offering loans to those who institute specific policies, or *structural adjustment programs* (205)

international relations   the interactions among various actors (states, international organizations, nongovernmental organizations, and subnational entities like bureaucracies, local governments, and individuals) that participate in international politics (2)

international society   the states and substate actors in the international system and the institutions and norms that regulate their interaction; implies that these actors communicate, sharing common interests and a common identity; identified with British school of political theory (85)

irredentism   the demands of ethnonationalist groups to take political control of territory historically or ethnically related to them by separating from their parent state or taking territory from other states (127)

League of Nations   the international organization formed at the conclusion of World War I for the purpose of preventing another war; based on *collective security* (37)

legitimacy   the moral and legal right to rule, which is based on law, custom, heredity, or the consent of the governed; with reference to a government, a state recognized by members of the international community (29)

levels of analysis   in international relations, the widely accepted notion and analytic approach that each level—the individual, the state, and the international system—matters; specific events can be described and explained according to each of the three different levels (60)

liberalism   the theoretical perspective based on the assumption of the innate goodness of the individual and the value of political institutions (63)

limited war   a war fought for limited objectives with selected types of weapons or targets; the objective will be less than the total subjugation of the enemy (177)

Malthusian dilemma   the situation that population growth rates will increase faster than agricultural productivity, leading to shortages; named after Thomas Malthus (253)

mirror image   tendency of individuals and groups to see in one's opponent the opposite characteristics as seen in one's self (140)

multinational corporations (MNCs)   private enterprises with production facilities, sales, or activities in several states (74)

multipolar   an international system in which there are several states or great powers of roughly equal strength or weight (55)

nation   a group of people sharing a common language, history, or culture (101)

nation-state   the entity formed when people sharing the same historical, cultural, or linguistic roots form their own state with borders, a government, and international recognition; trend began with French and American Revolutions (102)

national interest   the interest of the state, most basically the protection of territory and sovereignty; in realist thinking, the interest is a unitary one defined in terms of the pursuit of power; in liberal thinking, there are many national interests; in radicalist thinking, it is the interest of a ruling elite (67)

nationalism   devotion and allegiance to the nation and the shared characteristics of its peoples; used to motivate people to patriotic acts, sometimes leading a group to seek dominance over another group (29)

neoliberal institutionalism   a reinterpretation of liberalism that posits that even in an anarchic international system, states will cooperate because of their continuous actions with each other and because it is in their self-interest to do so; institutions provide the framework for cooperative interactions (64)

neorealism   a reinterpretation of realism that posits that the structure of the international system is the most important level to study; states behave the way they do because of the structure of the international system; includes the belief that general laws can be found to explain events (69)

New International Economic Order (NIEO)   a list of demands by the *Group of 77* to reform economic relations between the *North* and *South,* that is, between the developed countries and the developing countries (95)

nongovernmental organizations (NGOs)   private associations of individuals or groups that engage in political activity usually across national borders (212)

normative   relating to ethical rules; in foreign policy and international affairs, standards suggesting what a policy should be (9)

North   refers to the developed countries, mostly in the Northern Hemisphere, including North America, the European countries, and Japan (91)

North Atlantic Treaty Organization (NATO)   military and political alliance between western European states and the United States established in 1948 for the purpose of defending Europe from aggression by the Soviet Union and its allies (45)

nuclear proliferation   the spread of nuclear weapons or nuclear weapons technology; Nuclear Nonproliferation Treaty obligates nuclear powers not to transfer their nuclear technology to third countries and obligates nonnuclear signatories to refrain from acquiring or developing the technology (157)

organizational politics   the foreign-policy decisionmaking model that posits that national decisions are the products of subnational governmental organizations and units; the procedures and processes of the organization largely determine the policy; major changes in policy are unlikely (122)

opportunity cost   when a choice is made, the value of the best forgone opportunity (190)

pluralist model   a model of foreign-policy decisionmaking that suggests that policy is formed as a result of the bargaining among the various domestic sources of foreign policy, including public opinion, private interest groups, and multinational corporations; these interests are generally channeled through democratic institutions like legislatures or persons holding elective positions (124)

power potential   a relative measure of the power an entity like a state could have, derived from a consideration of both tangible and intangible resources that may be used; states may not transfer their power potential into actual power (106)

power   a relationship between two individuals, groups, or states in which one party has the ability both to influence the other and to force outcomes that the other party may not want (105)

prisoner's dilemma   a theoretical game in which rational players (states or individuals) choose options that lead to outcomes (payoffs) in which all players are worse off than under a different set of choices (64)

public diplomacy   use of certain diplomatic methods to create a favorable image of the state or its people; methods include, for example, goodwill tours, cultural and student exchanges, and media presentations (113)

radicalism   a social theory, formulated by Karl Marx and modified by other theorists, that posits that class conflict between owners and workers will cause the eventual demise of capitalism (71)

rational actor   in the realist assumption, an individual or state that uses logical reasoning to select a policy; that is, it has a defined goal to achieve, considers a full range of alternative strategies, and selects the policy that best achieves the goal (67)

realism   a theory of international relations that emphasizes states' interest in accumulating power to ensure security in an anarchic world; based on the notion that individuals are power seeking and that states act in pursuit of their own national interest defined in terms of power (67)

reciprocity   in international relations, treating the actions of other states in the same manner; if one side cooperates, the other cooperates; if one side engages in negative actions, the other responds in kind (65)

regime   in international relations, an all-encompassing term that includes the rules, norms, and procedures that are developed by states and international organizations out of their common concerns and are used to organize common activities (227)

sanctions   economic, diplomatic, and even coercive military force for enforcing a state's policy or legal obligations; sanctions can be positive (offering an incentive to a state) or negative (punishing a state) (113)

satisfice   in decisionmaking theory, the idea that states and their leaders settle for the minimally acceptable solution, not the best possible outcome, in order to reach a consensus and formulate a policy (124)

second generation human rights   social and economic rights that states are obligated to provide their citizenry, including the rights to medical care, jobs, and housing (positive rights) (266)

second-generation peacekeeping   the use of multilateral forces, both military and civilian, to organize governments, promote law and order, and offer humanitarian aid and intervention to states or regions experiencing conflict; used extensively in the post–Cold War era to try to mitigate the effects of civil and ethnic strife (164)

second-strike capability   in the age of nuclear weapons, the ability of a state to respond and hurt an adversary after a first strike has been launched by the adversary; ensures that both sides will suffer an unacceptable level of damage (117)

security dilemma   the situation in which one state improves its military capabilities, especially its defenses, and those improvements are seen by other states as threats; each state in an anarchic international system tries to increase its own level of protection leading to insecurity in others, often leading to an arms race (153)

Security Council   one of the major organs of the United Nations charged with the responsibility for peace and security issues; includes five permanent members with veto power and ten nonpermanent members chosen from the General Assembly (233)

socialism   an economic and social system that relies on intensive government intervention or public ownership of the means of production in order to distribute wealth among the population more equitably; in radicalist theory, the stage between capitalism and communism (42)

South   the developing countries of Africa, Latin America, and southern Asia, generally located in the Southern Hemisphere (91)

sovereignty   the authority of the state, based on recognition by other states and by nonstate actors, to govern matters within its own borders that affect its people, economy, security, and form of government (26)

state   the organized political unit which has a geographic territory, a stable population, and a government to which the population owes allegiance and which is legally recognized by other states (101)

stratification   the degree to which there is an uneven distribution of resources among different groups of individuals and states (91)

structural adjustment program   IMF policies and recommendations to guide states out of balance-of-payment difficulties and economic crises (205)

summit   talks and meetings among the highest-level government officials from different countries; designed to promote good relations, discuss issues, and conclude formal negotiations (51)

superpower   highest-power states as distinguished from other great powers; term coined during the Cold War to refer to the United States and Soviet Union (40)

sustainable development   an approach to economic development that tries to reconcile current economic growth and environmental protection with future needs (205)

system   a group of units or parts united by some form of regular interaction, in which a change in one unit causes changes in the others; these interactions occur in regularized ways (83)

terrorism   the use of violence by groups or states to intimidate, cause fear, or punish their victims to achieve political goals (178)

theory   generalized statements about political, social, or economic activity that seek to describe and explain those activities; used in many cases as a basis of prediction (59)

third generation human rights   collective rights of groups, including the rights of indigenous people and children, and the rights to democracy and development (266)

track-two diplomacy   unofficial overtures by private individuals or groups to try and resolve an ongoing international crisis or civil war (143)

transnational   across national boundaries; can refer to actions of various nonstate actors, such as private individuals and nongovernmental organizations (52)

Treaty of Westphalia   treaty ending the Thirty Years War in Europe in 1648; in international relations represents the beginning of state sovereignty within a territorial space (26)

unipolar   an international system where there is only one great power (55)

unitary actor   an assumption made by realists that the state speaks with one voice and has a single national interest (67)

universal jurisdiction   a legal concept that permits states to claim legal authority beyond their national territory for the purpose of punishing a particularly heinous criminal or protecting human rights (222)

universal rights   controversial belief that human rights are basically the same at all times and in all cultures (267)

Warsaw Pact   the military alliance formed by the state of the Soviet bloc in 1955 in response to the rearmament of West Germany and its inclusion in NATO; permitted the stationing of Soviet troops in Eastern Europe (45)

World Trade Organization (WTO)   organization to support the principles of liberal free trade; includes enforcement measures and dispute settlement mechanisms; established in 1995 to replace the *General Agreement on Tariffs and Trade* (208)

World Bank   a global lending agency to finance projects in developing countries; formally known as the International Bank for Reconstruction and Development, established as one of the key Bretton Woods institutions to deal with reconstruction and development (203)

INDEX